Deviant Desires

"When correctly viewed,
everything is lewd."
        —*Tom Lehrer, "Smut," 1965*

A TOUR OF THE
EROTIC EDGE

BY
KATHARINE GATES

DEVIANT

 powerHouse Books   BROOKLYN, NEW YORK

DESIRES

DEDICATIONS

The author would like to thank her original editor and publisher, Andrea Juno, without whose fearlessness and support this project would never have happened; Dan Gluck and the Museum of Sex for the opportunity to hone her approach to the subject; Midori for wisdom and contacts. Above all, the author is grateful to the many people who were willing to share their most intimate stories, and trust that they would be treated fairly and honestly.

This edition owes its cohesion and intellectual rigor to the colorful pens, legal research, and firm guiding hand of David Steinhardt, in association with Massive Publishing Enterprise.

On a personal note, the author would like to express her gratitude to her husband, and children, who aren't going to see this book until they're at least 18 if their mother has anything to do with it.

DISCLAIMER

Some of the activities described in this book are dangerous, and a few are illegal. Readers should not attempt any of the acts described herein. The publisher, author, and interview subjects accept no responsibility for any injury or damage caused by readers ignoring this warning.

Previous page: R'hyl, a unicorn warhorse
(see Chapter 2). Photo: Herb Ascherman

P. 8

Introduction

1 P. 14

Pedal Power:
Foot and Shoe Fetishes

Feet are the #1 Kink; Sweat Glands and Hormones; Levels of Fetishism; Difference between Kink and Fetish; Feet and Shoes in Action: Gas Pedal Pumping; The Erotic Equation: Pressure + Resistance = Excitement; Sidekink: Hair

2 P. 26

Ponyplay
Comes Out
of the Stables

Ponyplay in History; Sir Guy Masterleigh and The Other Pony Club, England; Major Themes: Power Play; BDSM Guidelines; The Equestrian Club, NYC; Piper Pony; Danny the Wonder Pony; Major Themes: Transformation; Paul Reed, *Equus Eroticus* Magazine; subMissAnn and the LA Pony & Critter Club; Kinky Fox Hunts; Sidekink: Pups

3 P. 68

Balloons:
A Pop Kink

Balloon Buddies; The Power of Odor and Memory; Latex + Pressure; Why So Many More Men Than Women?; Buster Steve, Gay Looner Icon; Poppers Vs. Non-Poppers; Top 10 Media Sightings for Looners; The Baroness' Balloon Fetish Parties; Domina Elle, Balloon Dominatrix; Looners United, Fetish Entrepreneurs; Sidekink: Sneeze Fetish

4 P. 92

Body Expansion: To Dream the Impossible Dream

Breast, Belly, and Butt Expansion; Nose Growth; BustArtist, Top BE Illustrator; Top 12 Media Moments for Body Expansion Fans; Squeak Latex's Inflatable Latex Clothing; Sidekink: Preggo

5 P. 106

Macrophiles: Attack of the 50-Foot Fantasy

Chuckcjc, Quintessential Macro; Ed Lundt, King of the Growth Fantasies; Magic Disc Illusion; Top 10 Giantesses in the Media; Ron H. and Ms. Zena: Black Giantesses Rule the Earth; SizeCon: A New Generation; Sidekink: Vore

6 P. 130

Suburbs of the Foot Fetish: Trample and Crush

Queen Adrena, Trample Goddess; Trampling Safety Tips; Crush Freaks; Jeff "The Bug" Vilencia; Ethics and Laws; Sidekink: Car Crush

7 P. 148

Wet and Messy Fun: Getting Down and Dirty

Splosh! Magazine; Wetlook; Mudlarking; Bill and Hayley's Tips and Tricks for Messy Fun; Rubber and Mud; Sludgemaster, Gay Messy Play; Quicksand and Stuck; Major Themes: Taboo; Pieface Mike and Pie Throwing; Candy Custard: A New Face of Sploshing; Sidekink: Clowns

8 P. 168

For the Love of Fat: Feeders and Gainers

Fat Phobia and Puritanism; Fat as a Core Fetish Material; Ned Sonntag, FA Artist; Gay Male Gainers and Encouragers; Top Ten Weight Gain Media Sightings; Heather Boyle Nymeyer and Supersize Betsy, Unapologetic Feedees; Funnel Feeding; Sidekink: Smoking

9 P. 188

Medical Play: Let's Play Doctor

Romain Slocombe's Bandage Fetish Photography; Laural Wood, MedicalToys.com; Medical Bondage; Catheters and Specula; How to Clean Insertable Sex Toys; Bob Flanagan: Turning Pain Into Pleasure; Saline Injection Play; Sidekink: Adult Babies

10 P. 204

Eat Me! Cannibal Play Feeds a Need

The Turkey Man Reprised; Armin Meiwes and the Limits of Consent; Megh Vaughan, Meatgirl; Muki's Kitchen's Tasteful Meatgirls; Gurgurant, Womaneater and Collector; Top Ten Cannibal Scenes in Popular Culture; The Cannibal Cop; Sidekink: Human Furniture

11 P. 218

The Sexy Fandoms: Slash Fiction, Furries, Robots, and Superheroes

Slash Fiction: Kirk and Spock Get It On; Cecilia Tan, Nerd Pornographer; Furries, Yiff, and Yiffsuiters; Plush Fetish; Robots, Mannequins, and Dolls; Top Ten Robot/Mannequin Sightings in the Media; Superheroes in Bondage; Pablo Greene; Sidekink: Female Latex Masks

12 P. 244

Over the Edge, In Conclusion, Kinkmap, and Bibliography

"*Rule 34 of the internet:
If it exists, there is porn of it.*"
—*Urban Dictionary, 2006*

Exhibition view of the author's *KINK: Geography of the Erotic
Imagination* exhibition at Museum of Sex, 2006–2007.
Exhibition design by Pentagram. Photo courtesy Museum of Sex

Introduction

Turkey Man illustration by Frank Gresham

In 1994, a New York dominatrix told me about the client she called Turkey Man, a traveling businessman who hired her to come to his hotel room and act out an unusual erotic ritual. He had a large brown cardboard box that was about three feet tall, three feet wide and four feet deep, with crudely drawn knobs and dials on the front of the box to make it look like an oven. It had a door that could be opened and closed. When the dominatrix arrived, he stripped off his clothes, leaving on only his socks, then climbed into the box and lay down on his back, his feet sticking up and arms tucked in to his sides, like an over-sized oven-stuffer turkey.

The dominatrix would then close the makeshift oven and perform a voiceover for Turkey Man's fantasy. "I'm turning up the heat. I'm setting it at 325 degrees. You're going to get really, really hot. You'll feel like you're suffocating. You'll feel your skin crisping and turning brown. In about 15 minutes, I'll come back and baste you in your own gravy. In a few hours, I'll carve you up with my carving knife. Then I'm going to eat you!" She described to me her client's total immersion in his role as dinner-to-be. His eyes would glaze over and he would tremble from head to foot. He was in an ecstatic trance. If all the right psychic buttons were pushed and in the correct order, Turkey Man would ejaculate right then and there without any kind of genital stimulation.

*The most important sex organ is
the mind, and it's what goes on in
people's heads that interests me.*

You won't find much actual sex in this book.
This book is about the erotic; all of the extra
trappings, rituals, conversations, fantasies, role-
play, and costumes that might come before or
around sex acts. For many here, "doing it" is an
afterthought or even beside the point.

The most important sex organ is the mind,
and it's what goes on in people's heads that
interests me.

In addition to exploring individuals' personal
relationships to their kinks, I am also fascinated by the creation of nonconformist erotic
communities. What happens when someone
with an unusual erotic interest finds out they
are not alone? Once they do find like-minded
people, what benefits might there be to
making these social connections? Are there
patterns in the development of these tribes?

As far as he or she knew, he was the only person
with this particular kink.

Turkey Man was the inspiration for my
decades-long journey to explore the lesser-
known backwaters of the erotic universe. Since
then, I've been an enthusiastic collector of niche
pornography, attending peculiar erotic rituals and
tracking down unexplored sexual subcultures.
I've pursued obscure kinks the way an ethnog-
rapher might look for rare folktales, seeking first
contact with the latest tribes of sexual misfits. I
never cease to be amazed at the inventiveness of
the human sexual imagination, at our capacity
to eroticize everything from Disney characters
and B-movie monsters to baked beans, party
balloons, even the act of driving an automobile.

This book is different from other books you
may have seen about fetishes and kink. For
one thing, it's not aimed at being titillating.
Neither is it intended as an instruction manual for erotic play, though there are a few
suggestions. You won't find interviews with
anyone in the medical or psychoanalytic
fields, as the notion of kink as an illness or
symptom has been explored elsewhere. I have
steered clear of the political inasmuch as it is
possible or desirable to do so. Politics is only
welcome in these bedrooms if it makes things
more exciting.

This book is also not about me and my own
journey of self-discovery; bookstore shelves
are stuffed with women's personal exposés.
I'm not being coy. My sex life really isn't all
that interesting and I won't bore you with
it. My goal was to listen to individuals with
messy, complicated, and idiosyncratic erotic
needs, and learn how they have had to be
inventive in order to meet these needs. I will
describe rather than prescribe. I tried to let
people speak for themselves.

It is outside of the scope of this book to address gender, sexual orientation, trans identity, and asexuality—all essential topics, but not mine. I also freely admit the book is mostly cisgendered and heterosexual. This is the population I am part of, and so feel I have some right to speak about it. (I heartily recommend reading other authors on this subject. Please enjoy the bibliography at the end.) I have no desire to make kinky trans folk invisible. Rather, the trans community has enough misconceptions to deal with, without my adding on images of trans people doing weird stuff and freaking out the straights.

And this book only addresses the kinks it addresses and does not pretend to be a complete encyclopedia of unusual sex practices. (There is already a very interesting book of that name by Brenda Love.) I'm more interested in delving deeply into the complexity of certain kinks than superficially describing as many as I could find.

I also purposefully did not include what I call "the Big 3": pedophilia, necrophilia, and bestiality. They are not only illegal, their practice ignores the fundamental requirements of safe, sane, and consensual. These subjects deserve attention, but I would rather not tar all consensual kinks by association with these three. Admittedly, there are places in this book where the lines of consent and safety get blurry, and I do find those lines interesting.

Like most works of cultural anthropology, it is an attempt to enlist the exotic to illuminate the universal. By looking carefully at others, we can sometimes find patterns and themes that illuminate things hidden within ourselves. I hope that by taking a deeper look at how niche kinks work, I shed some light on the function of the erotic imagination in all of us.

I hope that by taking a deeper look at how niche kinks work, I shed some light on the function of the erotic imagination in all of us.

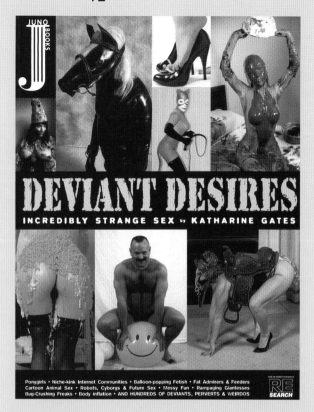

Cover of first edition of *Deviant Desires*,
published in 2000 by Juno Books

NOTES ON THE SECOND EDITION

The first edition of this book was the first to examine niche kinks like balloon fetish, giantess, ponyplay, and furries. After it came out in January 2000, I helped dozens of TV producers, magazines, and newspapers connect with the people I had interviewed. *Vanity Fair*, HBO's *Real Sex*, BBC, and Discovery Channel all later did features on these kinks with my help. One French magazine writer even translated chunks of my book word for word, then put her name on it. Thus, within only a few years of its publication, many of these kinks were old news. Furry in particular has become a major mainstream phenomenon.

In 2000, *Deviant Desires* documented a particular moment in the ongoing sexual revolution. The mid-1990s were the beginning of what I think of as the third sexual revolution. First came the feminist and gay rights movements, bringing awareness of gender and sexual orientation to the cultural mainstream. By 1996, technologi-

cal advances were making it possible for small groups of sexual minorities to connect and form communities. It's not so much that any of the kinks were new, but with the ready availability of desktop publishing software, anyone with a decent computer could afford to put together a zine and send it out to the world. The first erotic subcultures I explored were those I discovered from browsing zine racks in stores like See/Hear in New York or Atomic Books in Baltimore: *Equus Eroticus* for Ponyplay (see Chapter 2), *Giantess* for Macrophiles (Chapter 5), *Splosh!* for Messy Fun (Chapter 7), *Dimensions* for Feeders (Chapter 8) among many others.

The original editor and publisher, Andrea Juno, was one of the bright lights in this world of zines. She co-founded RE/Search books, a punk tabloid turned cultural tastemaker. Juno's *Modern Primitives* (1989) was, many believe, in great part responsible for the popular explosion of body modification and tattooing in the 1990s. Her *Incredibly Strange Music* (1993) had become a

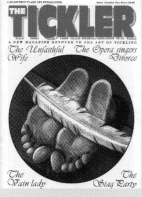

reference manual for anyone interested in collecting obscure vinyl. *Deviant Desires: Incredibly Strange Sex* was conceived as gonzo anthropology in the same vein: a funky patchwork of essays, interviews, illustrations and amateur photography, it abjured fashion-shoot slickness in favor of something more raw. Where readers might have expected titillation or a how-to manual, they found something else. People in the kink scene thought I didn't go far enough. People with no knowledge of kink thought I went too far.

For this revised and updated version of the book, I changed the subtitle. "Incredibly Strange Sex" now feels too freak-show. In 1999, everyone wanted to be a freak. The new subtitle, "A Tour of the Erotic Edge," is more precise. I cut dated material. I tried, where possible, to fix instances where I had not adequately examined my own sexual hangups. Many of the people I originally interviewed are either dead or have closed their businesses. Where they had valuable insights or relevant stories I kept them, especially those who

were founding fathers or mothers in the early days of their particular kink. This book might not provide as many surprises as it did 17 years ago, but I have added a few new kinks to freshen it up (gas pedal pumping, medical play, superhero, and cannibal play, among others).

It's amazing how much difference 17 years makes. In 2000, those households with internet dialed it up. In 2017, most of us have broadband access wherever we are. Isolation was the source of much suffering for people who feared they were alone in having a particular kink. Now it's pretty much a given that you will find someone out there with even more arcane eroticisms than your own.

It turns out Turkey Man isn't alone. In 2005, I met a bunch of other people whose fervent dream is to be transformed into someone else's meal… at least in fantasy. You'll have to wait until Chapter 10 to read about them.

Selections from the author's collection
of niche kink zines from the 1970s to the 1990s

Pedal Power:
Foot and Shoe Fetishes

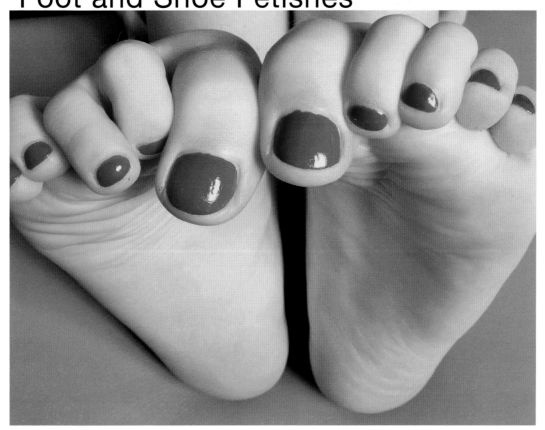

People often ask, "What's the most common fetish?"

In "Relative prevalence of different fetishes," published in the *International Journal of Impotence Research* in 2007, authors Scorolli, Ghirlanda, Enquist, Zattoni, and Jannin concluded that 47% of body-part fetishes are for feet.

In fact, feet surpass breasts, buttocks, and genitals as an erotic fixation. Bodily fluids came in second at a mere 9%, body shape (i.e., fat admiration) 9%, hair (head) 7%, muscles 5%, body modification 4%, and finally genitals 4%. Breasts came in at #10, under belly or navel and ethnicity, each at 3%. Legs and buttocks came up in the rear at only 2%.

Dian Hanson, former editor of *Leg Show* (circulation 200,000 at its peak), believes the foot is as natural an object of sexual desire as the breast. "I contend the foot is sexual in nature because it has apocrine sweat glands that produce glandular secretions like the armpits, the genital region, the anus, and around the nipples. These places all have the ability to arouse." Hanson points out that the pheromones from these glands communicate relatedness, fertility, and dominance. They can regulate female menstrual cycles and male arousal. Interestingly, humans have one of the highest concentrations of sweat glands of all mammals, and the most often eroticized body parts are also some of the sweatiest.

Not only do we respond subconsciously to the pheromones, we use odors as vital paths to memory and emotions. As infants, we form

Maya Kendrick's feet, from the foot porn site ATKingdom.com

Detail from the QuickFetish Mart
series, an imaginary walk-up store
for sniffing feet and dirty stockings by
DeviantArt user ffsf01

attachments to the odors and textures of our environment. Seeking out these familiar sensations is a matter of survival because they represent safety, food, and love. A child may reject a freshly washed plush toy because it no longer has its familiar, comforting funk. Odor stimuli bypass the cogitating forebrain and directly activate the memory and emotional centers, where they trigger conditioned feelings like comfort, fear, shame, and anger. In the erotic imagination, there's no such thing as a bad emotion; there are only ones that work for you and ones that don't.

My first year at summer camp, at 12, I was crushed by homesickness. In the dramatic way of preteens, I thought it would kill me. Then I found, discarded in the bottom of my camp trunk, a pair of my beloved older brother's gym socks. Sniffing them made me feel as if he were right there with me. I slept with them, tucked furtively into my pillow, for a week, until the homesickness abated. It wasn't sexual, but I was still ashamed. The socks comforted me, but the feelings they aroused were so intense and visceral they were frightening. I don't recall any genital tinglings, but then again, I was pretty unaware down there at the time. But if I had? Would I then have connected smelly socks with sexuality?

Foot fans don't necessarily want the feet to be smelly, by the way. Just the faintest whiff can do the trick for most. They want the feet well-groomed, clean, and nicely dressed; they may enjoy washing their partner's feet or giving pedicures as a form of erotic service and foreplay. Non-fetishists tend to assume some kind of disgust factor is at work in all foot fetishism; most cultures revile feet for their association with filth. When foot fetishists do prefer feet stinky and dirty, the conflict between a wired-in desire and a culturally driven resistance creates the kind of friction that makes them hot.

FOOT + LEATHER = SHOES

The authors of the 2007 study also examined the relative prevalence of erotic fixations on objects *associated* with the body. Objects worn on legs and buttocks (including stockings) took up 33% of all discussions in the Yahoo groups studied, and 32% of all groups were devoted to footwear. Only 12% were interested in underwear.

Stockings are particularly effective at absorbing and concentrating foot odors. Shoes not only have the special foot odor element but they also push the olfactory buttons for leather, another known touchy-feely smelly fetish material. Shoes coyly frame the foot, just as lingerie enhances the breasts or buttocks. Some straight male foot fetishists love to watch women dangle their shoes as a kind

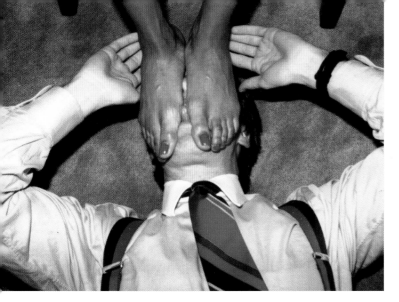

"Hi looking for guys to make videos of you jerking and cumming over pics of gf feet pm if interested and will send you pics!! Can do my wife's heels without her knowing they are taking cum and she's wearing them!"
—shoecumcpl, NY

of striptease. There's even a shoe manufacturer in Italy that specializes in creating high-heeled pumps with extra-short toe caps, so that the wearer's toe cleavage is shown to best advantage.

The style of shoe brings with it a whole slew of meanings, and opportunities for emotional intensification. Shoes send messages about the wearer's reproductive value. By far the most popular woman's shoe among straight men is the high-heeled pump; not only does it signify "adult female" more clearly than any other shoe, it also has the extra benefit of lifting and separating the ass cheeks—much in the way female apes display their vaginas when in heat—putting the wearer into position for mounting.

Yet there exist active message boards for any type of shoe you can imagine. Some men want to see women wearing nurse shoes, Dr. Scholl's orthopedic shoes, or tap shoes. The psychological oomph of the hurting/comforting nurse adds another layer of meaning on top of the core kink. In the gay male community, the most popular shoes are those that signify masculinity, such as athletic shoes or motorcycle boots, which bring the added frisson of the outlaw. Wesco Jobmasters are the go-to fetish footwear for the industrial hunk. But Oxford wing-tips (success, squareness) and Birkenstock sandals (freedom, peace) have their fans too. If there's a shoe style out there, someone gets off on it.

Ms. Zena and a foot slave.
Photo: Ron H. (see Chapter 5)

It's a bad idea to make assumptions about what someone means when they say they have a fetish. A woman could say she has a fetish for Manolo Blahniks, and simply mean she spends too much of her paycheck on the $1K+ shoes. Her compulsion to collect them might have an erotic component, but she probably doesn't use them for sexual purposes.

Someone else might say they have a shoe fetish and mean that seeing another woman wearing Manolos has their immediate attention–it's an enhancement to attractiveness. They might ask their partner to wear the shoes during sex: in certain sexual positions, the feet can be placed over the partner's nose and face to provide a full odor kick.

In BDSM play, the dominant may tape a pair of stinky shoes onto the face of the submissive for both breath play and humiliation. Some straight men might wear women's shoes to feel extra attractive and excited. When Manolos go on sale, the largest sizes—those suitable to be worn by cross-dressing men—are often the first to sell out. (It's important to be very clear that erotic cross-dressing or gender play is not the same thing as transgender. One is specifically for erotic purposes, the other is a core identity.)

Not all kinks are fetishes. Kink is the use of props, costumes, and role-play to enhance partner intimacy. Fetish is when the props, costumes, or role-play replace *the partner and the intimacy.*

4 Levels of Fetishism, illustration by Ned Sonntag

Yet another person may mean that they collect huge numbers of used Manolos, masturbate with them by fucking the instep, and have no interest in sex with a partner at all. The illustration at left, based loosely on the work of Havelock Ellis, shows some of these distinctions.

I've met foot and shoe fans on all parts of the fetish spectrum, and all I can say is that some end up with a hardcore fetish while others just use shoes for extra spice. Some move between different levels in their lifetimes depending on factors like relationship status or anxiety about work. Some people find little appeal in the bewildering complexity of intimate human contact. Objects and fantasy narratives fill a need that other people, for whatever reason, cannot.

Although the psychiatric establishment was in some ways founded on Sigmund Freud's fascination with finding a causal relationship between childhood presexuality and adult neurosis, this book is not concerned with medicalized narratives of kink. Self-identified origin stories are fun, and plenty are shared in these pages, but trying to solve the mystery of what causes fetishism or kinkiness misses the point. We no longer ask why someone is homosexual. We agree nothing went wrong. The better question is how does one find a meaningful and fulfilling erotic life in a world that continues to condemn sexual nonconformity?

True fetishism is basically a form of solo sex, a kind of auto-sexuality. Almost everyone masturbates, and it is common for adults to keep their solo sex life limited to images and fantasies that remain largely unchanged since puberty. Some people keep their solo sex lives and their partner sex lives separate, but many kinky folk consciously seek to share their deepest erotic selves with others.

To my way of thinking, not all kinks are fetishes. Kink is the use of props, costumes, and role-play to enhance partner intimacy. Fetish is when the props, costumes, or role-play *replace* the partner and the intimacy.

FEET AND SHOES IN ACTION: GAS PEDAL PUMPING

Feet are a perfect example of a "core kink"—the base material around which more elaborate layers of meaning and drama can be built. Most people with object-oriented kinks don't just want that object to sit there passively. They want it to DO something. You'll see several other examples of foot-related niche kinks throughout this book (see Chapter 6 on trample and crush), but for me the gas pedal pumping crowd is a perfect example of how people can build rich narrative dramas to intensify the visceral power of a core kink.

In 1996, Dian Hanson told me about one of her *Leg Show* readers who would write letters requesting she do a pictorial of a woman in red slingback pumps pressing the gas pedal of a particular model of American sports car. It just so happens that the gas pedal of this model passes through a hole in the floorboards, so you can see the pavement below. "He wanted to see her shoe press the pedal in and out, like the motions of a penis during intercourse." It had to be that shoe and that car, or it just didn't get him off.

You might think that was a niche interest, but there are thousands of hours of videos out there devoted to images of men or women pumping gas pedals. As a kink, it's a pretty lively one. Sometimes the drivers are revving an engine, sometimes they're grinding gears, sometimes they're cranking and failing to start an engine.

In other scenes, the brakes fail and the driver must tap the brakes repeatedly in a panic. The title of the videos are very clear on exactly what car it is and often what type of shoe: "Blahnik red strappy sandal pumping Chevy Impala '57." "Jetta driving 115MPH in pink Nikes." "Well-used Reebok sneaker cranking in distress." "Brown Oxford wing-tip stuck and spinning in mud; BMW S-Class." Each of the elements brings along a world of cultural, economic, emotional connotators, our love affair with cars on a whole new level. There's never any nudity–maybe some breasts jiggling inside tight shirts. The pumping gestures and the heightened feelings of peril, excitement, mastery, or frustration are the point.

I found Karl through his website, pedalpumping.org and his ebook, *Pedal Pumping—The Fetish*. Karl fondly recalls his "Aha!" moment when he was about nine and his older brother and his brother's girlfriend took him shopping in her 1988 Mercury Tracer Hatchback. "I remember vividly that I was in the back seat on the passenger's side where I had a clear view of her driving." He remembers specific details: she was wearing 1980s-style clothing and white Nikes. "My brother told her to hurry up… I watched her push the gas pedal to the floor. She had a standard, so she would let

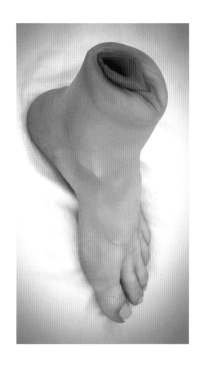

The Vajankle, from sinthetics.com. It is unclear whether this product is successful with foot fetishists

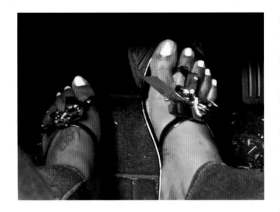

Still from video by Big Mo
Ebony Shoeplay

Still from "A Scenic Dive Through
Snow" by carstuckgirls.com

Still from "Pedal Pumping Cole Hahn
& Gold Toe Socks" by bootman

off to shift and then back hard on the gas pedal again." He watched the speedometer rise, his own libido revving in tandem. "Her foot stayed hard on the pedal after she was done shifting; the needle had gone past 85MPH and was pointing down past the numbers shown." Over 25 years later, and it still has to be specifically ordinary-looking women in Nikes. He knows his preference for athletic shoes maybe puts him in with 1% of the pedal pumper fans out there, but he didn't choose his kink and it works for him.

Karl is a revving and speeding fan, and wants to see a masterful, fearless woman showing full control of her machine. Best is when you can watch the tachometer's needle rise to the red zone over and over as the driver switches gears. The car is at the driver's mercy, engines squealing in distress, tires spinning, all to bring excitement to a full pitch. The videos are always shot from the passenger's point of view. If the pumping is a visual analogue to intercourse, then the driver is on top, pushing her partner into overdrive. In partner play, the driver may drive the car, pump the gas to max out the car's speed, and simultaneously give the passenger a hand job, her hand mimicking the motions of her feet.

Another pumping subfetish is cranking. Crankers want to see a man or woman having difficulty getting the car started, and grinding the starter while pumping. J Mottola is a cranker who volunteered this origin story: In 1972, when he was about 12 years old, a pretty and friendly neighbor would drive him to and from school in her 1966 Chevy Impala. "I would eagerly walk to her house in the morning, timing it right to see her come out the front door of her house as she clicked on her heels to the car." He would get into the back seat and lean up between the seats so he could watch her struggle to start the car. "It took on average three tries and about a dozen pumps before the car came to life." Then she would let it run while she adjusted herself in the seat. "Her right foot would shift to the gas pedal as she would rev it four or five times and away we would go. I WAS HOOKED!!"

One memorable day, she left him in the car while she got groceries. While she was in the store, he used an umbrella to pump the gas pedal. When she returned, he watched carefully as she inserted the key in the ignition and pumped the gas pedal with her high heels. She took her shoe off her right foot, and after three barefoot pumping and flooring efforts, he orgasmed. "I was afraid, embarrassed, and hooked, and could not take my eyes off of her stocking foot holding, pumping, slamming the gas pedal to the floor." Once the car started, the woman sighed with relief and laid her head back in the seat, as if it was good for her too. Ever

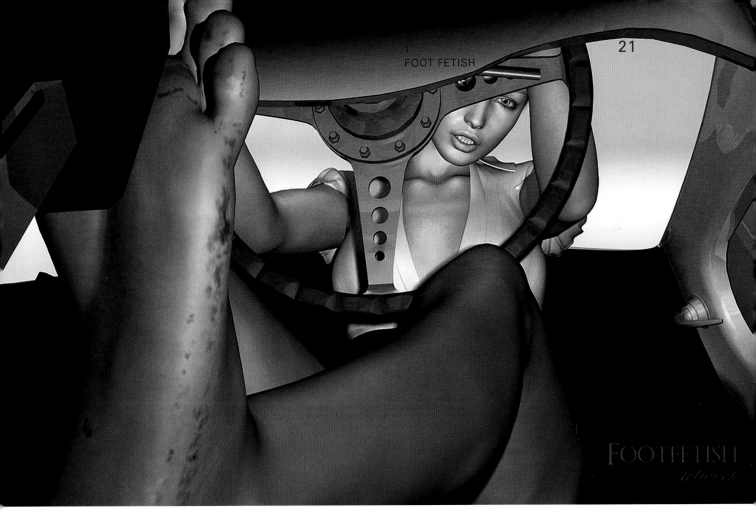

FOOTFETISH

POV computer image by ffsf01, on DeviantArt

since, for Mottola, it has to be bare feet and pump-starting.

Brake failures excite another subset of the pumping crowd. The driver might be going full-speed down the highway when the brake pedal suddenly stops working. (Karl insists that these videos are simulated, as actual brake failure would be too dangerous to film, but some makers do appear to push the limits of risk.) He explains, "The male typically becomes aroused by the female reaching high anxiety levels from the car not stopping. The female will usually become very vocal or exhibit panic/crying while she pleads with the car to stop." The car, like the sex partner, is out of control, helpless in the face of its trajectory towards orgasm. Many of these videos simulate crashes at the end—an orgasmic explosion.

And, while Karl's own interest is in female drivers, and himself as the invisible male passenger/

viewer, he's seen videos representing almost every possible combination of sexual orientation and gender: "male to male, male to cross-dresser, male to transgender, female to male, and female to female."

A small number of pumper fans prefer their drivers barefoot. This can add the extra sense of danger as apparently some states give out fines for driving barefoot. Thus the driver is being reckless or rebellious against the anti-barefoot driving (anti-sex) authorities.

Another subfetish of the gas pedal crowd is known as "stuck." The car is mired in mud or snow and the tires spin. The driver might switch between reverse and forward gears trying to get traction. Her fear or stress is exciting, as is the motion of her foot going back and forth between gas and brake: the driver is shown frantically trying to get the car going but repeatedly

Stills from a typical car stuck in mud video, note inset of shoe as it pumps ineffectually

"Her right foot would shift to the gas pedal as she would rev it four or five times and away we would go. I WAS HOOKED!"
—J Mottola

failing. She might be flooding the engine with gas and her pumping is so strenuous that her entire body is bouncing up and down. Or the car is stuck in mud and the driver keeps getting it stuck deeper. The driver, the car, her clothes, and her shoes get covered in mud (see Chapter 7 for more about the wet and messy kink). If the pumping is the act of intercourse at a symbolic remove, then the driver's strong emotional reactions to sexual frustration, the car failing to get it up, become a sexual drama.

Like most porn, pumper videos have only as much plot as is necessary to establish the dramatic tension. A healthy young woman late for her gym class. A woman angry from her breakup taking out her rage on the car's transmission. A master of the universe in wingtips in a rush to a business meeting. There are regional preferences: Southern folk prefer their drivers in pickup trucks. There are pedal pumping message forums just for school buses.

Each of these elements—the shoe, the car, the economic status of the wearer—adds a unique flavor to the narrative. Some pumper fans want to try all the different flavors in the smorgasbord of pedal pumping. Others demand the same thing every time. Much like with sex: some folks want it the same, while others crave variety.

In 1995, Karl decided to reach out and find other men with his interests. He was an early adopter of the internet, so he built one of the first websites where people could send him photos to share for free. In 1996, he added a membership area. "I started making a fair amount of money, but other sites started to pop up as competition." So in 1997, Karl figured out how to convert VHS tapes to digital and sell downloads. As payment for providing the gateway for video producers to sell the videos, he would get personalized videos from the models. In 2001, he began producing his own videos and selling them on Clips4sale, a portal used by many fetish producers to sell their material. One Australian gas pedal pumping

THE EROTIC EQUATION

FOOTFETISH
Artwork

In *The Erotic Mind* (1996), Jack Morin, PhD, interviewed hundreds of his sex therapy clients, trying to understand the common elements of peak sexual experiences. From straight and gay, vanilla to kinky, cisgendered, trans, and everyone else, he found what made any fantasy or scene truly exciting was the tension between desire and obstacle.

DESIRE + OBSTACLE = EXCITEMENT

In vanilla sex, we might find the process of seduction makes the prize more thrilling. Cultural taboos or sexual hangups provide additional obstacles that can add excitement. Making out in the back of your parent's car was extra thrilling because it was forbidden. For some people, sex before marriage is naughty enough. As long as you find just the right power balance between the forces, you generate pleasure. This mechanism works like a hydroelectric dam: Pressure builds up behind the obstacle, turns the turbines, and creates energy. Similarly, the erotic imagination incorporates narratives of pressure and resistance to generate sexual energy. Individuals have their own personal "sweet spot" where the tension hits just the right level to charge up their excitement.

Morin's equation works on many levels. Lingerie is more erotic than bare breasts because it forms a barrier to the desired body part. If the bra is tight, the body part strains against it and threatens to pop

out. If the briefs are small, the engorged penis presses against the fabric, threatening to rip through the obstacle. The tension adds to the interest. In the same way, for a foot fetishist, looking at a foot encased tightly in a beautiful shoe, or watching a bare foot press against the resisting gas pedal is the ultimate thrill.

PRESSURE + RESISTANCE = EXCITEMENT

My variant on the "Erotic Equation" is based on my interviews with many hundreds of people with niche kinks and my observations of the structure of erotic narratives. If you reduce almost any erotic fantasy down to its most basic structure, at its center is a simple mechanism of pressure and resistance, tension and release. In the world of kink, this equation can be found on every level of the fantasy, from arousal via physical pressure to the tension between one's fantasies and cultural taboos. In sexual fantasy and sexual play this pressure may be physical, such as tight embraces, tight clothing, trampling underfoot or pushing a gas pedal. It may be interpersonal pressure, such as seduction, dominance, or submission. Or it may be social pressure, like sexual taboos and our resistance to them.

I invite you to discover the Erotic Equation as it applies throughout this book.

Pedal pumping and macro combined
(see Chapter 5) by ffsf01 on DeviantArt

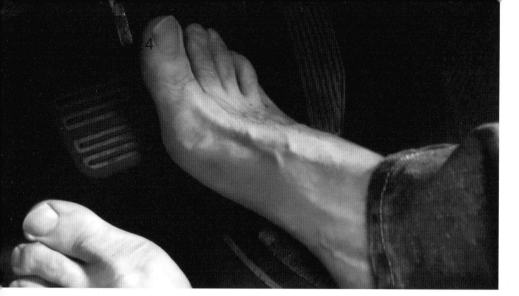

Still from "Pedal Pumping Bare Feet"
by Bootman540, YouTube

GAS PEDAL PUMPING IN BRIEF

TERMINOLOGY:
pumpers, crankers

CORE KINK:
foot

MAJOR THEMES:
power play

SUBTHEMES:
peril

SUBKINKS:
cranking, stuck

RELATED KINKS:
crush (see Chapter 6)

EROTIC EQUATION:
pressure on gas pedal

video producer told me that in his 14 years in the business he's made over $275K profit.

Custom videos are where the best money is. A woman with an Instagram account and the #pedalpumping hashtag can charge between $50 and $250 for a single custom 10-minute video. The highest dollars go to those willing to do the riskier scenes of speeding or create the illusion of brakes failing.

There's plenty of free content out there, too. Since it's not explicit and there's no nudity, you can find all kinds of pumping videos on YouTube, some of which garner hundreds of thousands of hits apiece or more. Some purveyors are proud that their kink is so nonthreatening; in fact, Pedalvamp, an Italian maker of pumping and cranking videos, refused to be interviewed for this book. He felt he didn't want to be associated with those "too deviating stuffs."

For Karl, this erotic focus is simply one part of his life. His wife is one of his models and she enjoys that she can now afford to buy any shoes she wants. "My wife has well over 50 pairs of running sneakers, thanks to me!"

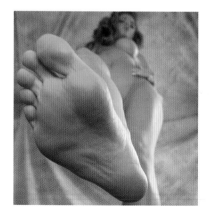

For more variations of the foot fetish,
see Chapters 5 & 6. Photo: *Leg Show*

Sidekink:
Hair

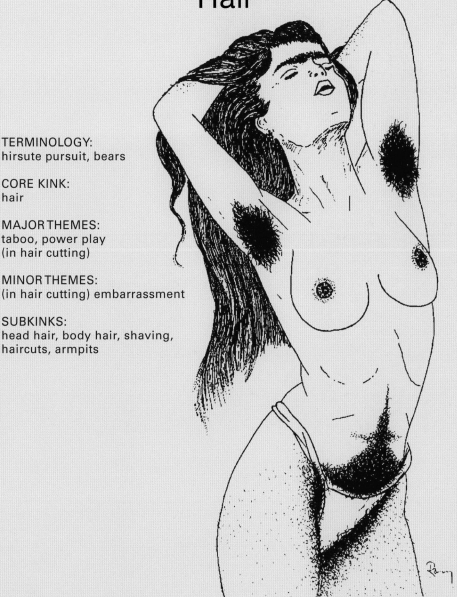

TERMINOLOGY:
hirsute pursuit, bears

CORE KINK:
hair

MAJOR THEMES:
taboo, power play
(in hair cutting)

MINOR THEMES:
(in hair cutting) embarrassment

SUBKINKS:
head hair, body hair, shaving,
haircuts, armpits

Hair captures pheromones; the hairiest parts of the body are often the ones with the most scent glands. On men, body hair represents masculinity; big, hairy men (bears) have been a significant subculture within the gay community since the 1970s. Head hair fans may wish to be whipped with long hair or have their penises wrapped with the hair. Some people eroticize particular hair colors, especially women with red hair.

Hirsute pursuit is a kink for lots of female body hair. *Hair to Stay* was a glossy zine of the 1990s that showed unusually hirsute women brave enough not to depilate. One reader expressed his ecstasy at seeing the wind riffle the blonde arm hair on a desirable woman. Hairy women are seen as powerful rule breakers.

Shaving and haircuts have their own fans. *Yankee Clipper* was a homemade zine of the 1990s devoted to stories and images of women being shaved bald. Shaving can also be an erotic act in adult baby play.

Illustration from *Hair to Stay*,
Winter 1997

Hair to Stay, Winter 1997

Ponyplay Comes Out of the Stables

Paul Reed, publisher of *Equus Eroticus* magazine, riding PonyLynn. Photo: Eric Kroll, ericdavidkroll.blogspot.com

I first learned about ponyplay in 1997 when I purchased the premiere issue of *Equus Eroticus*, "a publication for and about the world of pony girls and boys." The cover featured a woman in full-body leather, pony ears, bridle and bit, hoof-like platform boots, a fluffy blonde tail sticking out from her backside, and stirrups dangling from her waist. In an inset, a woman rode a saddled pony-girl wearing a pretty pink satin dress, dark stockings, white pumps, and matching white kneepads. Inside the magazine I found images of men in saddles, women and men pulling carts, first-person narratives of human pony dressage routines, and fantasy fiction about being transformed into a human pony. The editor's note explained that, "used as a form of sexual bondage or foreplay, this erotic activity can result in a special physical intimacy between loving persons." Many of my kinky friends had never heard of it.

Ponyplay boasts the oldest and noblest pedigree of all the niche kinks. For as long as humans and horses have lived together, people have explored the symbolism of human/animal transformation and the metaphor of humans harnessing animal power. Cave paintings at Lascaux in France suggest that Neolithic shamans impersonated horses in rituals of the hunt. The first clear representation of humans being forced to act as beasts of burden is a 4,000-year-old Assyrian frieze depicting a king riding into a conquered city on a chariot pulled by captive human ponies. Ancient Greek satirists claimed that the philosopher Aristotle delighted in giving ponyback rides to his domineering wife. In fact, early psychiatrists often referred to ponyplay as "The Aristotelian Perversion."

LA Pony and Critter Club Summer Cart Pull and Romp at Mile Square Park, 2015. Pony: Cardholder. Photo: Trainer Pollux

Now, 20 years since the first issue of *Equus Eroticus*, ponygirls, ponyboys, and their human puppy friends are a ubiquitous part of pride parades from Scottsdale, Arizona, to Sydney, Australia. Fetish events are incomplete if they don't boast a well-groomed human critter or two accompanied by their proud human trainer.

What's remarkable about ponyplay is its rich variety of possibilities for play, creativity, and sexuality. Quite a few ponygirls and ponyboys get their biggest thrills by trotting themselves out to grand competitions featuring variations on equestrian sports like racing, dressage, and choreographed show pony performances. For some, ponyplay is a variation of BDSM (Bondage and Discipline, Sadism and Masochism), a blanket term for a wide range of erotic practices involving consensual power play and the manipulation of sensory and emotional states. Ponies may not speak or use their hands, so bondage comes into ponyplay through the use of arm sleeves, harnesses, bridles, and bits. The ponygirl or ponyboy might be "owned" in a formal consensual arrangement; both human and pony discuss in advance all limits to punishment or sexual contact, negotiating their desires and expectations before every play session.

Few ponies consider their human-to-animal transformation to be a form of humiliation. Rather, most human ponies are proud of their animal alter egos; they see themselves as noble, beautiful, and powerful creatures, a treasured pet and an exquisite object of desire. They develop full pony personas by selecting their breed and pony name, and spend a great deal of time and money amassing beautiful costumes they wear out to public events.

Ponyplay is deeply erotic. It is sometimes—but not always—used as foreplay to more or less conventional sex between "human" and "pony" or two "ponies," but never between humans and real animals. The excitement comes from transformation, power exchange, and a kind of do-it-yourself make-believe world. For its participants, ponyplay is a perfect combination of childlike playacting, romantic drama, and erotic expression.

THE OTHER PONY CLUB, ENGLAND

In 1997, for the first stop on my tour of human pony culture, I visited Sir Guy Masterleigh of The Other Pony Club in Hereford, England. Perhaps I had been fooled by his aristocratic pseudonym, so I was a bit surprised when he picked me up at the train station in a well-used station wagon. Sir Guy wore what you might expect from a former defense industry engineer: khakis, plaid shirt with pens in the breast pocket, and Oxford shoes. He had a very tidy beard and a boyish but firm manner.

Phyllis Riding Aristotle, 1620, woodcut by
Hans Baldung Grien

French erotic postcard, probably from the 1930s

Raven Darknights and trainee
Ebony Midnight. Long Beach Pride,
2015. Photo by Iggy

As we drove past some 13th-century battlements, Sir Guy enthusiastically described his weekend hobby of dressing up and participating in historic reenactments as an official during the British Civil War. We parked behind a strip mall and entered an unmarked door to the cluttered and unerotic offices of The Other Pony Club. One of his female volunteers prepared us some instant coffee, and Sir Guy gave me the brief history of his personal interest in BDSM. When he was about 12, he read a number of children's books by an author named Arthur Ransome. The books were about English children playing together in the Lake District: "It's all very innocent, except that the kids are taking each other captive all the time." When he looked for other works by the same author, he found a whole different set of books that were about the author's experiences in pre-Revolutionary China. These dealt in some depth with the gruesome punishments that were meted out to prisoners, including putting them in cages and stocks and various other tortures. "It wasn't a 'scene' book, but he was spending a little too much time talking about the penal customs and the penalties than was altogether healthy!" Little Guy had discovered Dominance & Submission, which would turn into his lifelong avocation.

BDSM remained a part-time hobby throughout Sir Guy's college years and his successful career as an engineer in the British

Ponygirl illustration by John Willie,
Bizarre Magazine, 1946

From *The Muir Report*, Miss Prim's Muir
Academy kit list and rulebook

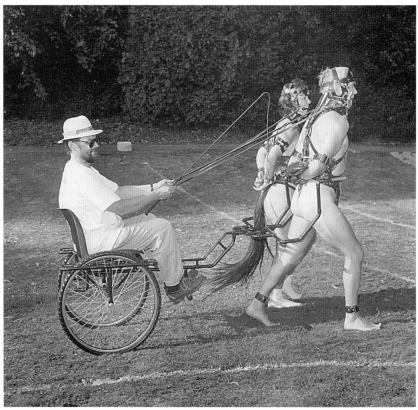

"They think, 'Well. I've been a maid, I've been a slave, I've been a schoolboy, let's try being a pony—see if it's any different.'"
—*Sir Guy Masterleigh*

defense industry. In 1987, he and his then-girlfriend (later wife) decided to start an erotic role-playing business called Miss Prim's Muir Reform Academy. The Academy offered weekend retreats for adults interested in reliving the humiliations of their childhood in the English public school system. Miss Prim treated them as schoolchildren, and they conformed to strict dress codes and plenty of complex rules and regulations. Careful attention was paid to proper uniforms and etiquette, and frequent and enthusiastic canings were meted out at the slightest infraction. No sexual contact was allowed in any form between schoolmasters and students, or between students and each other. Even masturbation was punished—probably adding to the repressive verisimilitude of the whole experience. (As far as I know, there's no such role-play reform school in the USA; perhaps it's the combination of native Victorian prudery and discipline-oriented British childrearing practices that makes this scenario so popular in the UK.)

When Margaret Thatcher's general layoffs put him out of work in the early 1990s, Sir Guy decided to start his own BDSM business based on ponyplay. Between its inception in 1993 and its closure in 2014, The Other Pony Club grew to several hundred members worldwide. The majority lived in the UK, but there were a few in continental Europe and the US and a scattering in Africa,

Sir Guy in action. Illustration: Fopp,
The Other Pony Express

Sir Guy with trainees. Photo: Ziegfried Brahm

the Middle East, Far East, and Australia. For a small fee, members received access to The Other Pony Express newsletter and website, photocopied erotic fiction chapbooks, and custom human pony equipment. Sir Guy also offered private training sessions for would-be ponygirls and ponyboys and organized occasional "Pony Weekends" in the countryside featuring racing competitions and barn accommodations for the human ponies and the occasional human piggy or human puppy.

The Other Pony Club (TOPC) was Sir Guy's full-time job and he just about broke even financially. People sometimes assume that these fetish types are making money hand over fist, but often, as in Sir Guy's case, it was more of a labor of love than a capitalist venture.

Sir Guy described his clientele: "They have imagination and strength of character; they're very rarely boring. They're people with complexity, and with depth. Usually they have a third degree of education and intelligence; they're wonderful people but very varied." TOPC membership was one-quarter cisgendered female, a far higher proportion of women than in most BDSM groups. Women interested in ponyplay are evenly split between would-be ponies and would-be trainers. According to Sir Guy, the women tended to be more active and involved in the scene than the men, and this helped to partially redress the gender imbalance. TOPC included several gay men and some bisexual men, though most of them were apparently game to "play horse" with partners of either gender.

Of the men, two-thirds preferred to play the submissive horse role and only one-third wished to be masters, trainers, or owners. About half of the would-be ponies wanted to be "geldings"—i.e., men costumed and treated as female horses wearing wigs, makeup and high heels under their pony equipment, a far higher proportion of cross-dressers than one finds in the American ponyplay scene.

According to Sir Guy, British ponyplay is almost exclusively devoted to cart ponies as opposed to riding ponies or show ponies. TOPC only had two members interested in being or playing with riding ponies and both were American men. As far as he knows, choreographed show pony performances are an exclusively American phenomenon. Sir Guy described a typical British-style cart pony training session: "Quite recently I had a woman who was brought here by her husband with the express purpose of making her a pony. I offered them coffee, I showed them the equipment, she took her clothes off, I harnessed her up, checked that everything fitted and everything was complete. She was wearing nothing but sneakers, underwear, harness, and the cape." Most training

PONYPLAY EQUIPMENT

Bridle: may include brass plaque for pony name, blinkers, pony ears, plume

Bit: may be made of leather, rubber, or metal

Tail: butt plug version optional. Tail may be dyed to match the pony's natural hair color

Arm restraints: for cart ponies and show ponies only. (Two-legged riding ponies must have free use of their arms to maintain balance.) German style: hands are locked at the small of the back. Spanish style: locked at the hips, facing forward. English style: attached at the front

Halter or corset: can be used to affix hands and make them useless

Cart: two-wheeled, preferably light and easily dismantled

Saddle: (riding ponies only) small "real" pony saddles with padding can be used. Two-legged ponies may have custom angled saddles made for them. Some male two-legged ponies wear backpack-style saddles

Kneepads: essential for four-legged riding ponies

Hoof gloves or mitts: another way to disable the hands

Hoof boots: optional for show ponies. They can make two-legged riding and cart-pulling difficult and dangerous, though

Whips and crops: optional

Hobbles: bungee cords or ropes may be used to limit the pony's steps while walking two-legged

Twitch: an optional disciplinary device that comes in many forms. It is either a clamp or looped chain that can be used to pinch a body part such as nipples, lips, or cock to get the pony's immediate and undivided attention

Ponyboy Silver Spurs and driver on an
English country road. Photo: Ziegfried
Brahm

sessions begin with some kind of grooming (undressing, examining and/or brushing, and caressing the pony) and tacking (putting on the costume). Since the pony as a rule can't use its hands, it is the trainer's job to put on the harness and bridle.

After the grooming and tacking, Sir Guy took the woman out into a secluded area of the countryside—with the husband tagging along. "We secured her arms behind her back so that she was quite helpless, and then we put a big cape over the top of her, and took her down to the woods." A pony's arms are usually bound or covered in large mitts to prevent human-like hand movements, and for the pleasure of bondage. "We harnessed her up to the cart and went out for a spin for a few miles. I trained her to respond to the reins and the whip. At the end of the day she'd enjoyed herself very much. She went off in a highly excited state with her husband."

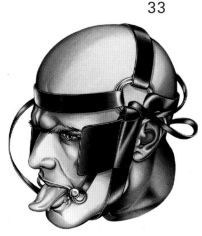

Snaffleman illustration René Habermacher

For some of Sir Guy's visitors, ponyplay was simply another spicy BDSM role-play option to try out. As Sir Guy put it, "They think, 'Well. I've been a maid, I've been a slave, I've been a schoolboy, let's try being a pony—see if it's any different.'" There is a natural translation between the equipment used in SM play and the equipment used to administer punishment to "real" horses. A whip translates into a riding crop; leg cuffs become hobbles; butt plugs are butt plug tails; blindfolds are blinkers; gags become bits; and nipple clips or clothespins become a "twitch"—a painful clamp sometimes used on horses' noses to make them behave. Ponygirl and ponyboy costumes work well for those with fetishes for leather and bondage; pony harnesses work like restrictive corsets; bridles and halters are similar to leather restraints; and the extremely high-heeled fetish shoe has its translation in the uncanny-looking "hoof boots" worn by some human ponies.

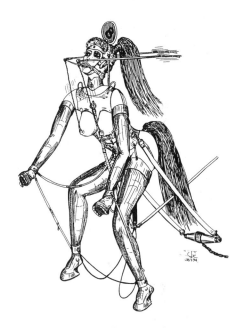

Fantasy ponygirl tack. Illustration: JG-Leathers

In traditional BDSM, much of the excitement comes from the tension between the wills of the dominant and the submissive, a dynamic, evolving exchange of power and trust. The dominant and the submissive may try to ratchet up excitement by pushing both their limits to the edge, by trying to overcome obstacles in the form of endurance, self-control, and mastery. In ponyplay, rigorous pony training becomes a form of control, an obstacle to the uninhibited animal self. This is ponyplay's version of the Erotic Equation.

For many human ponies, ponyplay is closely connected to a childhood fascination for horses. "One of the best ponygirls I've had recalls going out in the country with a friend and actually getting down on all fours and running around the field, jumping logs, and

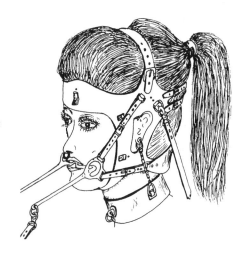

Harness illustration: JG-Leathers. jg-leathers.com

"*People don't want to
have the responsibility
of thinking about what
to do next... They
want it simple: Pull on
this rein—turn this way.
Pull on that rein—go
that way... They can
just be empty.*"
—Sir Guy Masterleigh

trying to see how it works. She remembers somehow getting excited playing these completely innocent games." Their horsey fascination had a distinctly sexual/romantic flavor; it's as if the horse
represented their own burgeoning animal sexuality—a sexuality
little girls are taught they must control and tame at all costs. By
keeping a horse identity (or by training a real horse) girls might be
able to own their sexuality without risking social condemnation.

For the ponies, at least, playing relieves them of adult human responsibilities and pressures. Guy explained: "People don't want to
have the responsibility of thinking about what to do next. They
don't even want to be told, because that means they have to think
about what's been said. They want it simple: Pull on this rein—turn
this way. Pull on that rein—go that way. They don't have to think;
they can just react. They can just be empty." In some ways, being an
English ponyboy or ponygirl is like being a kid again, with all of its
advantages and disadvantages. "Of course, they also love the reassur-
ance, the petting, and the sugar lumps."

The Other Pony Club's Pony Weeks in secluded farms in the Welsh
countryside offered would-be ponies an opportunity for full immersion; paying members could play in an animal or human role to
their hearts' content. These events had a distinct pseudo-aristocratic

Grand Champions Ms. Adelasia, Ponyboy Stormy
and Ponyboy Rusty at Camp Crucible 2012.
Stormy and Rusty are a bonded team. Photo: William

air, and guests were expected to wear evening dress at supper—unless, that is, they were eating their supper in the barn with the other animals. Depending on the rules set out in advance, human ponies could sleep in the barn on straw laid out for the purpose; eat oatmeal from buckets without using their hands; and urinate and defecate in their stalls. If they wished, ponygirls and ponyboys could participate in a slew of equestrian activities, such as racing, cart pulling, and vigorous public grooming. Cart racing competitions were a high point, and everyone got in on the game. For solitary male ponies, this was an opportunity to strut their stuff and try to attract the rare female trainer. An almost peacock-like exhibitionism prevailed, especially among the male ponies. At one event, a man dolled himself up as a multicolored body-painted human zebra.

Pony Weeks attracted not only human ponies and their trainers, but also would-be human puppies, piggies, and kittens. "Shep," a human who enjoys playing an Old English Sheepdog, regularly attended these events in costume and in role. Shep hung out with the ponies, played fetch, ate from his dog bowl, and howled for attention.

Domesticated animals appear to be much more popular than wild animals for BDSM role-play, probably because they offer more models for power games between "human" and "beast." It's a more relaxed form of power play, and individual creativity is far more welcome here than in more rigid BDSM scenes. Sir Guy's imprint, Masterleigh Books, published a number of fantasy stories featuring women becoming "cows," complete with milking devices and fattening diets; human foxes being hunted in a big foxhunt; and science fiction stories about body morphing.

As Sir Guy described the Pony Week events, it struck me that ponyplay is an extraordinarily sociable erotic subculture. The base metaphor that ponyplayers are working from—equestrian sports and horsey activities—are essentially very group-oriented. People attracted to ponyplay find opportunities for outdoor activities with other ponies and humans. Some ponies might be attracted to the idea of just running around in a corral with other ponies and nibbling on the grass, while others may want minimal physical contact, so they present themselves as cart horses. Whereas the "slave and master" scenario or the "lady and maid" scenario might suggest activities in one's basement or dungeon, the equestrian metaphor is wide open to fun outdoor sports. For Sir Guy's Pony Week participants, it was about coming out in the open and being publicly playful. From the photographs it's clear this made the players exuberant. Sir Guy added: "If you let go of the pony's reins a moment, they will take off, they'll bolt, just because they fancy

PONYPLAY SAFETY TIPS

Establish and reconfirm a safeword or signal before starting play. Some riding ponies use a double-tap of the right fore-hoof as a signal for the rider to dismount. The rider must comply immediately.

Be aware of your own limits. This is a strenuous activity.

Ponies with back problems should stick with cart- and show-pony styles.

Establish rules beforehand on limits to corporal punishment and sexual contact.

Ponies must make grooms, trainers, or owners aware of their dietary restrictions. For example, diabetic ponies should not be fed sugar cubes.

Four-legged riding: most ponies find that having the rider sit on the pelvis—rather than in the middle of the waist—helps to distribute weight over the legs and knees.

Four-legged ponies must always use kneepads.

When using metal bits, be aware of the possibility of dental damage. Some ponies wrap their metal bits with leather or rubber to protect their teeth. Leather can contain toxic chemicals and rubber can cause allergic reactions.

Be aware of your surroundings. When playing inside, survey the floor for tacks, splinters, or obstructions before play. When playing outside, know the terrain.

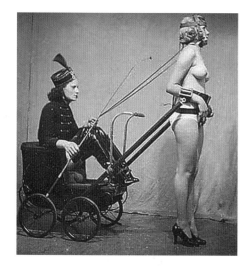

the other side of the field. They'll make you have to run after them to catch them again!"

This sense of freedom seems especially liberatory in the light of England's draconian sex laws. Operation Spanner was the name of an offensive carried out by police in the UK city of Manchester in 1987, as a result of which a group of gay men were convicted of assault occasioning actual bodily harm for their involvement in consensual sadomasochism over a ten-year period. In 1990, a number of gay men in the UK were given prison sentences for engaging in consensual SM activities that resulted in bruises or cuts "of a lasting nature" or "more than trifling"—less serious than injuries common in rugby and football, but, in this case, criminal. That these same laws were rarely applied to heterosexual BDSM activities makes clear that homophobia drove the laws. Nevertheless at the time of this writing, this precedent has not been revisited and continues to oppress nonconformist sexual play in the UK. It is a precedent upon which further law is built, such as provisions that ban possession of "extreme pornographic images."

Sir Guy always made sure that ponies had the power to refuse to consent to any act at the Pony Weeks and other private events. Ponygirls and ponyboys were strongly encouraged to set guidelines in advance of what they are willing to endure and what they wanted to experience. Sex between human and pony was only allowed if the pony agreed to it beforehand, and only with potential partners agreed to beforehand. Because ponies can't verbalize their wishes and owners can't always be present, Sir Guy created a logbook that the ponies affixed to their harnesses explaining who may do what, how often and when.

Sexual acts did happen, but in Sir Guy's experience people attracted to ponyplay see eroticism as a more diffuse, overall experience which does not have to end in orgasm. "If the players (both doms and subs) wanted the subs to simply be sex toys, they would be playing 'Sheik and Concubine' or the female dominant equivalent of harem games. It is much easier to get volunteers for that anyway. So why would anybody go to the whole pony paraphernalia if all you want is straight or kinky sex?" Ponyplayers get turned on, but use the sexual energy in other ways.

When I press for more sex details, Sir Guy explains that where the sex mostly happened was in the situations where a human has "contracted" to be an animal for longer periods of time under a lifestyle dominant. "They've been required to fellate their masters, suck their mistresses (both genders doing both) and/or been bug-

Vintage ponyplay. Source unknown

Shep the Old English Sheepdog, at one of
The Other Pony Club's Pony Weeks

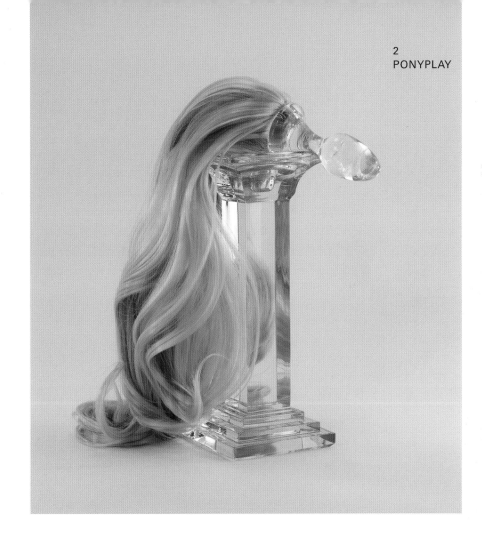

gered or fucked. Some have also been required to 'serve' a filly (or vice-versa) in front of others as part of a scene, the way horses are mated." Sir Guy also pointed out that quite a few of his participants apparently have no interest in sex acts at all: "'Shep' the human English Sheepdog wants to be a dog—but he doesn't want to be a sexually active dog."

There do exist people who think they want to be human ponies permanently. But, as Sir Guy pointed out, "The reality of the situation is that with twenty-four hours a day, seven days a week as a pony, very few people could stand the boredom." As a cautionary tale, he tells me a story about a gay man who lived as a pony for two years. At the end of the two years, his owner got bored of him, gave him his clothes back and dumped him at the train station. "I imagine he was pretty fucked up and spent a few years on skid row getting his humanity back together."

Towards the end of our meeting, Sir Guy showed me the custom-made human pony equipment he sold through his mail-order catalog. His enthusiasm for the minutiae of straps and fasteners brought out the former engineer in him—in fact, his persistence in showing me every one of his products made me miss my train back to London.

Twice he suggested that I try on various bridles and corset harnesses, but I respectfully declined. There was a harness with little individual bells to be hung from pierced nipples and from cock rings. Sir Guy displayed a very frightening butt plug ponytail that was made to match the customer's own hair. The internal plug-end was a long, dark brown, bumpy cast latex object that ended in a nasty sharp barb. It looked excruciating, but Sir Guy explained that the point is to keep it inside so it won't fall out in an embarrassing moment. Sir Guy also sold cute head harnesses with attachments for a plume and a

My Little Pony–inspired butt plug
by Crystal Delights, available in all colors
of the rainbow

Ponyboy Buck and Maîtresse Lisanne.
Buck owns Waterhole Leather,
a ponyplay equipment manufacturer

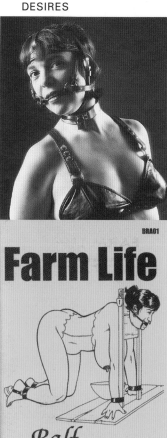

custom-engraved brass tag for the pony's name. He used leather bits rather than metal ones, "because I don't want to be responsible for dental repairs!" He also sold props for people who wished to play the human piggies and human puppies; he showed me a water-bottle drinker for one of the piggie girls, and some dog food. "They don't actually LIKE eating cat food and dog food, most of them. But they like being forced to."

Guy credits the 2000 edition of *Deviant Desires* for bringing about 90 new "high-quality" members to The Other Pony Club. The business and the scene were booming through the '00s, but in 2011, Miss Prim left Guy and things started falling apart. The mail-order business failed and Guy admits he was too slow to adjust to the internet. In 2014, a malicious scenester burned down Sir Guy's barn with all of his equipment, leaving him almost homeless. Sir Guy picked up the pieces and moved to Portugal where he

is now trying to revive the pony scene in the balmier weather there. Guy now advertises on FetLife for playmates who would be willing to put in elbow-grease to turn his ramshackle trailer rental into a pony play scape. He's a little disappointed in the new generation of would-be kinksters online, though: "They project out what they think they want, but they never follow up."

Nevertheless, Sir Guy has managed to attract several visitors—cisgendered females and cross-dressers—who have helped paint walls and hammer nails. He still has dreams of a permanent human animal farm with great gatherings of ponies, humans, and other critters. His vision is, as it has always been, ambitious. "As my father once told me, 'Why have ambitions that are too easy to satisfy?'"

THE EQUESTRIAN CLUB, NYC
From 1997 to about 2006, The Equestrian Club of The Eulenspiegel Society of New York was

"Automatic horse woman disciplining exerciser" by JG-Leathers

Ponygirl bridle manufactured by TOPC. Photo: Ziegfried Brahm

Farm Life, a fiction chapbook by The Other Pony Club, features cowplay as well as lactation, feeding, and weight gain. (See Chapters 4 and 8)

Major Themes:
Power Play

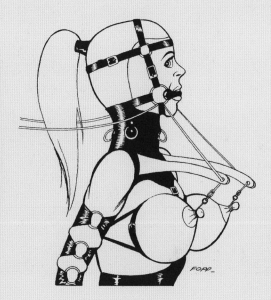

The erotic imagination harnesses aggression and fear to intensify sex. Dominance and submission can be found in almost every erotic fantasy. Humans are wired to mix sex and power: On the biological level, we all rely on androgens such as testosterone for our libido. Testosterone also drives the urge to dominate. In many mammal species, only dominant alpha males and females have access to sex and reproduction.

Among social mammals, submission brings a sense of belonging and the safety of the pack. Submissive animals lie on their backs and display their genitals. Animal submission is also accompanied by displays of fear. In humans, fear causes the release of adrenaline, which increases blood flow and can cause genital engorgement. Humans interpret these instinctual responses as specifically sexual.

BDSM has long recognized the erotic power of extreme sensory play. Pain causes the body to release endorphins—natural opiates—and intense impact play such as whippings and flogging can bring people into ecstatic altered states. For some, carefully negotiated scenes with trusted partners can be a means of transforming childhood trauma—as Dr. John Money once put it, "wresting triumph from tragedy."

The BDSM community developed the following set of guidelines to clarify the difference between BDSM and abuse.

CONSENSUAL
All participants must be sober adults of sane mind

Must have the mental capacity to fully understand consequences

Must engage in negotiation before, throughout, and after ("safewords")

Consent may be compromised if there are real-world power differences between participants (such as boss/employee, teacher/student, psychologist/patient)

SANE
Participants must know the difference between fantasy and reality

Participants must be willing and able to establish and stick to limits

SAFE
No permanent injury (viewpoints differ on piercing, tattoos, cutting, and branding)

Observe safe sex guidelines—bodily fluid awareness, no sharing toys

Self-education and awareness of risks (especially breath play and bondage)

Activities should not court arrest, loss of job, or loss of family (taking risks is hot, but going too far is not)

Arm restraints and headgear.
Photos: Ziegfried Brahm

Fantasy bridle illustration by Fopp,
The Other Pony Express

a driving force behind ponyplay on the East Coast. The Eulenspiegel Society, the oldest heterosexual-oriented BDSM organization in the United States, permits members to create specialized subgroups if they can find enough participants. Long-time TES member Lady Velvet Eagle had choreographed a prizewinning showpony routine for the first Equestrian Extravaganza at the Black Rose Tenth Anniversary Leather Retreat in 1996. (This is a weekend summer camp cum convention for pansexual BDSM players, featuring kinky crafts and whipping workshops, a flea market, and pony training sessions.) Velvet and company were so energized by that show that in 1997, they got approval from the Eulenspiegel board to create The Equestrian Club, a group for ponyplay, puppyplay, and role-play with other types of human pets. Known as TEC@TES for short, it had over 30 members at its peak. TEC's last meeting was in 2006, but it built a close-knit community of ponyplayers who continue to meet up at events such as Camp Crucible in the summer.

The first TEC meeting I attended, in 1998, was held in a bright dance rehearsal space with metal folding chairs and blinding fluorescent lights. The first person I met was fairly typical SM: a big man in black-on-black clothing, leather vest, gray ponytail, big hoop earrings and a scowl. But he was talking with a petite older woman wearing a red little-girl ballerina tutu, a red T-shirt, and red slippers—a surreal vision. Then I saw the guy she was with, a tall white man of about 45 wearing nothing but a pair of red briefs, a red T-shirt, a pair of red slippers, and a red headband that held a jaunty red ostrich plume. He skipped lightly around the room, occasionally coming to a stop next to someone, gently neighing, pawing the ground with his slippered foot, and moving on. The other members were affectionate with the red ponyboy in that instantaneously intimate way you might caress a dog or cat you've just met. Lady Velvet later explained to me that the red couple's game is to be circus pony and rider. They are a role-playing pair only—they do not have sex, and in fact both have monogamous

Ponygirl getting a sugar cube treat.
Photo: Efrain J. Gonzalez

TEC@TES meeting. Left to right:
Piper Pony, Red Safari (a circus pony),
and Codypony. Photo: Velvet

relationships with other people who do not mind their sideline hobby.

In one area of the meeting space, a crowd gathered around in a hushed circle to watch special guest Paul Reed of *Equus Eroticus* magazine demonstrate his training technique on a ponygirl called "Satin Doll." A girlish "filly" wearing T-shirt, jeans and thick kneepads, Satin Doll was crawling on the floor on her hands and knees. Paul Reed was sitting on her rump. Paul rested his feet in short stirrups attached to each other by a thin leather strap that he had draped over the ponygirl's middle. Satin Doll wore a leather bridle and a small rubber bit, which was attached to short reins that Paul held lightly in his hands. When Paul wanted the ponygirl to move forward, he would pat her on the butt and make clicking noises with his tongue, just like a cowboy.

Satin Doll crawled very slowly, and every movement was precise and careful. I could see sweat on her forehead and her total concentration on the task at hand. Every now and then she would buck her head and chew her rubber bit just like a horse. Occasionally she stopped in place, and rocked forwards and backwards on her arms and legs. When she stopped, Paul would lovingly wipe her shoulders and neck with a small cloth. At one point, he fed her a little carrot stick. Everyone in the room was watching her, rapt, and she was acutely and pleasantly aware of the attention. Her hip movements made clear she was sexually aroused. It was electrifying. In the awed silence of the crowd, a man in a gray business suit turned to me and said with hushed reverence, "Isn't she *perfect*?"

In another area of the space, a few men discussed ponyboy equipment. One young Texan man known as Codypony was wearing nothing but leather chaps and a string bikini bottom. He proudly showed off his new custom-made hoofboots—a pair of wrestler's shoes affixed to a metal high-heel armature and covered with

a leather "hoof." The hoof boots completely changed the shape of his leg, lengthening the appearance of his foot so that his heel transformed into a fetlock, forcing his knees forward and his ass backwards. Codypony discussed the pros and cons of butt plug tails with the pedantry of a university professor: "Few things add to the feeling of being a horse than having a tail swishing against your legs. One of the problems with butt plug tails, though, is that they sometimes fall out at inappropriate moments. They also come out of the body in the wrong spot for a proper animal tail, so you have to gather the lock up and attach it a little higher for the right effect. In any case, the butt plug has the added bonus of humbling the wearer and stimulating the sensitive anal area."

Ponyboy Silk, Velvet's long-term partner, shared what he had learned about modifying the bits and halters he buys at real equestrian tack stores. He warned that since metal bits can break teeth, leather can contain toxic dyes, and rubber can cause allergies, his solution was to wrap dye-free

Paul Reed riding Satin Doll at
Erotic Thoroughbreds '98. Photo: Lochai

leather around a chrome pony bit. "It's rigid, but it's soft so that my teeth won't get broken. And I can actually grip it and keep it in place even when it's being tugged on. I have another one I'm working on which has a deep U-shape in it that is more restrictive, pushing down the tongue, which will be used more as a punishment bit. It relieves me of the burden of speech." At this, other listeners offered their ideas and suggestions. It could almost have been a meeting of any hobbyists, if not for the powerful erotic charge in the air.

During the break, the ponygirls and ponyboys pranced around, neighed and whinnied, and nuzzled each other. One ponygirl later explained to me that she loves the fact that when she's in her pony persona, she can be warm and affectionate with total strangers— something she doesn't feel she can do in her human life.

When the meeting was called to order, Velvet asked everyone to identify themselves and their area of interest. (Human ponies were given special permission to speak in this instance.) Of thirty or so present, six were women. Of them, all but Velvet identified as ponygirls or switches. I met Satin Doll, a Palomino; Freya, a high-spirited young Scandinavian pony; Piper Pony, a Highland pony; and Sassy, a Caspian horse. At a later meeting I was introduced to Tugmaker, a trans woman who sees herself as a mule. Tugmaker used to prance around in the woods behind her house all alone for years before she found out about The Equestrian Club. Tugmaker drove over four hours to attend TEC's monthly meetings and be with people who understood her passions.

The men at the meeting split fairly evenly into would-be ponyboys, pony trainers, and observers. Most of the ponyboys were desperately seeking female trainers—and it was clear that they would probably have a long wait. Silk was the only stabled ponyboy this evening, and he described himself as an Arabian warhorse owned by Lady Velvet Eagle, the leader of the TEC group. Yet another man (the same man who had so breathlessly approved of Satin Doll) identified himself as a human pony veterinarian. His only prop was a stethoscope draped around his neck—though I half expected him to pull out armpit-length rubber gloves.

Under the direction of Velvet and Silk, a work group practiced their famous showpony dance routine. Silk explained the various two-legged pony gaits (walk, trot, and canter) and how they might be incorporated into a dancing human pony act. Silk also handed out a reading list of books about "real" horse training, in order to encourage maximum authenticity. He led several of the female and

Hoof boots by Etsy store Horseking

Hoof boots.
Photo: Ziegfried Brahm

Nighty, a kinky pony from Berlin.
Photo by pangur

*"I thrill at the thought of a
bit wedged crisply between
my teeth and lips, reins and
harnesses constricting and
controlling my body and head
movements, and the quiver
of my flanks responding to
the flick of my master's
(or mistress's) riding crop."
—Joni, a cross-dressed Utah
pony,* Equus Eroticus #4

male ponies in tandem skipping, occasionally
switching his leading foot and making a large
circle around the rehearsal space.

When I asked Velvet to describe her choreo-
graphic influences, she said, "It's kind of a cross
between Michael Flatley's *Riverdance* and country
and western line dancing—in pony costumes,
of course." One friend who witnessed their
original Equestrian Extravaganza later described
it as "a sort of kinky Esther Williams synchro-
nized-swimming-without-the-water Broadway
revue, with all sorts of people dressed up in
homemade pony costumes skipping around on
the stage." After a moment or two, he revised
his assessment. "Actually, at some points it was
more like a kindergarten school play." He wasn't
making fun of them; he found it a delightfully
refreshing change from all of the pouting, posing
humorlessness of conventional BDSM.

It's clear that for many of the American ponies,
there's no humiliation or shame in their play at
all—it's about fantasy, make-believe, and playful
sexual fun. The Equestrian Extravaganzas and
British Pony Weeks sound like erotic theme

parks for grownups, sexual versions of Disneyland
complete with costumed characters and cheesy
stage acts.

I met up with Velvet and Silk at her workplace
a few weeks later. They are a full-time lifestyle
SM couple for whom ponyplay is but one of
many erotic options. By day Velvet is a corporate
executive in the textile industry; by night she is a
lifestyle dominant with accomplished whipping
skills and a love of organizing theatrical scene
events. She is a real New Yorker—no-nonsense
and goal-oriented, but also cautiously friendly
and non-judgmental.

Velvet and Anthony/Silk have been lovers since
1996 and have been living together in a full-time
monogamous relationship since 1998. Velvet is
the dominant and Anthony is the submissive.
While Velvet is always Velvet, Anthony has many
erotic alter egos. Anthony might play Silk, the
Arabian warhorse; Sparky, a Dalmatian puppy;
or Antonia, a human girl. Velvet controls all of
Anthony/Silk/Sparky/Antonia's sexual hab-
its—from when he can masturbate to when he
can come to when he must service her with

Joni, a cross-dressed Utah Pony.
Photo: Greyline Service

foot massages, "oral worship" (cunnilingus), and sexual intercourse. Velvet makes Silk wear a little bell on the end of his Prince Albert penis piercing so that she can hear him if he tries to masturbate. At one TEC meeting, Silk wore a cock cage—a muzzle-like rigid metal framework that is attached to the penis and balls by leather straps. Velvet explained that Anthony had been misbehaving and needed a little added focus; the cock cage prevents him from getting totally hard but also chafes and arouses him at the same time. Velvet also whips him, beats him, and torments his cock and balls (by kicking, squeezing, or the judicious use of a single-tail whip) on a regular basis—as often as he needs and wants, but at least several times a week.

Velvet and Silk both came to ponyplay from a lifelong interest in radical sex. Velvet was a swinger in the 1970s and got involved in SM culture during the AIDS crisis. "I have been experimenting with some sort of sexual aspect of life since I was 12. I didn't necessarily seek this particular aspect—it's an acquired taste. I had reached a point in my life where it was important to be able to join a group that was involved

in sexual things but at the same time not anything that could possibly give you a disease." In 1989, Velvet joined the National Leather Association. Shortly after that she joined The Eulenspiegel Society and became an activist for sexual freedoms. Velvet always brought to her BDSM activities a sense of fun. "I found that when I first came into the scene, everybody was much too serious! God! Nobody laughed. I enjoy myself. I enjoy laughing while I'm spanking."

For Velvet, public ponyplay is a form of performance art; private ponyplay sessions are more blatantly sexual. When Velvet decides to initiate a ponyplay session, she'll alert Anthony by calling him by his pony name—that's his cue to get into character. Their session may begin with Velvet harnessing Silk up and putting him through his jumping and dressage paces. She may use a twitch, in the form of a nasty loop of chain on the end of a big stick, as a form of cock and ball torture, wrapping the chain around his cock or balls and twisting…very gently. She might whip him if he needs it. These private ponyplay sessions usually end in what Velvet and Silk call "stud service." Stud service is whatever Velvet

Lady Velvet Eagle leading Piper Pony
and Silk at a Click and Drag club horse night.
Photo: Lochai

desires at the moment, whether it be foot worship or pony-style fucking. On occasion, Velvet "rides" Silk by fucking his ass from behind with a dildo and pulling on his reins in rhythm to her thrusts.

When the sessions don't end in orgasm for Silk, Velvet sometimes beats the sexual tension out of him or kicks his cock and balls. "The other night we attached a braided leash to the tip of his Prince Albert. I used it as a whip and I whipped his balls and his cock for hours. It amused me to no end. I was feeling lazy so I hooked it into my foot and I pulled on his dick to try to stretch it." Silk explains that this is good enough for him. Velvet adds, "By the time you're finished being whipped, you are completely refreshed afterwards—all of your sexual tension has dissipated. There isn't necessarily a need for an orgasm. I enjoy keeping his sexual tension going for days."

Velvet sometimes has to fight against her own desire to pleasure her lover. "There's a part of me that just wants him to come as often as possible. It's part of my upbringing I have to fight against sometimes. Fuck him, blow him, whatever it takes

to make me or him come. That's the goal—getting off physically, where there's an actual fluid exchange. However, when we click into that role-playing space, that changes. Then it's my decision whether I want to deny him and I want him to hold it for a day or a couple of days." Charles Gatewood, the fetish photographer, once described this philosophy of sexual denial to me in spiritual terms. "It's about getting the high

> *"I like to think of what we do as performance art. I'm going to put on a costume and be whatever I've decided to be for that particular day. Today I'm Mistress of the Ponies. Tomorrow I'll be Mistress of Whips."*
> *—Lady Velvet Eagle*

Velvet riding Silk. Photo: Lochai

Silk performing mock "stud service" on Ponygirl Sassy. Photo: Lochai

really going and not having an orgasm…they call it having an SM orgasm. In other words, they build that energy until its about to explode and ride it, and keep it inside; people stay high for hours or days or longer doing this. It's a whole different way of looking at it. It's more tantric, more about playing with the energy."

DANNY THE WONDER PONY

Danny the Wonder Pony enjoys celebrity status within the pony-play community because he was the first to take his ponyboy show on the road. A fixture of The Vault and the Hellfire clubs in New York in the 1980s, Danny rigged up a backpack-style saddle, a bit and stirrups, then he would approach women at the clubs and offer to give them ponyback rides. Annie Sprinkle, the porn star–turned performance artist and one-time Queen of Kink, once told me: "Danny's saddle always had a wet spot!"

I finally had my chance to ride Danny when he was guest speaker at a TEC@TES meeting. He showed up in full Wonder Pony regalia: black Lycra spandex biker shorts, kneepads, wraparound shades, and a saddle decorated with black light reflector strips. I was impatient to ride him, but I had to wait my turn. TEC shares its meeting night with Age Play, another special interest group—adult babies in diapers, Lolitas, and the like. At this particular meeting, two of the "six-year-old" girls were having a birthday party, complete with cupcakes, party hats, and party games. The birthday girls insisted on having their pony rides first.

Rainbow of pony butt plug tails
by Crystal Delights

HUMAN PONY GAITS
(developed by Silk and
Lady Velvet)

WALK: slow gait where one foot is on the ground at all times

TROT: faster version of the walk

PASSAGE: slow-motion trot lifting legs high and kicking outwards

CANTER: both feet are off the ground simultaneously (skipping)

GALLOP: all-out running gait in either trot or canter

LEAD: the leg that starts the gait

CHANGE OF LEAD: changing the lead leg in the canter

ONE TEMPE: change of lead every step during canter

TWO TEMPE: change of lead every other step during canter

PIROUETTE: 360° turn in place

PIAF: pirouette in slow motion

BACK REIN: backing the horse up

NEWEST BREED IN ENTERTAINMENT

DANNY THE WONDER PONY
The One True Rocking Horse

Bachelorette Parties, Clubs, Photos
Private Riding Sessions
For The Only Equestrian Sex Symbol
Call (973) 674-0007
Have Saddle - Will Travel

At last it was my turn. Danny handed me the reins and knelt down on the floor just like an elephant or camel does when kids ride them at the circus. I swung one leg over his shoulders and sat down in the saddle. He slowly stood up and put my feet in the stirrups. Then, as I held tightly on to the pommel, Danny started bouncing and bucking and swinging around in circles. I would have to describe the experience as a cross between the 25-cent kiddie rides and one of those *Urban Cowboy*–style buckin' bronco machines. Once I relaxed, I realized Danny's practiced moves were geared to getting my girly bits to rub in just the right way against the pommel and the saddle. I was grateful that he had added a shaped foam cushion to the saddle, "so women don't get blisters from the ride." (Danny's saddle does come equipped with a vibrator, but most of the women in the night-clubs find that a bit too much.) Danny gives his moves a little variety by occasionally leaning over a stool and doing longer slower swooping motions. "You have to figure out how to do what they want, so that they'll come back," he explains. By the end of my two-minute ride, my face was quite flushed and I had some difficulty speaking and concentrating. After the ride was over, Danny kissed my hand and thanked me. "No, thank YOU!" I said.

Danny dropped out of the SM scene in the late 1980s. Not that he had given up being the Won-

der Pony; on the contrary—he'd taken his act to the masses in mainstream vanilla nightclubs like Limelight and Tunnel. "That's part of the turn-on for me—being a professional wonder pony. I want to be paid to do it." For a while, he had regular paid gigs at several straight New Jersey night-spots. For Danny, much of the fun comes from freaking out the normals. Danny also had a fairly active sideline business performing at bachelorette parties. "I guess they just got tired of the same old strippers. I offer them real interaction."

Quentin Tarantino saw him on the Springer show, and invited The Wonder Pony to be an extra in his B-Grade exploitation flick, *From Dusk Till Dawn*; you can catch a glimpse of Danny onstage in the Titty Twister nightclub scene surrounded by bikers. Danny was a bit anxious about how the hundred-or-so real bikers would treat him, but he found that most people just shrug and smile when he explains, "It's amazing what a guy will do for money." Americans respect that kind of ingenuity.

So, have women orgasmed while riding him? Danny is quite certain they have. "I get a real kick when that happens or when I know that's what they're going for. When they yell 'Don't stop! Don't stop!' that's a good indicator. Or 'Danny, please keep going a while longer.' A lot of them are very verbal, while others do the shudder thing. And all of a sudden after they've been so excited about the riding,

Danny the Wonder Pony's business card

they'll suddenly say, 'OK Danny, that's enough, that's enough!' It happens more often than you might think!" Danny never knows which rider is going to come. "You might think that the wild stripper would be the one that gets off, but it's the mousy little ones you have to watch out for."

For Danny, the Wonder Pony act is hot, thrilling, and sexual, but he doesn't really have any interest in fucking the women he gives rides to. "I don't think of pony rides when I'm having sex, and when women ride me I'm not thinking of making love to them or tearing their clothes off. This isn't foreplay; it's its own thing." Danny has a fiancée he has been dating for years. He keeps his Wonder Pony act and his love life completely separate; she never rides him in private, and she is the only woman he has actual sex with. "It's more exciting for me to think of her in real sexual terms." Danny doesn't think it's necessary to find a woman who wants to be his permanent rider. "You know, I realized that you can't base a relationship on sexual compatibility. If she enjoys it, that's great. But if she doesn't, it doesn't mean she's not the woman for you. This might be the woman for you, she just isn't into that."

When I reinterviewed him in 2017, Danny calculated that The Wonder Pony has given about twenty to thirty-thousand ponyback rides over the last 27 years. As you might imagine, it's a strenuous workout, and he's had to cut back pretty seriously. What will happen when he gets too old to do it anymore? "Maybe I'll have to start walking around with a wheel at the front. I mean, there are some very old athletes and they're amazing. I might have to start putting a hood over my head so that people aren't afraid of hurting the old man. If they don't know I'm an old man, maybe it will still be OK. You'll see— my costume will start having a hat or a helmet!"

PONYGIRL PIPER PONY
Piper Pony is the Highland pony alter ego of

Michelle Rollman, an accomplished artist whose sculptures and drawings have long explored her erotic fantasies of human-animal hybrids. (See her illustration in the Vore Sidekink, Chapter 5.) Michelle's earliest sexual fantasies were of being a caged animal or an animal being trained to perform.

Michelle had been involved in BDSM for several years before she found out about ponyplay—and when she did, it clicked. "An animal has its own spirit. It's something different than being a slave in that you are not totally subject to somebody else. An animal is treated in a different sphere of control and yet they get some respect and some individuality." Michelle and her then-boyfriend/ pony trainer Dana immediately decided that she would become a Highland pony because it is stocky and powerful. They named her Piper Pony after the pony Michelle had as a little girl.

Danny the Wonder Pony and rider at The Baroness' Fetish Retinue Party, 2012. Photo: Mark McQueen

R'hyl is a unicorn warhorse who enjoys intense impact
play (whippings). He and his partner, who produce
costumes and accessories professionally, also attend Furry
and Sci-fi conventions. Photo: Herb Ascherman

Major Themes: Transformation

The erotic imagination creates tales of magical transformations, transporting us out of our rule-driven, routine lives and reconnecting us with ecstasy.

The erotic imagination, like pagan myths, is crowded with humans transforming into gods and animals, men turning into women, and living things becoming statues. In kink, these transformations are realized through consensual role-play, storytelling, costuming, and art.

Costumes liberate us to act in ways not permitted in our ordinary lives. Adults interested in costuming are dismissed as childish, but pagan cultures have historically made a place for these impulses in orgiastic communal rituals. Rather than severing sex from spirituality, these transformation dramas incorporate the erotic, fulfilling a human need for aliveness and transcendence.

Illustration: Marquis de Panasewicz

Rubber Pony, aka Bryan Milhoud in a self-built costume begun in 1978. Photo: Paul Reed

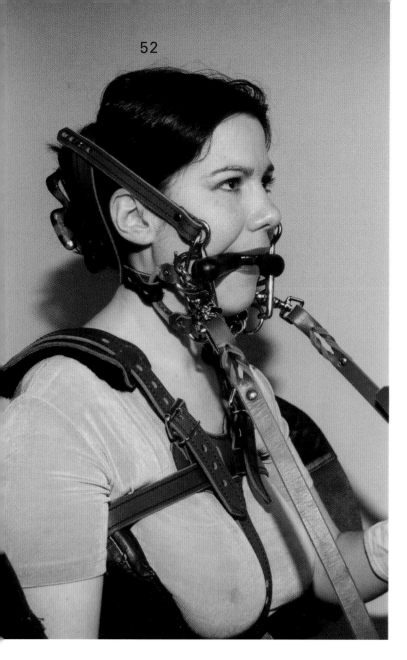

One of Michelle's most memorable ponyplay experiences was a weekend she spent at the country farm of Maîtresse Lalique, a professional dominant specializing in training ponygirls and ponyboys. Piper Pony spent the night in the barn on the straw with Lalique's real horses, and spent the whole next day giving rides, pulling carts and getting petted and groomed. Towards the end of the day, after a particularly taxing round with the cart, Lalique and her assistant began whipping Piper Pony. "They would whip my cunt from underneath and around the front to my breasts. They were whipping me that way and then they came around and were giving me kisses and patting me and being affectionate. They whipped me a little bit more and they brought me to a climax." From her expression it's clear this was a real knee-buckler.

Michelle recalls another weekend she spent at a New England bed and breakfast run by "Master R and Madame Sang"—two professional and lifestyle BDSM players. This B&B has monthly parties where they invite 30 or more people up for a weekend of BDSM play. They have a two-room dungeon in the basement for the use of the guests. One very enjoyable evening, Piper Pony got whipped and raked with spurs. "I like being marked. I'm always proud of marks." Another time they acted out a more elaborate fantasy. "They blindfolded me and there were three of them grabbing and clawing at me and making ravenous wolf noises as if they were a pack of wolves eating me. It was really so much fun!" (See Vore Sidekink, Chapter 5.)

Piper Pony climaxed in an entirely new way when Madame Sang began fingering her mouth. "She was doing this thing with her fingertips back inside the very tender soft part of the roof of my mouth, just behind the gums. It's a soft tissue area that's the same as in your vagina, and it's very sensitive. She was getting me off in the roof of my mouth! I had a real orgasm!"

Dana is a foot fetishist and cross-dresser, and Michelle is happy to play along. On occasion, they've invited other ponyplayers over to her apartment to play the role of groom; Piper Pony wouldn't mind being "bred" pony-style with a ponyboy, if that were her master's wish.

When she's in role, Piper Pony usually wears mesh stockings, a satin leotard and tap shoes—a cross between little girl and burlesque queen. Piper Pony is well-known among ponyplayers for her uncanny ability to make realistic—and surprisingly loud—horse noises. "I love to neigh. I'm generally the one who just shuts up, so it's my chance to be the center of attention."

Piper Pony's custom bit and harness.
Photo: Dana

Since our original interview, Michelle and Dana got married, moved to rural New Jersey and bought a real horse, Rosa, whom they board at a nearby stable. Michelle has won awards as a pony trainer, and runs the annual pony camp at Camp Crucible (an annual BDSM summer camp) which attracts around 20 ponies every year.

PAUL REED, *EQUUS EROTICUS* PUBLISHER

After I witnessed his electrifying training session on Satin Doll at the New York TEC@ TES meeting in 1998, I traveled down to Paul Reed's home near Washington, DC, for a follow-up interview. A former beauty pageant photographer and director, and at the time I met him a full-time television producer, Paul Reed's true lifelong passion has always been women transformed into riding ponies. He is one of the most successful ponygirl trainers in the world and from his start in 1968 to the time of this writing in 2017, Paul claims to have ridden over 500 ponygirls.

Paul's glossy full-color magazine, *Equus Eroticus*, was my first introduction to ponyplay. A product of the desktop publishing revolution, it was for its run, from 1997 to 2010, the only magazine devoted exclusively to human ponies and pets. Although *Equus Eroticus* contained articles and photographs by people representing the many distinct "takes" on ponyplay, it was still strongly influenced by Paul Reed's particular style. Paul is not interested in the harder-edged SM approach to the practice and sees his ponygirls as treasured pets rather than slaves to be whipped. This may explain his extraordinary success at attracting women to allow him to ride them.

PREMIERE ISSUE

EQUUS EROTICUS

$12.00   A PUBLICATION FOR AND ABOUT THE WORLD OF PONY GIRLS AND BOYS

SPRING 1997
Number 1

Horse Woman

From Woman to Horse

"Rubber Pony"
A Profile About Bryan Milhoud

A Pony Named Sarah
Young Lady Explores Her Fantasy

PLUS

4 Pages of Pony Girl Photos

Special
Pony Girl "Tame Down"

Column, Story and Photographs

Pony Boy "BUCK"

An Interview with Mike Derrick

ADULTS ONLY

Issue #1 of *Equus Eroticus*

Paul Reed's photographs of ponygirls have a wonderfully idiosyncratic and unfashionable quality about them. He likes his ponygirls to wear girlish pink satin French maid outfits, taffeta crinolines, traditional feminine lingerie, high heels and stockings, and long satin gloves above the elbows. He also likes to add the occasional cute touch, such as colorful matching head-plumes and bunny-ear headbands.

I spent an afternoon with Paul witnessing one would-be ponygirl's first training session. Paul's modest two-floor condominium was in the center of one of those labyrinthine middle-class residential communities in the DC suburbs. The lawns are ruthlessly manicured, there is fresh pavement in each of the marked parking spots, and every corner looks alike. Paul greeted me wearing a plaid, button-down, short-sleeved cotton shirt with pens in the breast pocket, chino pants, and dark sneakers. He is quiet, steady, and polite, and talks very slowly and carefully with a flat Midwestern accent.

When I entered his living room, I recognized the place immediately as the site for all of his photos—same carpet, same drapes, and same fireplace. The walls of Paul's apartment are covered with beauty-pageant contestant head shots from his days as a pageant director and photographer. They're autographed, too. "Thank you so much Paul! I love my look! Love, Danielle." Each of the girls displays all of the conventions of American ideals of female beauty: robust milk-fed health, big hair, big teeth, and big smiles—not unlike his photos of ponygirls.

Paul and his new ponygirl, whom I'll call Dawn, had already been training for several hours. Dawn is a big woman, and when I arrived she was sweating in her T-shirt and black tights, which she wore under white athletic kneepads. After we introduced ourselves, Dawn returned to her hands and knees and Paul draped his pair of stirrups over her waist. As he slowly sat down on Dawn's back and she began

her slow crawl on the carpeted floor, I asked Paul about how he got into ponyplay. "I grew up on a farm in Iowa. I kept asking for a pony and I never got one." Paul thinks that there is a strong connection between ponyplay and childhood: "I think part of the fetish is that little children love to ride things. They like to ride on Mommy and Daddy; they love to ride those mechanical horses outside of Walmart. I'm feeling like a little kid and being aroused too. I'm thinking, 'Oooooh! I finally got my pony!'"

Paul believes he began to fantasize about riding women when he was about 12 and had begun to notice girls. "I just transferred my desire for a pony onto girls. I don't want to ride guys, so the only thing left is to ride women." It was at this critical point in his development that he saw an advertisement for an Off-Broadway production

Ponygirl Satin Princess. Photo: Paul Reed

> "It's getting to the point now where I enjoy this more than the sex; that's what makes it a fetish."
> —Paul Reed

of Jean Genet's *The Balcony*. The ad featured a photograph of a woman dressed up as a horse in a very sexy outfit—the prostitute acting out a customer's ponygirl fantasy. This was Paul's eureka moment; he knew then and there that he wanted to have a ponygirl when he grew up.

As he told me his story, Paul frequently wiped Dawn's neck and patted her head. Because this was their first training session, she took frequent breaks to rest her arms and wrists. I expected that Dawn's back would hurt, but because Paul rides so far back on the ponygirl's hips, her knees actually carried all of his weight—this is why kneepads are very important in four-legged riding. Paul takes safety seriously. Before he gets on a new ponygirl, he makes sure they don't have back problems. Paul explained: "The secret is to take things slowly. We've all seen female bodybuilders. They don't train one day and compete on the next. It's a slow process. The first session is usually pretty short, and you slowly build up to it. Over time, her muscles develop."

Paul begins each training session by teaching the ponygirl his safe

Ponygirl illustration by Matt

signal: "She has the right to stop the session at any time. They usually have a bit in their mouth, so you can't depend on a voice signal. If they do the safe signal—two taps on the floor with the right front hoof—then I'm off of them in a flash. That signal means 'Get off of me right now!'" Paul has found that it is difficult to get some ponygirls to use the safe signal, even when they're on the verge of collapse. "Unfortunately, a lot of submissives will refuse to give you the safe signal. If they start shaking, that's a pretty good indication you've got to get off."

During their breaks in the session, Paul asked Dawn to rock back and forth to give him the pleasurable feeling of continued riding. Paul explains, "The rocking is for the rider's benefit, not for weight training. She doesn't mind doing it, but it gives the rider the tactile illusion of movement. It prolongs the riding experience,

because she's not expending energy crawling, so it's to my benefit that she does this."

Although he prefers four-legged riding, Paul trains some ponygirls two-legged style, especially if they have knee trouble. With two-legged riding, balance and center of gravity become the main issue. Usually the ponygirl must lean fairly far forward and the rider must grasp the ponygirl's neck or shoulders to keep from sliding off. Two-legged riding requires a saddle custom-fit to the curve of the ponygirl's back. Most of these saddles work like a backpack, and have shoulder straps which help the ponygirl keep her balance and keep the weight over her legs. Paul has noticed that most male ponies prefer to give rides two-legged. "Men tend to be stronger in the upper torso than women. I know one particular ponyboy who insists that his rider ride him on his shoulders—he doesn't want to be ridden

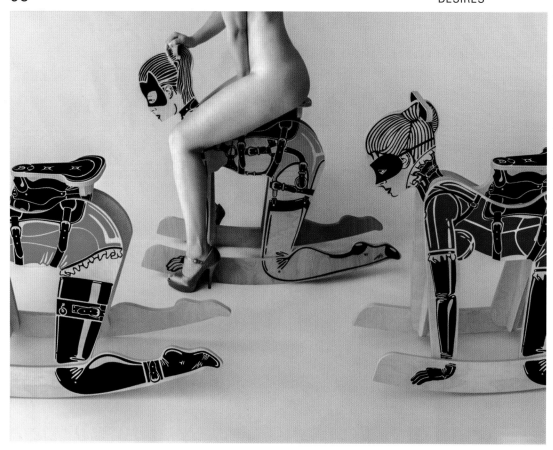

on his back at all. That takes care of the center of gravity problem, but it's also intimidating for the rider to sit that high up."

Paul Reed's personal journey to ponyplay continued in his teens. It wasn't long after 12-year-old farm boy Paul saw the photo from *The Balcony* that he saw another image representing a wonderfully bizarre historical curiosity called The Siege of Weinsberg: a tidy, winding line of almost a hundred women carrying men piggyback through the town. The caption described a festival that commemorates when, on December 21, 1140, King Conrad III offered terms of surrender to only the women of the town, following a siege against the Saxon townspeople of Weinsberg who had defended their prince, from the royal House of Guelph, against the conquering Hohenstaufen monarchs. "The king said, 'The women can leave in safety, but they can only take their most prized possessions with them.' So the women huddled together and agreed to the terms, returned to

the castle and picked their husbands up on their backs and carried them out!" Paul found the story absolutely enthralling and inspirational. The castle ruins are even today known as *Weibertreu*, which translates to "wifely loyalty."

The connection between horses and women seemed natural to young Paul: "I find horses to be the most beautiful animals—they're powerful and they're sleek. I think women are gorgeous and I love women. When you put the two together, then you really have an erotic, beautiful, unbelievable creature. You have the best of both worlds." Paul ultimately named his publishing company Magic Pony Productions to express this idea: "There's something magical about a ponygirl. It's the ultimate animal to me. It satisfies every need that I have."

When he started out, Paul tried to convince his high school sweetheart to "play horse" by at first taking the role of the pony himself. As he says,

A few of Peter Jakubik's 8 ponygirl rocker designs, peter-jakubik.com

"The best dominant has been a submissive. You have to see what the other person is going through." It wasn't until after he got out of the army in 1968 that Paul managed to convince an ex-girlfriend to give him a ride. "As soon as I got on her back, I said, 'Ooooh, yeah.' Of course, I didn't have any equipment and she did it because I wanted her to. I don't think she cared one way or the other. I think the first 10 or 15 girls that I rode were just doing it to be nice to me. I don't think they particularly enjoyed it." Paul's ponyplay practice was incorporated more or less into relationships with girlfriends, but it wasn't until the mid-1970s that Paul started meeting women specifically in order to ride them. He was living in an apartment building, and he noticed that the two women who lived next door were into riding horses. "I said to them, 'Gee, I understand that some humans like to be ridden too.' You sort of bring it up in casual conversation to see what the reaction is. You throw an off-handed remark out and see how it is received." These women became his regular ponygirls and also provided the first objects for his pony equipment collection. "They thought it sounded intriguing so they took an actual horse bridle and they modified it for a human face."

As I watch Paul riding Dawn, I can see that she is positively glowing with pleasure. Paul explains his affection. "She's my pet, and this is what you do with pets, you pet them!" I can tell that Dawn is sexually aroused, but she also seems terribly grateful just for the attention. She stops crawling and says, "At one point Paul was squeezing my sides. Oh, I really liked that! And he said, 'Not as much as me!'" Dawn feels comfortable with Paul. "I can feel what he likes and he knows what I like. It was pretty much an immediate bond. I knew immediately just from the phone calls that he was safe to be with." Paul's calm and steady demeanor, his very clear approach to the process, and the way he keeps communication open are very attractive. "I haven't lost a ponygirl yet!" he boasts.

Dawn never had any interest in horses as a girl, but she always enjoyed the sensation of carrying heavy weight on her back. "I remember when my nieces and my nephews were younger, I loved just lying on the floor and having all five of my nieces sitting on my back and watching TV. I just loved that feeling of having something on my back." Dawn had originally been drawn to ponyplay because of an interest in BDSM, which she had discovered in the late 1980s through the ubiquitous Anne Rice *Sleeping Beauty* books. She had been in a brief relationship with a traditional BDSM master, and had been excited by the idea of feeling pleasantly humiliated, but she got affection instead. This seems to have caught her pleasantly off guard—in fact, she seemed to me almost starved for it.

PONY GIRL

Satin Princess

TYPE OF PONY GIRL
Riding (Western & English)

FAVORITE PONY TREAT
Yogurt

FAVORITE HANGOUT
Around Stallions

PONY GIRL

Gigi

**ENDURANCE LIMIT
WITH A 190 POUND RIDER**
Hands & Knees – 4:47 min.
"Piggyback" – 4:05 min.

GOAL IN LIFE
Racing in the Kentucky Derby
...& Winning

Sample stats on Paul Reed's Pony Girl
Trading Cards, 1998

"Sex wasn't something that a 'good' girl did. But being able to go out and ride a horse with that constant thump, thump, thump, it felt good."
—*Ponygirl Frisky*

The first day Dawn got on the internet, her initial downloads were pictures of human ponies. When she began posting some pictures to her personal web page, she was contacted by a friend of Paul Reed's who suggested they correspond. Paul interviews each pony-girl for at least an hour before beginning the training. In his first sessions, Paul allows the pony to speak freely, human-style: "If you don't keep the pony happy, you're not going to have a pony."

After the initial interview, most ponygirl training sessions begin with grooming and tacking. Sometimes the ponygirl will begin completely nude, other times with some lingerie on. Once she's started her role as ponygirl, she cannot use her hands, so Paul must costume her himself—and that's a huge part of the fun. "Sometimes what you'll do is groom her and brush her down while she's nude and then dress her up a little bit. There's no set procedure. That's the other thing that makes it more erotic—you never do anything the same way twice." For grooming, Paul uses an actual horse grooming kit he bought at a tack store. The kit contains several different curry brushes that he uses to brush down the ponygirl. "I love to brush the mane of the ponygirl, and to use a

Pony Tindala and Mistress V playing in the Nevada desert, 2012. Photo: SN Jacobson

curry brush all over her body. I actually use a hoof-pick sometimes on their feet, the way you might on a horse's hoof. It's almost like tickling, in a way; you just rub the pick on the back of the pony-girl's foot. Some ponygirls like that a lot. I had a ponygirl who was very turned on by that." Paul also sometimes grooms after a riding session as well: "I've taken a hose and turned it on and hosed her down just like a real horse. That's very erotic also."

When it became apparent that Dawn was tired of carrying his 160-plus pounds, Paul suggested I give ponygirl riding a try. I gingerly climbed up on Dawn's back, and my legs had to stretch far apart and open up to get around her. My crotch bone rubbed against her tailbone through my jeans. I was not prepared for how strangely intimate it felt.

For Paul, the most intimate rides are bareback ones. "Whenever she breathes I can feel it. In a way, we become one animal, and that's an erotic thing in itself. When she coughs, I know it. Saddles are mostly for public show. I don't use them in private that much because they put a barrier between me and the ponygirl." Paul finds that riding a ponygirl is much more fun than training a cart pony. "It's such an intense personal feeling. There's a real bond that develops between a ponygirl and a rider, and I think it's a bond that wouldn't develop with a cart pony or a show pony."

Paul's love of ponygirls is directly sexual, and he usually has an erection during his riding and training sessions. "It's getting to the point now where I enjoy this more than the sex; that's what makes it a fetish." While sessions do not end in sex, Paul does occasionally have orgasms while riding. Before he began working with his newest ponygirl, Frisky, Paul had never met a ponygirl who could endure more than 12 minutes of continuous riding. Frisky recently gave him a ride for 50 minutes and he had a huge orgasm. "Duration helps, but it's other factors too. The eroticism continues to build throughout a ride. It's the attitude of the pony too. I can tell when the pony is trying very hard to please me—that's very erotic. If I can sense that the pony is aroused, that's even better."

Paul isn't very interested in the bondage and discipline aspects of ponyplay, and he says he probably wouldn't have anything at all to do with B&D if it weren't for his erotic interest in riding women. In fact, Paul didn't even hook up with the BDSM community until the mid-80s. He had seen John Willie's ponygirl illustrations in *Bizarre* in the 1970s and felt his own idea of ponyplay was completely different from the bondage/torture/whipping approach he'd seen in that magazine. Once he learned more about BDSM

"Being a horse is not being lower than being a person... a horse is not humiliated by having to urinate when it needs to urinate. When I am a pony, if I've got to go, I'm gonna go right where I am."
—Ponygirl Frisky

Master Robert and PonyLynn demonstrating a different riding style. Photo: Anna's Erotic Art

"The hobbles force me to move very carefully and deliberately, which makes my hips sway and my tail brush the backs of my legs and cheeks. I do my housework wearing my tail, my hobbles and my high heels and nothing else."
—*Ponygirl Frisky*

and its credo of consent and communication, Paul realized there was a connection—though he still feels that he's not a traditional master. "I've trained a few ponygirls whose masters have brought them over and I could tell they weren't really enjoying it. They were doing it simply to please their masters."

Paul sees his interests as quite different from some BDSM relationships. "I don't really consider her a slave. I consider her to be a pony, and a pony should be treated a lot better than a slave. I always treat animals with respect, so why wouldn't I treat a ponygirl with respect?"

Paul has noticed that some ponygirls use their submission as a way of attaining altered consciousness. "There are a lot of things going on below the surface with ponyplay. It's very complex. A lot of ponygirls love being ponygirls because they don't have to think human anymore. They can let go of their human thinking and just be an animal. To some people, that's a tremendous release. It's a way of shedding their conventional thinking; it's almost euphoric."

Since our original interview, Paul and Frisky have gotten married. In 2005, Paul and Emily Reed retired to a 20 acre ranch near Dallas, Texas. Paul occasionally still trains riding ponygirls at the

Paul Reed and his now-wife, Frisky

Beauty and trainer at Folsom Street Fair, 2015.
Photo: Adda Dada

ranch. Even after nearly 50 years of training ponygirls, he still finds it as exciting as it was when he trained his first one. Emily has retired from active ponyplay but is still involved via her art business, FirePony Artworks. She has a studio where she creates resin and fired fetish art and custom jewelry as well as pony harness brasses and stall plaques.

Equus Eroticus continued through the mid-2000s, but competition from the internet made it difficult to keep afloat. "After a few years, there were so many websites devoted to ponyplay, people decided they didn't have to depend on the magazine for information and they let their subscriptions lapse." In the beginning he had four distributors around the world, but then when Tower Records and Books went under he knew the days of print were numbered. *Equus Eroticus* ceased publication in 2008 after 22 issues.

A NEW LEADER: SUBMISSANN

After TEC@TES closed, *Equus Eroticus* stopped publication, and The Other Pony Club moved to Portugal, the ponyplay scene desperately needed new leadership. That void has been filled by subMissAnn, a lifestyle and professional submissive who has been bringing her love of petplay all around the country at established events and at her own EQUUS International Pony Play event in Los Angeles.

Like many, subMissAnn came to ponyplay through BDSM. She had started exploring BDSM with a friend in the 1990s, without any connection to the larger BDSM community or much in the way of guidelines. "I was really sheltered." When she finally met an experienced master who realized she had no real education in BDSM, he required her to fill out a long playlist and negotiation form, and to read the BDSM classic *Story of O* and Anne Rice's *Training of Beauty*. "That put the hook into me!"

Then photographer Ken Marcus invited her to do a cover shoot for Issue #22 of *Equus Eroticus*,

and she began the long process of gathering gear and learning how to play. Finally in 2006 at Stampede, an annual ponyplay event, subMissAnn met professional human pony trainer Rebecca Wilcox. SubMissAnn began to pay Ms. Wilcox to train her as a pony. "She let me live my fantasies. We went to Sequoia National Park, to Yosemite, and to the beach, and I would pull her in my cart." It was a strictly professional arrangement, no sex. "I chose Rebecca because she offered a very clear relationship, a neat and tidy exchange without baggage."

Rebecca Wilcox named subMissAnn's pony-self Beauty. "I used to go deep in pony headspace. When Beauty takes over, she's her own spirit. She's more outgoing than I am. She's very funny. She has qualities I want to have. I learned how

subMissAnn in her trainer mode.
coshlandphoto.com

Pink Pony and Phyllis Serene, a Thailand-based sex educator and Oracle, showing off their blue ribbon, 2012 Jamboree. Photo: coshlandphoto.com

to listen. I learned how to obey without hesitation. Learning a quietness and a peace of mind, not having conversations going on inside of my head." She never gives Beauty over to someone who would demand sex, though. "Those aren't my values."

By 2007, it was clear that many of the founders of US ponyplay were stepping away from their roles. TEC@TES was winding down and *Equus Eroticus* was preparing to publish its last issue. Although Rebecca Wilcox had published a book about pony training and had purchased the rights to the *Equus Eroticus* web domain (since inactive), she was planning to move to Sweden. "We were concerned that ponyplay be an enduring scene, because it was always one person at the center who was into it and if they disappeared the scene would disappear." The two of them made a wish list of events to which subMissAnn would bring her equipment and skills. "I hit the

road, actively sought out to bring ponyplay to all of these communities and events." She has since crossed all of them off her list: Camp Crucible, Desire, Sin-in-the-City in Las Vegas, Leather Heat, Great Lakes Leather Alliance, Brimstone, DomConLA & The Pony Show in Los Angeles, Thunder in the Mountains, Leather and Leis in Hawaii, and more. She has been crowned "Grand Champion" at numerous pony events, both as Beauty (handled by Piper Pony) and as a trainer.

Even though subMissAnn is a submissive, she will train ponies if they are compatible. "I have to know that they have qualities that I appreciate. They could be a good pony and a not so good human. It has to be a good match. Training is going to be like doing ballet together. There is effort and hard work. That turns me on, I'm getting moist right now." She has given her collar to only a select few whom she has known for years.

In 2008, subMissAnn founded the LA Pony and Critter Club, where human pets of all kinds can hang out and play at regular playdates, as well as train and enter in various competitions. She corrals the 168 members into a wide variety of activities, from monthly cart and sled pulls in public parks, Human Derby Day, the Saturday Pony Show at DomCon in Los Angeles, August's EQUUS International Pony Play event, and the semi-annual Fox Hunt in Ojai, CA. She offers classes in Advanced Pony Training, "The Woo of Pony Play (Animal Totems and Energy movement: how they may be applied and incorporated into to your Pony Play to bring it to another level)," and "Pony Play in Small Spaces." SubMissAnn fiercely defends anyone's right to interpret ponyplay exactly how they want. "Any way you want to do it is OK!"

In 2014, she published her first book, *Ponyplay with subMissAnn,* and since 2015 she has been producing EQUUS International Pony Play Event, a major pony event in Los Angeles.

One of the highlights of the year at the LA

Phantom Pony and Raven Darknights.
Photo: Trixie LaFontaine

Pony and Critter Club is the semi-annual Fox Hunt, which takes place in a National Forest in California. It's "a live-action role-playing game of wit and wile, prowess and pursuit, where a human fox (or other prey) attempts to outwit teams of human hunting dogs, ponies, hunters, handlers, and trainers in an outdoor setting." A group of at least 20 people gather in the campground, with communal responsibilities for food and shelter. It's quite a production: in addition to the five human foxes, they must have enough human puppies to chase them, and human ponies and riders to follow and capture the fox. Each fox, puppy, and pony must have a human handler who monitors them and keeps them safe. "We had to take the precaution of having humans attend the foxes in case they get too deep into the headspace." In an early event, foxes got lost and another became so terrified of the baying human puppies that he forgot how to come out of hiding. "The foxes

are running for their lives, their heart is racing." One year, a fox was even treed.

At about 11 a.m., the foxes get a head start. They each carry 50 to 100 flags, which they use to "pee scent" their trail. Each flag must be placed within visual range of the last. After a little while, the human puppies and their handlers chase the foxes using the flags as guides. After the puppies run the human ponies and their trainers. All of the handlers have horns they use to signal each other throughout the three hours of the hunt. Foxes can "win" by sneaking back to their cages without getting caught, and quite a few have been admirably foxy in tricking the puppies into chasing after false leads. Once a fox is caught, the human trainer collects the tail, after which everyone returns to the campsite for a feast. "We've had foxes who lose and have terrible grief from 'dying.' Aftercare is really, really important always." Sometimes, the end of the hunt might

PONYPLAY IN BRIEF

TERMINOLOGY:
ponyplay, human critter play

CORE KINKS:
leather, sometimes rubber,
bondage

MAJOR THEMES:
power play, transformation

SUBTHEMES:
animal transformation

SUBKINKS:
puppyplay, cowplay, piggyplay,
and other human pets

RELATED KINKS:
BDSM, furries

MAY BE COMBINED WITH:
age play, erotic cross-dressing

EROTIC EQUATION:
physical pressure of bondage and
weight, interpersonal pressure of
training and control

culminate in a negotiated BDSM scene symbolizing the ritualized dismemberment in the spirit of fox hunting.

Her most recent lesson learned was that furries (see Chapter 11) can make good foxes, but "we have learned that wearing bright orange fursuits makes them too easy to find. Successful foxes need to wear colors of the terrain, like their bio mates do."

A fox on the run at the 2013 LA Pony and Critter Club Fall Fox Hunt. Photo: coshlandphoto.com

Sidekink: Pups

Veronica Vixen and Pup.
Photo: Marj Borjorquez

TERMINOLOGY:
pup

CORE KINK:
leather or rubber

MAJOR THEMES:
power play, transformation

SUBTHEMES:
animal transformation, rarely humiliation

RELATED KINKS:
ponyplay, furries, pups, and superhero fetishists often hang out together

EROTIC EQUATION:
pressure of bondage, interpersonal power

Since 2000, puppy play has become an increasingly popular variation of BDSM, especially within the gay male community. Pups wear leather or rubber masks, collars, leashes, and often hand-binding gloves. As with ponyplay, pups may not speak or use their hands.

Obedience training may include various forms of submission, including being kept in a cage or eating dog food. Mostly, however, pup play is an opportunity for play and affection; pups may play fetch, run around, cuddle in dogpiles, and get belly rubs and treats from their human owners. Doggy-style sex may or may not be expected.

A pup frightens caged fox Fancee at the LA Pony and Critter Club Spring Fox Hunt 2012. Photographer unknown

Balloons: A Pop Kink

Buster Steve, gay looner icon.
Photo: Leo M.

When I first viewed the Balloon Buddies website over 20 years ago, I assumed it was a hoax. Here was a fetish no researcher had documented. The medical literature on paraphilias made no mention of it, and Brenda Love's *Encyclopedia of Unusual Sexual Practices* missed it entirely. Balloon Buddies didn't even look like a fetish site—more like some kid's birthday party. On the opening page, a bouquet of animated balloons bounced around on a series of Crayola-colored backgrounds. When you rolled the cursor over the balloons, they popped.

The whole site was happy and friendly and lacking the usual slick gothic quality of typical fetish material. You'd probably never even imagine it was sexual at all, if it weren't for the fact you can't get any deeper into the site without passing an age statement warning. When I did, I struck

the mother lode of kink. I had made first contact with an entire community of people who proudly call themselves "balloonatics" or "looners."

Looners are the thousands of men and women, straight and gay, who have a lifelong sexual passion for collecting, fondling, inflating, and popping balloons. Although a few folks log on with tales of boinking vinyl pool toys or bouncing on special butt-plug-fitted Hoppity Hops (big rideable rubber balls for kids), the vast majority of looners just want to play with regular old latex party balloons. They like to rub up against balloons, jerk off while inflating them, or fuck them in various rather ingenious ways. They love to share balloon porno, downloading JPEGs of models sitting on, blowing up, or popping balloons with various implements like high heels or cigarettes. Most of the pictures

Maggy BerLoon, looner and balloon entrepreneur. André Krenz photography

"I love seeing the neck of the balloon start to lengthen. The longer it gets and the closer it is to popping, the more turned on I am. I start to feel scared, my heart starts beating very rapidly, and I get a very stiff hard-on."
—Mark

aren't remotely naughty—no nudity or even suggestion of intimate acts—yet the subjects still have the black strip over their eyes that implies forbidden thrills.

People like to claim that there are no new kinks under the sun, but the balloon fetish proves them wrong. Every era seems to have a fetish that is uniquely its own: In the Victorian age, some men developed a sexual fascination for watching women wring the necks of geese—certainly a powerful psychological experience for children in that period, but a rare occurrence in this day of prepackaged meats. Quite a few British schoolchildren who grew up during World War Two developed a fetish for the rubber gas masks they wore during air raids. The anxious situation, combined with the strong smell of rubber and a feeling of almost suffocating containment, cemented gas masks into their psyches. The gas mask demographic is weighted heavily towards British folk who were kids during the war. The balloon fetish could only be relatively new; after all, rubber latex toy balloons were only invented in the 1920s, and have only been a routine part of the American home since the 1950s.

Balloon Buddies was the very first looner organization, founded in 1976 as a mailing list by a man called Buster Bill. Buster gathered together the first 100 Buddies by taking out ads in straight and gay male fetish magazines. Membership swelled slowly over the years, but the balloon fetish really exploded when Buster put it all online in 1993. In the first several years alone, Balloon Buddies expanded to over 2,000 members, including a handful of women. A separate gay male list called The Buddymen started up in 1995; in 2000 it had over 1,000 members. In the summer of 1999, the female balloon fetishists founded their own group. Balloonatics now have a choice of at least 100 websites, chatrooms, IRCs and newsgroups, including 25 pay sites selling videos and hot, live, one-on-one

Zeppelin blow to pop.
Balloongirls, 1980s

balloon action geared to the particular interests of a looner audience. Even now, Buster Bill regularly gets messages from lonely looners who have finally found their way home, no longer thinking themselves the only person in the world who gets off on balloons.

Everyone knows about shoe fetishes and leather fetishes—they're almost fashionable at this point—but balloonatics are still just emerging from the toy closet. A balloon can be a terribly embarrassing fetish to have. Even though latex is now a popular, well-known kink, balloons are not. And the association with kids' birthday parties brings a whiff of pedophilia that looners must constantly explain to vanilla folk: no, they're absolutely not interested in children, it is the balloons they want. For many, signing up with Balloon Buddies is their first opportunity to talk with intelligent, sane, and successful people who share similar fantasies.

One of the first things looners discover when they join the Buddies is that they are part of an extraordinarily diverse group of people. Looners are as complex and varied a crowd as any other random bunch of humans. I met a sheep farmer, a professional architect, a corporate lawyer, several artists, a talk-show host, and a college professor. There are looners in Australia, Germany, Japan, the United States, and Britain. And, although male members still outnumber females about 30 to 1, Buster Bill finds that the internet has made women far more comfortable about opening up and talking about their desires. "I hear from at least three or four women a month now, as opposed to three or four a year in the past."

This rich archive of online material consists of far more than jerk-off fodder—it's also a gathering place for some fairly serious conversations. Looners share childhood stories about how

Drawing by Buster Steve. Buster copies images from porn magazines, then adds the balloons

Taking Off. 1950s pinup

One Australian looner handcrafts
balloons, then has a professional
photographer shoot portraits

Movie poster for *The Stripper*,
a Joanne Woodward film of the 1960s

they discovered their fetish, and speculate about why they developed the way they did. Some share their efforts at making their own balloons by hand, and receive enthusiastic encouragement. Older looners offer sage advice on how to come out to friends and lovers, and how to bring balloon sex into relationships with non-looner partners. Looners agonize among themselves about balloon play with someone other than their spouse—even if there's no sexual contact. "That's what I consider sex, so is it infidelity?" They also argue at length about the ethics of tricking unsuspecting strangers into inflating or popping balloons. These conversations strike me as eminently healthy.

What is it about balloons that makes them such a perfect fetish object? Part of the answer lies in their smelly, touchy-feely material, perfect for that tactile, olfactory memory cascade discussed in Chapter 1. You could call the balloon fetish an estranged cousin of the latex fetish (which includes rubber clothing, rubber masks and rubber sheets), but most looners have no interest in rubber other than balloons. One looner told me, "Latex clothing is a BIG turn-off to me, don't ask me why. A waste of good rubber you could be inflating?"

Looners find the smell of balloons a powerful sexual trigger. Jeff, a 46-year-old gay male looner, mailed me an extraordinary 3,000-word essay on the sensual joys of balloons. He devoted five hundred words alone to the various odors and flavors of latex. A true balloon gourmet who enjoys combing through his collection of thousands of different balloons, Jeff effused about the wide world of excitement available to the true latex connoisseur: "Different manufacturers and tempering methods make every rubber unique. Some are oily and sweet, others bitter, sharp, or musty. Balloons are usually treated on the inside with a drying, mildly antiseptic talc. Though never 'perfumed,' each talc has its own savor."

At the time I spoke with him in 1999, Jeff had been married for nine years to a non-looner man. An avid reader of contemporary British fiction, his vocabulary for balloon odors is almost as rich as an oenophile's lexicon. "Certain old, much-used balloons release a briefly overpowering 'hyper-rubber' scent, or an ominous musk that seems to threaten early explosion but often means the balloon will grow larger than any ten of its same make... I've had some balloons 'perfume' my hands, face, and body so strongly that a day could go by, and I'll still have a thrilling, memorable reek." Jeff recognizes this connection between balloons and other fetishes: "Perhaps this is the 'hardest' fetish aspect of balloons—a close, earthy crossover to mainline fetishes. Balloons have an unmistakably

Why So Many More Men Than Women?

Sexologists estimate that only one in 100 fetishists are female. Among the balloon fetish crowd, the average appears to be more like one in 30, and the gap is closing rapidly. The explanations for this discrepancy are complex.

The primary reason why sexologists' estimates are inaccurate is a cultural one: fetishistic women are far less likely to visit a sex clinic—and be counted in these statistics—than men are. Men with fetishes may be more inclined to seek medical advice because they feel more pressure to perform sexually than women do. If they require a fetish object for arousal, they may feel somehow deficient, dysfunctional, or unmanly. Women, on the other hand, are still discouraged from expressing their sexuality at all, let alone a deviant sexuality. Women are capable of having intercourse even if they're not aroused—and tragically, many women simply tune out rather than address their own dissatisfaction.

Women may be more likely than men to shut their sexuality down altogether if they find their own erotic urges strange or frightening. The shockingly high number of women who have little or no sexual response might in fact conceal sexual nonconformists who repress their erotic impulses rather than risk exploring them. Women are made to believe if they step outside conventional modes of female sexuality, they will be labeled whores. They may even be targeted for rape.

In the last half-century, women have demanded more options for sexual expression. More women now consume pornography, pursue their erotic dreams, explore the sexual fringes, and feel safer doing so. The anonymity of the internet allows women to feel safer expressing nonconformist sexualities, and allows fetishistic women to come out of the closet without risking rejection, while also fostering connection with like-minded others. Although cultural factors are most likely to contribute to the differences in how women and men express their sexuality, it's possible biological factors play some role between male and female tendencies to fetishism. It's always dangerous to suggest biological determinism, though. Biology evolves just as culture does, and cultural changes may affect biology.

Scientists believe testosterone is the primary hormone governing libido in both men and women. On average, men have higher testosterone levels than women do, apparently contributing to more aggressive and more focused sexual urges. Of course, some women have higher testosterone levels than the average man. This wide range itself is entirely normal.

Dian Hanson, the publisher of *Leg Show* magazine, once experienced suddenly elevated testosterone levels while being treated for a thyroid condition. She felt a tremendous jump in sexual aggression, urgency, and focus. She felt compelled to go out and get some sex, right now, and it had to be exactly the way she wanted it. Johnny Science, a transgender man, told me when he's taking his testosterone he feels much more focused on objects and things during sex.

Drawing by Buster Steve

Maggy BerLoon, photo courtesy
Looners United

non-animate smell. But it's also a 'gentle' chemical processing twang akin to the odor of tanned leather (i.e., shoes, vests, chaps, harnesses, whips, etc.) or cloth (lingerie, uniforms, ropes, etc.)."

I hadn't had much contact with balloons since I was a kid, so I went to a party store and bought a package of Qualatex brand 16" round toy balloons (the brand and size most recommended by looners). When I ripped open the package, that instantaneously recognizable balloon odor insinuated itself into my nostrils. It's very intense, and kind of nauseating. If I had to describe it, it's a cross between vanilla beans and old people's sweat—like a yummy dessert and scary grandparents rolled into one.

I suddenly remembered scenes from my childhood I thought I'd forgotten. All at once I re-experienced the anxious sugar-buzz hysteria of a birthday party when I was eight. I relived the terrible feeling of loss when the precious balloon tied to my wrist got loose and flew away. This odor made me uncomfortable; it is too intimate, too close to home. I also remembered the strong sour reek of the pathetic shriveled little helium balloons I'd kept carefully for weeks in my room, protecting them from being popped or discarded, a memory associated with shame. I may not have the directly sexual response looners have to balloons, but I understand how hardwired that smell response can be when it hooks in to childhood experiences.

Some looners' very first memories are of sleeping with balloons as if they were teddy bears or security blankets. The balloons' vaguely body-odor-like smell probably helped cement the emotional bond, just as an infant's body smells infuse a beloved blanket or toy and make it an extension of itself. Infants are deeply sensual creatures who can experience sensory pleasures from anything available. We say they are "polymorphously perverse"—every object is new sensory terrain to explore through touch or taste or feel, and it's all thrilling. With our deadened adult senses, we've lost a lot of that. But for looners, balloons instantaneously open a door to that pleasurable period of belonging and of full-body sensuality.

Every looner I spoke with mentions some treasured early balloon memory they return to over and over, with the smell of the balloon bringing it back in sharp focus. Doug was a 20-year-old looner who remembered balloons as friends: "From my first memories as a child, I remember loving balloons. Not necessarily sexually, but loving them truly from my heart." Like Doug, Mac's emotional attachment to balloons transformed into an erotic one at puberty: "It turned erotic for me at the age of 12. I was behind the locked door of the bathroom, in the tub with an old friend, a well-used 20" Tilley balloon. I didn't know what I had done to myself, but I knew I liked it! This was my first orgasm."

Of course, the touchy-feely quality of latex evokes human skin—especially the velvety silky skin of our most private parts. Jeff describes the tactile joys of the balloon's caress: "Balloon 'skin' has a delicious silky give that becomes slicker and firmer the larger they get. In the first stages of inflation, they have a huge amount of give coupled with a marvelous resistance. You can crush them and your hand/arm (leg/knee, etc.) sinks deep into that spongy texture, all but surrounded by it. Once they're larger, you can wrap your arms around them and press their flanks into yours." Jeff describes how larger balloons

Top Ten
Media Sightings for Looners

(compiled by Inflate123)

1. *Abbott & Costello Go to Mars* (1953). The two morons end up on Venus, where they find a society of Amazon women who give them "truth balloons" that burst if they become sexually aroused.

2. *Employee's Entrance* (1933). Loretta Young. A party in a hotel, the hotel is filled with balloons, she pops them with her cigarette—a good one!

3. *Insignificance* (1985). An artsy film about a fictitious meeting between Albert Einstein and Marilyn Monroe. In a prolonged scene she digs her nails into three white balloons. One pops. (Highly recommended!)

4. *The Man with the Balloons* (aka *The Breakup*) (1965). Marcello Mastroianni plays a man who, depressed by the end of a love affair, becomes obsessed with figuring out how much air a balloon can take before it explodes. Clearly a looner story. An obscure film, apparently later removed from distribution at Mastroianni's request.

5. *Let's Spend the Night Together* (1982). The Rolling Stones seem to appreciate balloons. Of special note is a 3-second scene of one of the inflater girls popping a huge 20" pink balloon. Looner gals will enjoy the scene where Keith pops one over his head. Huge drop scene at the end.

6. *Roger Rabbit Short Cartoon*. Baby loses balloon at amusement park and gets into trouble trying to get it back. Live action blonde cutie offers cartoon baby a real balloon. Cartoon baby pops it with a cigar. She lets out a nice shriek.

7. *The Soupy Sales Show* (1960s). Live kids' TV show that once featured a practical joke on Mr. Sales in which an exotic dancer unexpectedly appeared from backstage holding two strategically placed 12" balloons. (Now famous scene often appears on bloopers-type shows.)

8. *Benny Hill Show*. Mr. Hill was one of us! In one skit, Mr. Hill plays a naughty boy with a slingshot who goes into a burlesque bar where a nude dancer is doing a dance behind a 20" pink balloon. He pops it. The scene was later censored.

9. *Three's Company*. In the first episode after the pilot, Jack hasn't moved in yet and needs a shave. Chrissy borrows a straight razor and tries to prove she can safely shave him by inflating a 12" red balloon, covering it with shaving cream and shaving it. She pops it—spraying them all with cream. A+ for effort!

10. *Hogan's Heroes*. For the gays and gals in the audience. Schultz visits a circus near the camp and buys two enormous helium balloons for his nieces. One of Hogan's gang pops them.

Movie poster for *The Breakup,* also known as *The Man with the Balloons,* 1965

Sally Rand, the famous "Original Bubble Dancer" from the 1930s–1950s

can be warm from breath, and how the thin, delicate membrane of an overinflated balloon can tremble at the touch. It's as if he's describing a lover's body.

Balloons are successful fetish objects not only because of their latex material, but also because their shape has the capacity to call up powerful images. The fetish object is, before anything else, an aesthetic object. Like an abstract painting, it works only if it is able to hold many meanings at once and mean different things at different times; the best fetishes are opaque and flexible, much like balloons themselves. And, depending how looners use them in masturbation sessions or with lovers, balloons can be nurturing like breasts, empowering or threatening like engorged penises, or even receptive and containing like anuses, vaginas, or wombs. A balloon can be a whole body as well—a fragile reminder of our mortal selves.

The one human body part that balloons most obviously suggest, with their pear shape and

nozzle, is the female breast. Doug, who slept with balloons as a child, now uses them as breasts in his regular masturbatory practice. He inflates exactly four 16" latex toy balloons to semi-hardness; he puts two under his shirt to simulate women's breasts and the other two in close proximity to his penis. "While masturbating, my right hand jacks off while my left hand caresses the balloons under my shirt." The balloons are part of a subtle cross-dressing ritual, as well as a way of creating a female sexual partner he does not have.

Doug, like many non-poppers, has an almost anthropomorphic identification with balloons. The balloon is a lover or friend. "The idea of the balloon bursting while I am masturbating with it scares the heck out of me. I have never gotten over the fear of popping balloons. I don't even like to do it in non-intimate backgrounds (like kid's games, parties, etc.). I guess I like to give the balloon a chance." After he climaxes, Doug deflates the balloons and puts them away. "Then I light up a cigarette and think 'Boy, that was great!'"

Some guys literally fuck balloons. One young straight looner likes to wrap long thin clown-type balloons around his erection to get off. Jeff has seen gay men press their cocks between the inflated ears of a Mickey Mouse-type balloon. Buster Steve, married gay architect, uses the nozzle as an orifice. One of his favorite ways of getting off with a balloon is to blow up a large 18" or 20" round one as large as it will go. "Then, holding the neck carefully closed, I spit on my throbbing cock and pull the neck of the balloon down over the shaft of my cock like an inflated condom." This takes practice, he explains. "Then, with the hard tight balloon bobbing on the end of my cock, I take the balloon in my hands and shake it violently, so my cock slaps back and forth inside. Then I proceed to punch, slap and tap the balloon back and forth so that it 'works' the head of my cock while bouncing and rebounding from my attacks. The sensation is out of this world!"

This looner's handcrafted balloons generate lots of praise on the balloonbuddies listserv

Carrie, a 35-year-old astronomy student and single mother, likes to use balloons like a vibrator, rubbing them between her legs. "The sensation of the cool tight skin feels so wonderful, always with my fingers holding and squeezing it as close as I can. If I am close to orgasm the feel of that will finish me off instantly almost every time."

The phallic shape of the long airship or zeppelin balloons appeals to gay men and straight women alike. Jeff explains, "When these balloons are near their full inflation, they're also very dramatic. You stare down a seemingly endless expanse of taut, glittering rubber."

 The balloon works as a fetish not only because it suggests all sorts of body odors and body parts, but also because it can perform the allegorical drama of growth, tension, and explosion. The process of inflation, the spectacle of balloon tumescence, can mimic the looner's own sexual tension and arousal. Watching a balloon expand is certainly as mesmerizing as witnessing a penis or labia or nipple "magically" inflate when aroused—and the balloon nozzle gets slick and wet and firm and spongy just the way breasts and penises and vaginas do when sucked.

Jeff gleefully pointed out how blowing up a balloon is like sucking cock. "For us gay men, there's the sense of having a penis to suck on! You can run your lips up and down it, exactly as you would the shaft of a cock, since most balloon necks stay more or less taut during inflation. What's more, they often get quite wet, and you have to stop blowing to wipe the neck and your mouth before you continue." Buster Steve agrees how hot this can be: "I love how the balloon grows tight and hard in my grasp, swelling and stretching. I love the way the neck swells out once it is overinflated, and pushes towards the lips." (You know, I always wondered why we call fellatio a 'blow job'—after all, it's more sucking than blowing, isn't it?) And not only gay guys get off on the cock-sucking model: Carrie thinks her love of inflating balloons relates to her joy for fellatio. Straight male looners particularly enjoy watching women giving balloon "head," and actively trade JPEGs and video clips.

Jeff may be gay, but he also thinks it's like breastfeeding: "There's the feel of the neck on and between your lips. It's definitely infantile in one sense, a continual pacifier thrust into your mouth." And the nozzle of the balloon becomes engorged—just like a nipple—as you mouth it. It's a comforting, nurturing feeling, a very oral pleasure.

You'll find the theme of growth throughout this book. Kids just love seeing things get bigger and bigger. Small children are almost

Jan BerLoon, fetishist and balloon entrepreneur, courtesy Looners United

Maggy BerLoon, courtesy Looners United

TOP 10 REASONS, WHY LOONERS MIGHT BE THE LUCKIEST PEOPLE IN THE WORLD
by Will Blown, reprinted with permission from Looners United

1. People with a balloon fetish get so much pleasure and so much joy from a simple object that is very common and not very expensive.

2. Since we can satisfy our basic human sexual needs/desires with an inanimate object, the risk to our partners that we will seek this in the arms of another is greatly reduced.

3. If we are lucky enough to be able to share our fetish with our partners, we share a very intimate secret that makes our relationship stronger.

4. Balloons intensify our sexual experience with our partners making something that is already amazing only that much more fantastic.

5. When our partners are not in the mood, for any number of reasons, we can always turn to our balloons who never say no.

obsessed with size differences in a world where everyone but themselves seems gigantic; kids often feel small and impotent compared to adults. Adult eroticisms tap into this sense of wonder.

Balloon inflation is an excellent illustration of the Erotic Equation: breath forced into the balloon presses against the resisting latex skin, and as the tension builds up, so does the excitement. The huffing and puffing are a critical part of the thrill—the in-out motion of the air is sexual, in a similar way to a foot pumping the gas pedal of a car. This may be why oral inflation is by far the most popular method, though a few looners will settle for watching women or men using helium tanks. None of the looners I met had any interest in water balloons.

Blowing up a balloon is an intensely intimate act: one looner enjoys exchanging breath with the balloon as it inflates—a kind of "kiss of life." Inflating a balloon can make your heart beat faster and your blood flow harder—physiological effects not unlike sexual arousal. Doing it quickly can cause hyperventilation, and people sometimes purposefully induce oxygen deprivation to increase arousal and make orgasms more extreme. (Autoerotic asphyxiation and self-strangulation are some of the more dangerous methods.) The rubber fetish in general is often associated with breath play: gas mask fetishists enjoy the panicky feeling of being smothered by the powerful odor of rubber, and some rubberists wear tight masks with little balloon-like squeeze-bulbs that a partner can use to fill their lungs with air.

Drawing by Buster Steve

Buster Steve showing his balloon fucking technique. Photo: Leo M.

Some looners can get off just from the very sound of someone else blowing up balloons, listening to the crackling and squeaking of the latex as pressure increases. Buster Steve has had phone sex with partners who inflate balloons next to the receiver. Kaboom explains his fascination with balloon sounds: "The flesh tingles, the mind races: Who is blowing up that balloon? Where are they? Is it a pretty woman? Is she good at blowing them up? In any case, I have an immediate urge to go find that balloon!" Hearing these sounds in public can be frightening as well: "The urge is tempered by two fears: the fear of getting too close to a scary situation, and the fear of being too obvious about my interest."

For Mac, the apex of tension—the moment just before the pop— is the height of orgasmic pleasure. "Most of the non-poppers like myself agree that the tighter the balloon gets the more turned on they get. This is right up to the point the balloon will hold no more. We try to make the orgasm happen at the time the balloon is at its max." In Mac's case, slow and deliberate inflation (a kind of balloon fetish version of long slow lovemaking) is the true erotic art form. Mac especially enjoys watching his wife blow up balloons. "Before I told my wife about my fetish, I found I would have trouble with my erection from time to time. Now all my wife has to do is inflate a balloon in front of me and I get the BIGGEST, LONGEST, WIDEST, HARDEST, throbbing, pulsating erection!" Balloons aren't always a part of their sex life, though. "Sometimes I just don't want the interruption. I also think my wife needs to know I'm in love with her, not the balloons."

The most emotionally heated arguments on Balloon Buddies happen over the issue of popping. Some looners feel extremely protective towards their beloved fetish object, and would be devastated if it were destroyed. Others just don't see the point of balloons unless they pop. As one looner said to me, "If it doesn't pop, I don't pop!"

Non-poppers like Mac can get quite defensive about what poppers want to do with their beloved friends, and online chatrooms can get a little contentious around the subject. Buster Steve explains, "For non-poppers, loss of your balloon is purely unpleasant, a mortifying, heartbreaking theft or bullying." Ric Blue Eyes is a non-popper of this defensive school of loonerism. "As a non-popper, all I see after a balloon has popped is rubbish. If I am wanking with a balloon and it pops, I normally don't finish what I am doing—I give up." Ric feels poppers are simply bullies—not only in their desire to pop balloons, but in what he sees as their tendency to oppress non-poppers. "Poppers are very rude and put down the non-poppers. And for some reason this is very much the

"I remember during puberty looking up the words 'balloon' and 'pop' secretly in every dictionary I came across, just like other teens look up 'sex.'"
—Carrie

6. When it comes to a sex partner so to speak, balloons are always a perfect 10—okay not all balloons are perfect but I have never been with a balloon that was less than a 9.5 on the sexually attractive scale.

7. As far as fetishes go, balloons are quite innocent and do not involve much more than blowing them up. I don't judge anyone's fetish, and why would I, but especially for our partners who usually do not share our fetish, balloon play is something that most are willing to do for us. Balloons are fun and playful.

8. Balloons, when they are not inflated, are small so we can secretly carry them around in our pockets and sneak a little pleasure throughout the day without anyone even knowing.

9. Balloons are everywhere and we will usually see at least a few when we are outside our homes especially if we live in cities.

10. The balloon community is supportive, rarely judgmental and filled with many wonderful people who share something with us. Even if we live all over the world and our views and life situations are completely opposite we share a common characteristic that brings us together.

case with the guys from the USA! Almost all the poppers think they are shit hot! You know, butch as butch can be."

Some poppers fluctuate between non-popper and popper activities, depending on their emotional state. Jeff's approach is a rich variation of sexual play. "There are times I couldn't blow up a balloon to explosion to save my soul. In such cases, I exhibit all the 'preservation' behavior of a non-popper…and STILL get my rocks off. Other times, no balloon can reach my lips, fingers, or feet without soon exploding. In those instances, I can be a wild man who goes on for hours! Other times, I just don't want to deal with balloons at all."

For Jeff, blowing up, playing with, and popping balloons are an integral part of regular enthusiastic sex with a hot man. "That would include the full spectrum of male-male sex acts—which need no description here—and the same balloon-related activities I usually enjoy: Blowing them up, lying on them, crushing them between bodies, popping them in various ways. Boy meets boy, boys get out dicks and play, boys get out balloons and play with them while also playing with dicks. (For 'dicks,' please read ALL possible body parts/combinations/activities.)" At the time I interviewed Jeff in 1999, he had been with his non-looner spouse for nine years, and balloons had been openly discussed and included in their sex life that entire time. "He does balloons for me, but not because they have anything like the erotic kick for him they do for me." Jeff finds non-looner sex extremely exciting: "Regular (non-balloon) sex is just as exciting as it ever was, which is PLENTY!"

For some poppers, the thrill of balloons is to teeter on the edge in a constant state of expectation of that frightening, explosive BOOM. The tension, anticipation and anxiety is what makes it hot, and the violent explosion like sexual release itself. Balloongirl gets off by riding 36" balloons to their climactic pop. "I like the suspense of knowing the balloon may or may not pop at any moment… It's the anticipation." She enjoys the thrilling play between control and loss of control. "I like to pop as it gives me a sense of power. To some extent, but not always, I control when the balloons pop. I don't like to deliberately burst the balloons, but I do like the anticipation of knowing a balloon I am riding may pop at any moment." Balloongirl surrenders herself to the balloon's explosion and to her own orgasm.

For Balloongirl, riding balloons to the point of popping is a regular part of sex play with her boyfriend. They have sex while riding on the larger weather-type balloons. "My boyfriend is not keen on popping and asks me not to pop the big 36-inch ones when we

Photo: Buster Steve

Balloon bondage at The
Baroness' Fetish Retinue Party,
2006. Photo: Mark McQueen

ride them—they scare the pants off him. This just fetches the little devil out in me." Balloongirl doesn't have to think about balloons to get aroused, but when she does think about them, it works every time. "The more open-minded my partner is, the more balloons take a part and the more I enjoy it."

Carrie is another female looner whose balloon practice centers on fear of the explosion. "I hate the noise, I need the noise!" She much prefers playing with her boyfriend over solo balloon sex, because she likes the idea of surrendering to the experience. "Being out of control really seems to be one of the primary elements, and when the balloon is in my hands I have a much better sense of how much more it will take before it goes. The tension of not-knowing rules my strongest fantasies." In her ideal scenario, her lover would gently tease her. "He tantalizes me and pushes my limits, forcing me to do what I rarely dare to do myself but so wish to do—but with no malice or desire to hurt me." He would wrap her hand around the balloons, push the balloons against their bodies and her lower back, and between her legs at the critical moment. For Carrie, her lover needs to exhibit strength and fearlessness "and empathy and love and a goodly sense of humor about the whole thing!" The whole scene needs to be done in play, "but with the seriousness of children at play."

Carrie doesn't have to think about balloons to get aroused, but they do always "flutter through her head" in sexual situations. "When I'm in a normal state I think about balloons pretty regularly." Although when I spoke with her she had been with her boyfriend for two years, she had only gotten up the courage to suggest balloon play with him eight times. He just hadn't picked up on how much it meant to her, and she was too embarrassed to press him further.

"I like the squeak and the crackling sound it makes right before it pops. Some balloons go 'bang,' 'boom,' 'snap,' and even 'poof,' depending on the size and the tightness."
—Mac

Pin pop. Photo: Balloongirls.com
from the 1990s

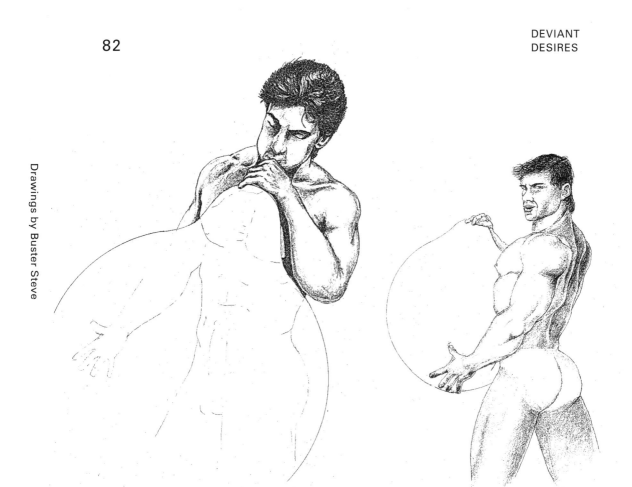

Even people who have not had a lifelong balloon fetish can still come to feel some of the thrill looners do. John discovered the joys of balloon play when he was 21 years old and dated a looner woman. "We had saved bunches from a dance and would untie them and reinflate them. The only time she would pop one was if it were damaged. With the addition of new balloons, our 'balloon encounter' lasted over two months." He had no particular childhood memories of balloons and felt that his fetish had everything to do with how he associated that original woman with balloons. John told his wife about his balloon fetish on their third date. "We were about to dispose of some condoms because we felt they wouldn't be needed anymore. She proceeded to blow one up and I told her how much it turned me on. She took me right into the bedroom and blew up the rest. Needless to say, I suffered premature ejaculation!" John's balloon fetish is now intimately connected to his wife. "When my wife and I make love, one will often pop a balloon just as the other is reaching orgasm."

While Kaboom and Carrie like the overinflation and the "slow squeeze" popping style, Mark takes a "wham-bam" quickie approach. When he's alone, this college professor performs a rather elaborate masturbation routine. First, he blows up anywhere from 5 to 50 balloons—depending on mood and time available. He then spreads pictures from adult magazines on the floor. "It is really the juxtaposition of the women and balloons that is necessary for me to be turned on." He rubs his genitals with the balloons, then he works himself up to popping. "Since I still feel some fear associated with popping, the first one is usually the hardest and I have to goad myself into it. But once it pops, I tend to get really turned on and will really get into popping." He likes it when women sit on them, but he generally uses a needle for the popping. Once he gets going, "Everything becomes focused on popping the balloons. I usually save one at the end to be sitting on when I come."

In adolescence, when sex is at its most terrifying, Mark connected his fear of pops with his anxiety about girls. "I made an association between the object of my interest [balloons] coming into close contact with interesting parts of their bodies in order to do what I most feared—popping the balloons by sitting on them." When Mark discovered the Balloon Buddies in 1997, he had been married for nine years to a woman who had no knowledge of his fetish. "Discovering the group and discovering I wasn't alone transformed my view. I didn't have to be as embarrassed about it. Knowing he wasn't alone released him from guilt: "After six months, with helpful encouragement from fellow Buddies, I finally told my wife. She was very accepting, and instantly agreed to take part in my fantasies."

Some looners combine their balloon popping with other core kinks. You can find videos of women pressing stiletto heels into the fragile latex skin, much as the pedal pumpers press the gas pedal. The heel bounces up and down, indenting the skin until the final penetration and pop. Smoking fetishists want to watch someone bring the red-hot end of a lit cigarette closer and closer to the balloon; the slow approach ramps up the excitement. Buster Steve likes to imagine a masculine man slowly moving the lit end of a cigar towards the balloon. "The tension mounts and my groin tingles as I await the imminent bang."

Some looners bring power games into their balloon scenarios. Dan is a New York artist whose deepest darkest fantasy is to be physically restrained, unable to cover his ears, as a woman teases him and frightens him with inflating and popping balloons. "The strongest, most pervasive fantasy I have is to be in the company of a woman who is completely nonchalant and unperturbed while blowing up, playing with, and popping balloons. A woman who has the ability to handle balloons without fear is awesome and devastatingly sexy."

As an adolescent, Dan was horrified by his desires, convinced that he was all alone, a "sick little pervert." His fetishism may even have played a role in his early decision to drop out of school and become an artist. He bicycled across the country alone, and homesteaded an apartment in a burnt-out building in one of the city's roughest neighborhoods. His paintings, incidentally, are organic abstractions with lots of jewel-like balloony colors, but he denies there's any connection. "The first time I discovered I was not alone was when I found Kaboom's Toy Balloon Heaven website. It changed my life." Knowing he was not alone changed Dan's looner practice as well; he felt

Vintage looner, possibly at Fort Dix.
Bought on eBay by Looner Dan

1950s vacuum cleaner advertisement
showing how it can be used to inflate
party balloons

"A balloon in my lover's hands is my soul in his hands. I must trust completely, give in completely."
—*Carrie*

less compulsive and more in control of his desires. He began to masturbate less with balloons, and began to think about coming out to others. Most importantly, the internet put him in touch with the BDSM community; he read Gloria Brame's seminal book on BDSM, *Different Loving*, and now thinks the motives behind his fantasy are very similar to those behind other kinds of BDSM role-play. "Rather then whips, paddles, and restraint devices, we are fixated on balloons."

Buster Steve has a leather-daddy balloon popping scenario. "I like the image of a rough and tough man, idly and gently playing with a large tightly inflated balloon, bouncing it gently around and roughly scraping his hands across it to make it squeal. I like to imagine him wrapping his rough hairy hands around it, distorting it out of shape and bursting it with sheer muscular force as if to prove his masculinity." Steve's favorite masturbation fantasy has him spread-eagled and naked tied down on the bar top in a leather bar, a big clear balloon bobbing from the end of his cock. He imagines big leather men taking turns at "torturing" the balloons. "I will come very close to coming this way, and then I slow down the 'torture' and very slowly and lightly tap the balloon across the head of my cock, as I feel the juices swelling. Just the vibrations of the balloon as I thump it, traveling through my cock into my groin, are enough at this point to bring me over the edge! Then I'll violently grab the balloon with both hands and mash it into my groin, while thrusting my exploding cock deep into the balloon! I love to make it bust just as I'm coming, the shock of the explosion intensifying my orgasm, making cum fly everywhere!"

Buster Steve's Dominance & Submission scenario reenacts one of his most traumatic childhood memories. Balloons were Steve's favorite childhood toys, and he remembers how his stepfather used to enjoy teasing and torturing him by popping his balloons. "I was about 11 or 12 and he loved to tease and aggravate me. He was a real rough and tough kind of guy, and found I didn't like it when balloons popped, so he didn't miss an opportunity to pop my balloons. One Christmas I received a stocking that had a bag of balloons in it. They were really big and I didn't want them blown up because I was afraid of them popping. My stepfather took one and blew it up as large as he could get it. I watched with fascination from a safe distance while it grew tremendous. He then began rubbing his huge hands across the tight rubber, making it chirp and squeal. I covered my ears and protested, but he would only drive his fingers deeper, laughing until it would finally burst. He then took another and this time blew it up so fast and hard it would expand and burst before he finished. I

remember him straining out the last bit of air, he had bent over and the balloon had swollen right up to his lips and suddenly burst with a loud bang." One must wonder whether Buster's stepdad was aroused by this.

For a surprising number of looners, the balloon-popping fetish is closely connected to a severe childhood fear of loud noises. Abject terror can develop—through careful self-mastery and practice—into a pleasurable sexual surrender. Tina, a New York business lawyer in her 30s, has had a lifelong fear of fireworks, gunshots, thunder, and balloon pops. As a girl, she was so scared of loud noises that she would never have any balloons in the house. Even now, she can become ill at children's birthday parties from fear of uncontrolled popping.

Balloons developed a sexual angle when Tina was about 13; she was spending the night at a girlfriend's house when she noticed an uninflated balloon on the girl's dresser. "As soon as I saw it I quietly swiped it, not for any intimate purpose but because I didn't want even a chance of her deciding to blow it up. ('WHAT

IF IT POPS?' was the thought screaming in my mind.)" Later, in the bathroom, Tina noticed the balloon in the pocket of her skirt. "With my heart pounding at about 1,000 miles per hour I put my lips to it and started to inflate it—I have no idea what possessed me." It was the first balloon she had ever blown up herself. "I just blew it up a little bit, and the anxiety and fear started to be mixed with the same kind of feeling that I got from touching myself." She began to wonder how it would feel if she blew up the balloon and touched herself at the same time, so the next day she rushed home and tried it out. "I could not believe how much the anxiety of playing with balloons added to my sexual feelings!"

Tina is now conditioning herself out of her phobia by masturbating with balloons. Some psychologists treat phobias by introducing the person to their phobia object in safe situations, gradually building up confidence and pleasurable associations. Tina is using the same technique to change a source of misery into pleasure. Mastering her fear adds another erotic element. "When I pop a really loud balloon

Still from a public service advertisement campaign against smoking. Both looners and smoking fetishists love this one

BALLOON PLAY TIPS

Never put balloons inside you! If they break they can cause embolisms.

Popping balloons on or near your body can hurt and the flying shards of latex can cause short-lived red marks. Of course, some people enjoy the pain.

Some people are allergic to latex and to the talc that is used to keep them dry. You can find non-latex substitutes in specialty stores. Talc itself is carcinogenic.

Oil-based lubricants will break down the chemical composition of balloons. Use water-based lube, especially if you want to reuse them and if you don't like balloons popping unexpectedly.

If you are male, and you want to fuck balloons in the open nozzle, be careful about the circulation in your penis. The neck of the balloon can be a very powerful cock ring, and can be very difficult to get off once it pops. Have a razor or some other sharp knife so you can cut the balloon off if necessary.

Even non-looner couples can have fun with balloons: Try inflating a few and rolling around on top of them or placing them between you as you make love. Do this on a soft surface as when they pop you land hard! Be sure to discuss beforehand your feelings about how and when balloons should pop.

Baking balloons will improve their stretchiness.

without going to pieces I find that the feeling of empowerment is terrifically exciting."

Tina travels a lot for her work, and has developed an elaborate hotel room balloon ritual. Tina prefers to use very small (8" to 12") balloons, and she likes to play around with them by sitting on them, overinflating them and squeezing them tightly to the point of popping. She may simultaneously use a vibrator and read erotic fiction, watch an adult film, or look at computer images of balloon play. "The images I enjoy are non-pornographic (and typically involve fully clothed people) have both male and female subjects, and show people having fun blowing up or otherwise playing with balloons."

Recently, Tina added an extra element to her balloon sessions—she now dresses up in schoolgirl uniforms or cheerleader costumes. "The look was a bit silly, but I could absolutely not deny that being dressed like that heightened the vividness of the fantasy enormously,

Candle popping. Balloongirls.com, 1990s

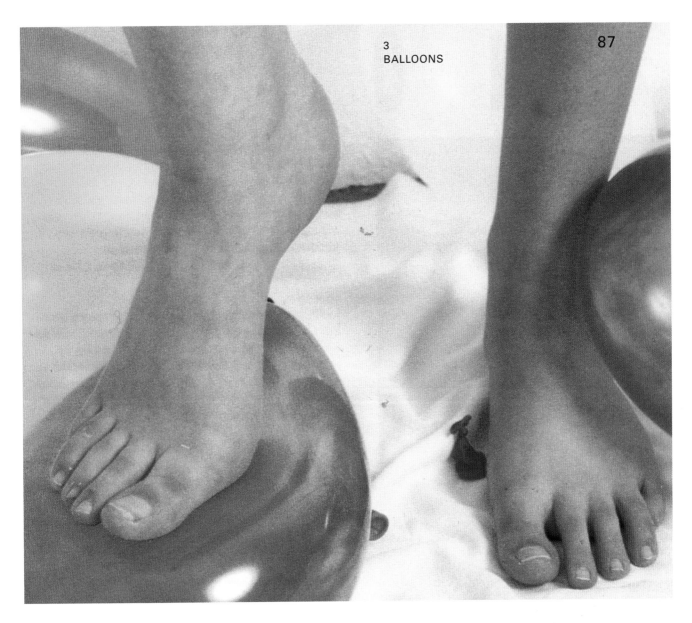

and it made for a truly pleasurable afternoon (if a bit embarrassing to me)!" She feels her interest in pretending to be a young girl partially has to do with the innately childish nature of balloons. "Mostly, I think that I enjoy the feeling of 'appropriateness'—I mean, it is not really appropriate for an adult to be playing with balloons, but for a child it is fine! Also, it seems more acceptable to be frightened by the noise of a balloon pop if I imagine myself as a young girl. So the juvenile element is relaxing in the sense that, to some degree, my fear and fascination with balloons is 'normalized' a bit."

Does Tina think there's a big difference between female and male looners? "I have been amazed by the amount of knowledge that some guys

have on balloon subjects (for example, knowing which factory manufactures which brand names, and knowing the difference between 'jewel green' and 'emerald green'). I have noticed that some (not all) of the men tend to fixate more on one element or practice: One guy is only interested in watching women pop balloons with cigarettes, one guy prefers to see large breasted women blowing up huge balloons, etc. For me, the interest tends to be a little more generalized."

In recent years, there have been efforts to expand the balloon fetish into other kink communities. The Baroness, a latex fashion designer and New York event organizer, had been unaware of the balloon fetish until the first edition of this book came out in 2000.

Foot popping, *Footsy*, 1997. (See Crush, Chapter 6)

The Baroness' Fetish Retinue Party,
2004-2006

Within months she decided to put together a balloon-themed event at her monthly Fetish Fashion Revue. She talked with Looner Dan about how she could make the party fulfill his greatest dreams. "We decided to leave out hundreds of balloons which the guests could inflate and pop. I was really looking forward to having him be there," she told me. "I just wanted to see his head explode from excitement!" But the guest of honor was too terrified to be around so many balloons and so exposed in public, even in a non-judgmental environment. He never showed up.

Nevertheless, The Baroness continued having balloon-themed events. In 2004, she found a looner named Balloonhead who brought along his compressor and oversized balloons so that partygoers could climb inside and experience the sensation of being contained within the fragile latex membrane. "Suddenly everyone wanted to get in," she says. "People have to twist and turn trying not to pop the balloon. It gets quite hot in there and you're completely engulfed in that chocolatey smell." The Baroness' last Fetish Fashion Revue was in 2011.

Denver-based Domina Elle is a pro-domme who also discovered the joys of balloons through this book. She had been a latex fetishist since she was 21, but when she started playing with balloons she had an immediate physical, emotional and psychological reaction. "I like to lick and kiss them, put my mouth on them, hold and squeeze them." Then she went to one of The Baroness' parties and it really clicked. Her first

Domina Elle and client at a balloon
pool party at Montreal Fetish Fest.
Photo: slave Rolonda SuMac

The Baroness whips the balloons off a woman.
Photos: Mark McQueen

experience inside a balloon was frightening. "I'm claustrophobic, to be honest," but the feeling of being pressed up against the delicate membrane, trying not to pop it, smelling the natural smells coming off the latex, got her hooked. "I now have cases and cases of different balloons. Classic toy balloons, doll-shaped balloons, Mylar balloons, pool toys." She's spent over $10K on balloons in the last two years. She has also worked with couples, one of whom is a looner, trying to help them navigate to a place where they can relate.

Balloons are the focus of Domina Elle's free public art performances in clubs. "I like spreading my love of balloons to other people. I like challenging them." She makes it a collaborative sport, to see how many people she can fit and has managed to get 13 people into a balloon before it breaks. She's found she can push straight men's boundaries by making five or six of them climb into a balloon together. "They have to strip down to their undies [so nothing sharp punctures the latex]. They were getting weirded out, pushed past their comfort zone having to touch all these other men," she says, with a cackle. "Then, if it pops, everyone

is crushed together without air until I can cut them out." The purpose, for her, is to bring joy. "Afterwards, strangers are hugging and laughing."

Her latest inflatable purchase is a giant bouncy castle, which she keeps in her large studio. She's filled it to capacity with 36" balloons. "I use a garden hose with a tiny stream, and a thin layer of water-based lube so that everyone can get in and do naked lube wrestling." Domina Elle has noticed that the looner community can be contentious. "They always ask me, 'Are you a REAL looner?' They see themselves as being judged." She gets tired of the online wars between poppers and non-poppers, Mylar and latex fans. "They can be picky, protective, judgmental, and intolerant." But Elle just ignores all that and has fun with what she does. "I want to be an example of someone who is not afraid. I want to share and inspire."

Domina Elle's looner client Catasta
Charisma. Photo: Domina Elle

Domina Elle and her doughnut balloon.
Photo: Slave Rolonda SuMac

THE BALLOON FETISH
IN BRIEF

WHAT THEY CALL THEMSELVES:
looner, balloonist, balloonatic

CORE KINK:
latex

MAJOR THEMES:
growth, transformation,
explosion, sometimes power play

SUBKINKS:
poppers, non-poppers

RELATED KINKS:
body expansion (see Chapter 5)

EROTIC EQUATION:
interior pressure from inflation,
exterior pressure from squeezing

UPDATES

Buster Steve has become a star in the gay male looner crowd. Although he's devoting much more time to his day job and his family, he has developed a following for his holiday-themed live-cam balloon events, where he fills a room with balloons and pops them using feet and cigars. "I would say there is a greater awareness of balloon play today than 15–20 years ago." Steve has conducted balloon play workshops at gay fetish events around the country. "I frequently run into folks online who say they got into balloon play last year."

A new company, Looners United, is now producing and distributing high-quality balloons specifically for the looner community. The owners, a German looner named Jan and his wife Maggy, believe in being positive and upbeat about the fetish. Their stylish website includes guest blogs from looners about coming out to partners and tips and tricks for getting the most out a balloon. There's even an interview with Danilo Catallo from CATTEX, scion of a family-owned Italian balloon manufacturer since 1964. Danilo is completely comfortable with the fact that his products are some of the most popular among balloon fetishists for their unusual large sizes, exotic shapes, and durability. "We appreciate that our product is giving so many looners so much pleasure!"

Maggy BerLoon of Looners United
and their custom "Fuck You" balloons.
Photo: Looners United

Sidekink:
Sneeze Fetish

Vintage sneeze, origin unknown

TERMINOLOGY:
sneeze fetish

CORE KINK:
noses, nostrils

MAJOR THEMES:
metaphors of arousal
and orgasm

MINOR THEMES:
explosions

RELATED KINKS:
vomiting (loss of control),
guns (explosions)

EROTIC EQUATION:
the pressure of the
impending explosion

Sneeze fetishists love to hear people of their desired gender sneeze, preferably uncontrollably. Excitement builds as the sneezer attempts to stifle the impending explosion. Fans may collect and share mp3 files of the best sneezes, though preferences vary between ladylike, stifled sneezes and full-on unashamed wet ones. Images often exaggerate the reddened, flared nostrils. In the sneeze fetish forums, artists tag their drawings with the reason for the sneeze: illness, allergy, induced, and level of embarrassment. Sounds are transcribed: "hih...he'NGXTSHU!"

I interviewed one female sneeze fetishist who gets off on her own sneezing; she and her partner induce sneezing during intercourse—they find the involuntary spasms intensify orgasm. Both sneezes and orgasms release tension and endorphins. Some people involuntarily sneeze when sexually aroused.

Fan sneeze art (Mycroft and
Lestrade from *Sherlock*)
by VoOS, a Swedish woman artist
on Sneezefetishforums.com

Body Expansion: To Dream the Impossible Dream

Detail from "Succubus",
(grOw/stOry#15) by BustArtist, 2015

Sexual fantasies realized exclusively through make-believe, costumes, and cinematic special effects bridge the quaintly childish and totally contemporary. For body expansion fans, the apex of pornography could be a Disney kid's movie or a Hollywood screwball comedy—as long as it features people with body parts that suddenly inflate to monstrous size. Think of the Eddie Murphy remake of *The Nutty Professor*—where the scientist explodes out of his clothing when the effects of his slimming potion wear off.

Body expansion is a catchall category of fantasies covering a range of subgroups devoted to specific body parts. The most popular sub-genre is breast expansion, and enthusiasts of this scenario call themselves "BE" fans. The typical BE fantasy might feature a woman tied up to an air compressor that inflates her breasts to impossible pro-

portions. The "B2E" category covers folks who like a combination of breast and belly expansion or breast and butt expansion. They might imagine a soothsayer cursing a woman so that the more sexually aroused she gets the bigger her belly grows, or they might fantasize that some mysterious potion transforms a woman into an immense Venus of Willendorf.

Another small but rapidly growing crowd enjoys penis expansion fantasies—as you might expect, these mostly attract gay men and straight women. I even found one labia enlargement story, apparently written by a female. Obviously, all these scenarios have the same magical growth appeal as the balloon fetish, except here the body part is literal. One guy even has an entire web page devoted to female nose growth fantasies. He morphs publicity shots of porn stars and

From EL Publications' *Barbara's Bewitched Boobs*. Artist: LoSarro

Inflatable latex blueberry suit by Squeak Latex

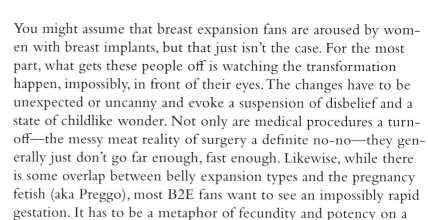

stretches their noses. He eroticizes the idea of them being exposed as "beautiful liars," and their imagined embarrassment at their involuntary nasal tumescence.

You might assume that breast expansion fans are aroused by women with breast implants, but that just isn't the case. For the most part, what gets these people off is watching the transformation happen, impossibly, in front of their eyes. The changes have to be unexpected or uncanny and evoke a suspension of disbelief and a state of childlike wonder. Not only are medical procedures a turn-off—the messy meat reality of surgery a definite no-no—they generally just don't go far enough, fast enough. Likewise, while there is some overlap between belly expansion types and the pregnancy fetish (aka Preggo), most B2E fans want to see an impossibly rapid gestation. It has to be a metaphor of fecundity and potency on a mythic scale; breasts become big enough to fill a room, penises too immense to fit through doorways.

In general, what makes these fantasies thrilling is that they are outrageous. The body expansion fan has to create make-believe situations and special effects. The most popular downloads are home-made comic strips, animations, and cheesy fiction stories. The story premises tend to rely on classic science fiction and fantasy devices: potions, elixirs, aliens, and malevolent witches. Body expansion folk especially love collecting and trading video clips of special effects from movies, television, and advertising—and you might be surprised how many there are. In recent years, some BE artists have begun live-streaming their art-making process, so fans can watch the images being made and live-comment the results.

If breast expansion were just guys jerking off to pictures of giant tits, I'd call it male adolescent breast fixation. But it isn't always men, for one thing—I've met straight women aroused by BE stories; they get off on both the idea of other women's and their own breasts becoming engorged. Quite a few straight male BE and B2E fans fantasize about their own bodies inflating, and the fiction usually describes the process from the perspective of the person whose body is growing.

A surprising number of these fantasies have the men morphing, through air inflation, into a woman. At least one fourth of the stories in the Breast Expansion Archive (an internet library of BE fiction) involves male-to-female gender transformation. Wren, who has been collecting BE stories and art since he was 23 (he's now in his 40s), imagines himself inflating by seeing himself as a woman. "I'm heterosexual, but I probably have some latent transgender

Porn star Angel Wicky morphed
by Tumblr user Pornocchia

desires, as I can't really imagine myself inflating except into a female form. I can't say I wouldn't be thrilled if I woke up tomorrow transformed into a girl who could inflate." He figures the female body is a natural choice: "Given the blossoming of hips and breasts through puberty, and bellies during pregnancy, women are kind of inflatable already."

Wren talks me through the experience: "Imagine you're inflating. The first thing you probably notice is your clothes getting tight. You feel a pressure from within. Perhaps something like the sensation of having just eaten a large tasty meal, but spread out all over your body. Eventually, you outgrow your clothes in a thrilling display of seams bursting and buttons popping off. You might be inflated too large or too tight to move at this point.... Rubbing your skin is going to squeak like latex and thumping skin is going to make you resonate like a hollow balloon. And you have no idea when or if the inflation will stop, or if you're going to pop."

Body expansion scenarios often incorporate BDSM plower play. Some plots are about control and forcible inflation, where a woman is tied to an air pump or transformed against her will. Wren likes the idea of a dominatrix using magic to transform her slave into a living blow-up sex doll. "Not only would she be immobile, but her fun parts would be larger and more sensitive!"

The thrill comes from imagining how helpless the woman feels at this strange thing happening to her body. Some stories incorporate fantasies of vengeance, with hackneyed plots about nerdy guys inventing secret spy formulas to get back at their ex-girlfriends, while a few body expansion fans enjoy the idea that the growing body renders the woman more powerful and potent. They might imagine being enveloped and suffocated by the gigantic breasts or belly. Wren adds, "Even with immobility, there can be a sense of dominance that comes from being at least twice as big as everyone around you, so it's perfectly feasible to inflate a dominatrix to grandiosity, with her every need seen to by those who worship her."

Wren's fantasies began with a childhood fascination for balloons and a passion for shoving stuffed animals into his pajamas. "It felt good, so I kept doing it." When he was about nine, Wren started experimenting with inner tubes and beach balls. When he got his first backyard kiddie pool, "I would go out there and sit in it wearing sweatpants or a sweatshirt, but I would have an inner tube hidden underneath the sweats. I'd leave the hose running and fill it up while I was sitting in there… From there, I managed to get up to air mattresses under baggy sweats, and went on to explore lots of other inflatable fun."

Wren made the connection between inflation and women's bodies when he hit puberty. Girls

were "busting out" all around him. "My inflation fantasies became focused completely on the female form at that point." Wren sees body expansion as a metaphor for the weird, terrifying, and fascinating changes that happen to one's own body in puberty: "Your body is changing, and neither you nor anyone else can do anything to stop it. The difference is, this is like puberty out of control—you get the thrill of helplessness that one gets from bondage, but there are no restraints in inflation. Your own body is restraining you. Your own body stuffs you full, tears your clothes off, takes you to new peaks of sensation."

Helia Melonowski is the punny alias of a female breast expansion fan I interviewed in 1999, when she was 23. She remembers as a young girl being transfixed by the cows on her grandfather's dairy farm. She found herself thinking about gigantic udders, and the suction machines and the hormones the farmer gave the cows to make them even bigger. "Later on, my friends and I played 'farm' and I played a big fat cow with a big fat udder." When Helia turned 17, her fantasies became reality: she suffered from macromastia in which her breasts ballooned in one year from flat-chested to 44GG. "Whoever said 'Take care in what you wish for,' knew what they were talking about."

Helia writes popular BE stories as her character, whose breasts enlarge when she gets sexually excited, her condition caused by an old witch's curse after being insulted by Helia's grandfather, owner of a latex factory. "I have always returned to inflation-type stories only because of my real life condition. At the same time, I felt somewhat odd and slightly guilty about it." Helia's fiction stories sometimes employ the idea of forced growth or Dominance & Submission, as long as it's never cruel. "I like the idea of being a victim if it isn't violent. In most of the stories, the girl is inflated and rendered helpless. Again, this doesn't bother me as long as no one gets hurt."

Kelly is a 35-year-old mother and part-time massage therapist whose BE fantasies began when she was nine and playing at a friend's house tormenting the friend's well-endowed older sister Julie. When the two younger girls were banished to the bedroom, the friend pushed a pillow up Kelly's shirt. "She said, 'Now you look just like Julie!' and I just stared. Something just clicked. I could hear her laughing, but it was as if she was a million miles away." When she finally brought herself back to reality, Kelly yanked the pillow out of her shirt and ran home. "I proceeded to have my very first orgasm. That's how strong it was. Zero to orgasm in ten seconds!"

Cowgirl photomorph
by CowTransformer on DeviantArt

From a BE story by E.L. Publications.
Artist: LoSarro

As an adult divorcée, Kelly took the pseudonym JulieKat (a nod to the girl in her childhood experience) and became chatroom monitor for the BE archive. She is bisexual, and her sexual fantasies feature either her own breasts inflating or another woman's breasts expanding and smothering her.

Kelly is one of those rare people who has managed to connect romantically with someone with the same obscure kink. She met him through the BE archive. He is a professional illustrator whose breast expansion drawings—under the nom de plume BustArtist—consistently win him "favorite artist of the year" awards in the BE community. In the late 1990s I had dinner with Kelly and BustArtist in Greenwich Village and saw a very happy couple. They are now, 17 years later, married and still involved in the BE scene. He makes a decent side income from selling access to his illustrated stories online.

BustArtist's BE fantasies combine with a healthy love of fat women, and Kelly is delighted to find a man who loves her big body. She enjoys the power when she acts out his fantasies. When she pretends her breasts are growing, BustArtist literally drools. Kelly's

> *"You have no idea when or if the inflation will stop, or if you're going to pop."*
> —Wren

Scenes from *Milking the Plot* by BustArtist

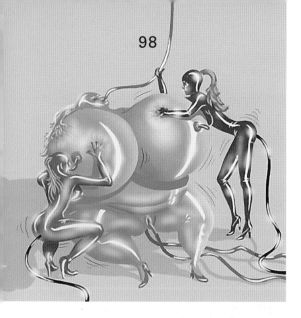

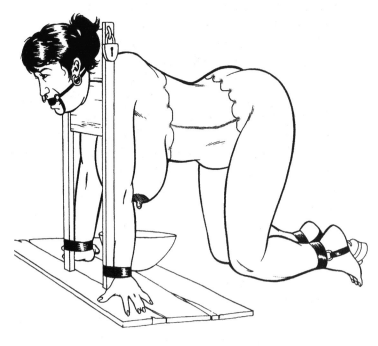

"This is like puberty out of control—you get the thrill of helplessness that one gets from bondage, but there are no restraints in inflation. Your own body stuffs you full, tears your clothes off, takes you to new peaks of sensation."
—*Wren*

fantasies may involve a woman being "subjected" to the transformation, "But in the end, who's got the real power? She does. Because she has become the object he wants so badly." BustArtist agrees there's something in the breast expansion fantasy that relates to male sexual potency: "I sometimes see it as an extension of when you're at that peak of orgasm and all of the blood is rushing to one spot. You're inflating in a way."

Both Kelly and BustArtist feel the healthiest body expansion fans are those who keep their fantasies fantastic, rather than those who focus on photos of body parts. She sometimes gets depressed by the yammering on the BE chatlines from guys who just want to talk about big tits.

Over the 18 years since I first met them, Kelly and BustArtist have seen changes in the online scene. Where in the early days Kelly often found herself one of the only women in chatrooms, and the women who did show up might have gotten harassed by the men, now women are getting stronger and more confident. "These days, women are raised with a different mindset. They don't put up with misbehavior."

Inflate123, a former child actor and founder of one of the first sites devoted to the BE fetish, has had inflation-related fantasies for as long as he can remember. It started out as a fascination for

Transformation into an inflatable love doll.
Illustration: Larry Latex

Cover illustration from *Farm Life,*
published by The Other Pony Club

balloons. His very earliest memory, from when he was two years old, is a dream where he imagined himself as a red balloon floating away into the sky. As a young boy, he made drawings of balloons and experimented with stuffing balloons inside his clothing—just like many of the looners. "I remember stuffing some inflatables down my shirt and ripping the seams on the sleeve, then panicking because I didn't know how to explain it to my parents. 'How did you rip that shirt?' 'I was...blowing myself up?' " His powerful imagination led him to misread a 1970s comic book advertisement for photo enlargements that read BLOW YOURSELF UP. "I stared at those three words for hours and replayed that dim memory of my dream over and over. I told my sister I wanted to blow myself up, and when she realized what I meant, she laughed at me for what felt like hours."

Inflate123's interest in balloons led him to become one of the first members of Balloon Buddies when it went online. He helped Buster set up the site. Inflate123 founded his own separate body expansion fantasy page a few months later, when it became clear that looners absolutely did not want to hear about real body parts inflating.

If there's one thing all body expansion fans have in common, it's their love of *Willy Wonka and the Chocolate Factory* and the character Violet Beauregarde, who grows into a giant human blueberry. Violet's stomach expands slowly at first, then her belt pops off and she eventually becomes completely spherical—her little head, hands and feet stick out and wiggle helplessly. Inflate123 explains: "This scarred pretty much everyone in the [BE] group—and we collectively love it...and our parents let us watch, the fools!" (Interestingly enough, most balloon fetishists find this scene way too scary and unpleasant.) It was, for body expansion fans, "Eureka!" Wren calls the movie the Holy Grail of body expansion, and Inflate123 sees Violet as his personal patron saint.

For fans, Violet's experience was terrifying and thrilling. When Inflate123 saw the film at five he cried inconsolably. "I was scared as hell—this girl not far from my age blowing up quickly." By the third time he saw it he just shut up and kept his fascination to himself. "It was the first external 'proof' of the concepts already swimming in my head." Inflate123 didn't care whether Violet was supposed to be filling up with blueberry juice. To him, she was just like a balloon. "Her belt giving way is still a powerful image to me—something pops, but the event's not over." Inflate123 is what might be called a body expansion version of a non-popper. "It's more melodramatic to have the inflation stop just at the nick of

Fannybelle, aka Bozella the Clown, just one inflatable clown alter ego of Sofonda Silicone, a body expansion fan and amateur clown

Inflatable immobilization suit
by Squeak Latex

*"I remember stuffing
some inflatables down
my shirt and ripping
the seams on the
sleeve, then panicking
because I didn't
know how to explain
it to my parents."*
—Inflate123

Mr. Blowup relaxing at home.
Photo: Mr. Blowup

time. Or if someone is going to explode from the pressure, I want to keep my last mental image of that last second before the pop."

In the years since our interview, Inflate123 has moved away from the Violet Beauregarde crowd online. "They are really into the color and the juice parts of the fantasy, whereas I was just into the inflation." And the single-mindedness of some of the Violet fans is a little off-putting: "There are now a zillion people named Violet Beauregarde on Facebook now with status updates that are pretty much first-person descriptions of that scene. I don't get it."

Inflate123 has managed to incorporate body expansion fantasies into his sexual relationship with his non-BE-fan wife. She sees his fetish as a personality quirk, and has helped him to get over much of his guilt and discomfort. "She said, 'It doesn't hurt anybody, it makes you happy, it's all rather innocent, and I don't mind it—so why are you upset?'" They might go out to dinner and start their fantasy game there: "I will mention that my drink tastes funny and ask if she'd put anything in it while I wasn't looking. She'll pick up on the lead and give me a 'you'll find out' look while denying everything, and the next hour or two are fun for me because I get to anticipate." Once they get to the bedroom, she will set him off with a few "potent" word choices: "swelling, balloon, inflate, pressure"—combined with some appropriate touching, which includes stroking the bottom of his stomach. "That's usually what inflates first in my fantasies. In my female fantasies, it's breasts first—but I don't have them, so..." The whole fantasy can be so powerful that he loses control of himself. "I shake with excitement, and my wife always knows she's got me in the palm of her hand when my teeth chatter uncontrollably." Inflate123 is deeply grateful he can trust his wife with his desires. "The fetish is a

Top Twelve Media Moments for Body Expansion Fans

(compiled by Inflate123 and Wren)

1. *Willy Wonka and the Chocolate Factory* (1971, and the 2005 remake). Easily the most famous inflatable fantasy scene ever committed to film! In the original film, look for the hose by her ankles—the tank is strategically hidden behind a crowd of onlookers.

2. *The Bliss of Mrs. Blossom* (1967). Sir Richard Attenborough plays a brassiere manufacturer who creates a "universal bra" that will give all women the chests they want and thereby alleviate world crisis. Due to sabotage, the inflatable bra goes horribly awry at the item's debut fashion show. The scene culminates with about twenty women with volleyball-sized inflated bosoms rising to the ceiling.

3. *Son of Flubber* (1960). The sequel to *The Absent-Minded Professor* finds the professor inventing Flubber Gas. The story's climax involves a football game where an unsuspecting friend wears a rubber diving suit that's inflated (and eventually, of course, overinflated) with Flubber Gas.

4. *An Evening With Kitten* (1985). A 40-minute or so collection of short comedy sequences featuring Kitten Natividad. In one sequence she plays a street bum who stumbles across a bottle of "super-grow" formula—upon drinking it she inflates, Hulk-style, to her famous Kitten proportions which launches her career as we know it.

5. *Saramandaia* (1976 and 2010 remake). A Brazilian telenovela with a character named Dona Redonda who is prone to overeating. Her lover envisions her swelling up and floating away like a balloon.

6. *Class of Nukem High* (1986). Crissy becomes pregnant with a mutant baby. In one scene, she's in bed asleep in a skimpy top and a bikini bottom. Her stomach starts to swell up and soon she looks nine months pregnant. The stomach looks very real—it's even the same color as her skin and doesn't look like rubber at all. It pulls open all but one button on her top and it pushes her bikini bottom down as it inflates.

7. *Leprechaun 3* (1995). The leprechaun punishes a woman who stole his gold by enlarging her breasts, then her lips, and finally her butt. Eventually she gets caught in a doorframe and explodes. Great sound effects (gurgling, swishing, stretching).

8. *Gilligan's Island*, "Castaway Pictures Presents" (1965). In an early episode, the Skipper and Gilligan dive down to the wreckage of their ship. Ginger and Mary Ann pump air into Gilligan's wet suit, which inflates and he bobs up to the surface.

9. *Harry Potter and the Prisoner of Azkaban* (2004). Harry accidentally magically inflates his Aunt Marge in the opening scenes of the book/film. Inflate123 has noticed that J.K. Rowling uses a lot of inflatable adjectives. "Listening to the audio book was at times a bit awkward." Of course, some in the community immediately assumed she's one of us!

10. *Epic Movie* (2007). Carmen Electra as shapeshifting X-Man Mystique, in a rubber outfit with stretchy sound effects.

11. Kary Perry's Plumpify CoverGirl Mascara ad (2016). Over the 90s tune "Pump Up the Jam" Katy Perry wears a latex outfit (and later, an inflatable skirt) while wielding an air pump and making all kinds of interesting faces.

12. Nintendo games like Super Mario World with the Power Balloon power-up. The item's effect is to make whoever picks it up swell up like a balloon and become Balloon Mario or Balloon Luigi, causing them to hover in the air.

Still from the original *Willy Wonka and the Chocolate Factory*, 1971

frighteningly powerful thing to me, and if my wife weren't so understanding and compassionate, she could use it against me in really nasty ways. So far, she just uses it against me in fun ways that she knows I'll enjoy."

It's vital for Inflate123 to involve his wife in his fetish and keep his focus on her. "The technical definition of a fetish is a fixation on an object or idea rather than your partner, and I've always wanted to avoid going in that direction if I can help it. My wife is voluptuous and I find her sexually attractive without the fetish—but when it's added in, I enjoy her on two levels." He doesn't need to think about inflation to get aroused, but it works every time when he does. Generally, he goes through phases. "Sometimes I 'need' it more than others, very much like an itch. Sometimes I only think about it and nothing else, have a big inflatable 'production' as my wife has termed it—just get immersed in the fantasy with props, build-up, and the whole bit." Other times he wants to concentrate on "normal" sexual themes and block out the fetish elements, "But ultimately, I'm more apt to use it than not—sometimes, when I don't

want to think about it, it sneaks in anyway just at the point of climax. Like it or not, it is ingrained now."

Like many BE fans whose fantasies started with a love of balloons, Inflate123 has explored the world of inflatable rubber clothing. In the late 1990s, he bought an inflatable black latex catsuit from a British fetishwear company in the hopes it would give him the sensation of pressure and inflating he was seeking, but "it made me look like a biker Santa Claus, which was not what I was after." The costume was also hellish to get into: "I had to coat myself with corn starch before slipping into it, because the perfumes in regular baby powder would damage the rubber. Plus the latex was cold and I was usually already trembling with excitement, so every nerve was always standing on end—it was a little painful." He bought a small compressor from Sears expressly for the suit, but only the front part of the suit inflated. The worst part of it was that he couldn't even reach his crotch to masturbate. "It turned out to be logistically difficult to bring myself to orgasm inside the thing." It sprang a leak after only about five tries. Inflate123 now laughs about the whole thing whenever he uses the compressor to inflate his car tires—"How mundane!"

For Inflate123, low-tech solutions have had perfectly acceptable results. He enjoys the feeling of pressure and containment he gets from wearing tight clothing, and feels sexy wearing bike shorts or a spandex wrestling tunic. "Squeeze bulbs or bicycle pumps connected to large latex balloons laid beneath spandex clothing work better than the catsuit—you feel it, you see it, and you can get out of the outfit in a hurry if you need to."

An inflation-oriented friend has perfected the art of wrapping inflatable mattresses around himself and hooking up an elaborate network of tubes under a spandex bodysuit, so he can inflate himself and enjoy the sensation of pressure. Overall, Inflate123 has a wonderful sense of humor. "Every day, I realize how patently silly the whole fetish is, how unrealistic, and how harmless it is. I'm sure there are people who see my web page and laugh at me—but I'm laughing at me too, because it's a ludicrous interest."

SQUEAK LATEX'S INFLATABLE COSTUMES

Latex inflatables have come a long way since Inflate123's catsuit fiasco.

Blowup Boy is the 30-something gay male founder of Squeak Latex, a fetish clothing manufacturer specializing in inflatable costumes. Blowup Boy is himself a long-term fantasy body expansion and inflatable clothing fan, and is fortunate enough to be married to a man who shares these interests. Like so many others, his fascination started with Violet Beauregarde in *Willy Wonka* and an inflation moment in *Who Framed Roger Rabbit*, and feels his brain has "simply always been wired to be attracted to the act of inflating." He never had any interest in pool toys or balloons though—it was always the idea of his own body inflating that excited him.

Blowup Boy's personal fantasy involves unexpected or unwilling inflation, usually in front of

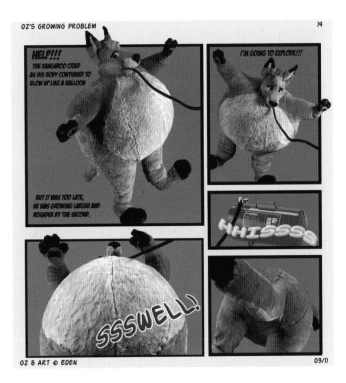

others who comment about it from the sidelines, "The loss of control and humiliation plays a large factor. It is in most part a laughable/comical sight to behold, followed by the helplessness and restriction. Once inflated it becomes hard or impossible to move, you're at the mercy of the situation and those around you." Like others, he has certain visual cues that push his buttons: buttons popping off, belts bursting, flailing about, panic, and so on.

Over the years he has played with inflating scuba suits and hazmat costumes, but like so many others, Blowup Boy was frustrated that there were so few inflatable costumes and the ones that did exist were overly expensive. He is also a furry (see Chapter 11), and the costumes he envisioned just did not exist. So, in 2010, he founded Squeak Latex to meet the demand. His first suits were the standard black latex, a fox, an inflatable raccoon and an inflatable blueberry, complete with exploding belt. He's sold over 100 copies of the latter. "Lot of blueberries waddling about around the world!" His dream is to make a blueberry suit where the wearer can be rolled around, just like in Willy Wonka, but after several

Detail from *Oz's Growing Problem*, showing a furry inflatable costume in action. Illustration by Eden

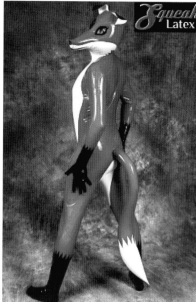

BODY EXPANSION IN BRIEF

TERMINOLOGY:
BE, B2E

CORE KINK:
latex, breasts, ass, sometimes
noses

MAJOR THEMES:
transformation/growth,
sometimes power play

SUBTHEMES:
embarrassment, sometimes
explosion

SUBKINKS:
breast expansion (BE),
breast and butt (B2E), penis
expansion, nose growth

RELATED KINKS:
balloons (see Chapter 3),
macrophiles (Chapter 5),
weight gain (Chapter 8),
preggo

EROTIC EQUATION:
interior pressure from
inflation

failed attempts it's clear he may have to use a different material than latex to support the person inside.

Since 2010, Blowup Boy has gone on to create hundreds of suits, sent to all parts of the world, including professional commercial work for music videos, TV commercials, TV game shows, and stage shows. He points out that, kink aside, inflating costumes and inflating body parts is a classic gag that has appeared in various media for years. "Even some of the earliest silent films feature body inflation gags!"

Blowup Boy does wear his inflatables to furry conventions, but only the ones that would pass a PG rating. "The old saying goes there is a time and a place for everything and my mind is in a non-kinky place when I'm out in a public space performing." Unfortunately, some of his customers have not shown the best judgment in wearing the more R-rated costumes—those with crotch zippers or inflating breasts—to cons. "This has caused some conventions to ban the use of latex suits, one or two ruining it for the rest of us."

That said, he's happy to fulfill customer requests, no matter how extreme. "I've always been a strong believer in never judging or kink-shaming anyone. We're all adults and people will use some of these suits during sex. I'm happy to accommodate."

Sample inflatable costumes sold by
Squeak Latex. Photos: Squeak Latex

Sidekink: Preggo

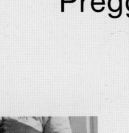

Mpreg selfie

Preggo fans get off on pregnancy, and enjoy the sight of hard, distended bellies in the last months of gestation. Some enjoy fantastical narratives of extreme, sudden belly growth with impossible quantities of fetuses. Others imagine their own bodies growing hopelessly huge. Male pregnancy fantasies are called mpreg. Preggo fans are generally not interested in the medical realities of the situation, like the act of childbirth or anything to do with the fetuses inside.

While much of the appeal lies in a universal attraction to fertility, some preggo fans want the pregnant person to be ashamed of her state (an unwed mother) or to be engaging in forbidden behavior, such as smoking or drinking.

CORE KINK:
belly

MAJOR THEMES:
growth, taboo

SUBTHEMES:
embarrassment

SUBKINKS:
mpreg

RELATED KINKS:
lactation, body expansion, fat

EROTIC EQUATION:
pressure of growth from within

Sudden multiple pregnancies.
Drawing by Marrazan, DeviantArt

Inflatable pregnancy suit
by Squeak Latex

5

Macrophiles:
Attack of the 50-Foot Fantasy

"Amazing Colossal Soul Sister" by Ron H., *Black Giantess* magazine

Of all the erotic growth fantasies, perhaps the most outrageous is wanting to see someone shoot up to 50, 100, or 1,000 feet tall and wreak Godzilla-style havoc. It's like *Attack of the 50 Foot Woman*, but it's also primo porno for macrophiles.

Macrophiles get off on stories about gigantic people eating, engulfing, and sitting on normal-sized folk. They imagine themselves smothered between a giantess's gigantic breasts, popped like a bug between her red lacquered fingernails, or trampled by her monstrous feet. They might masturbate to fantasies of riding gigantic penises or being exploded from the inside out by the ultimate mega-cum shot.

Of course, myth, folklore, and popular culture abound with godlike giants and giantesses

who dominate humans, as well as tiny people in a world of normal-sized folk. The ancient Greeks envisioned their gods as gigantic versions of human beings and created oversized sculptures to bring Olympian scale to earth: the bronze sculpture of Athena in the Parthenon is believed to have been nearly 50 feet tall; the Colossus of Rhodes over 100 feet, nearly as big as that modern giantess, the Statue of Liberty. The hero of the European folktale "Adventures of Tom Thumb" was constantly being swallowed and stomped by normal-sized people. In *Gulliver's Travels*, the hero experiences both sides—being a giant in a world of tiny people and tiny in a world of giants.

In contemporary culture, these magical figures are mostly limited to science fiction and chil-

"The Weaker Sex," turn-of-the-century satirical illustration by Gibson, of "Gibson Girl" fame. From the Currier & Ives catalog

Tiny POV, from GiantessKatelyn.com

dren's literature. The theme has been mined again and again in the nuclear age, from the original 1950s films to their various remakes. Children—tiny people themselves in a land of giants—love the theme of growing and shrinking, from *Alice's Adventures in Wonderland* to *Honey, I Blew Up The Kid*.

Although giantess worship is ancient, fantasies about giant men and women as a specific genre of erotic literature has a fairly short history. In the 1950s and 1960s, fetish illustrator Eric Stanton often pictured a dominatrix towering over her diminutive male slave. It has only been since the late 20th century that an entire body of narratives and images devoted to erotic giants and giantesses has come into its own.

Like so many of the kinks researched for this book, giantess fandom enjoyed a sudden growth in the late 1980s through the late 1990s due to the desktop publishing revolution. Ed Lundt began publishing the offset magazine *Giantess* in 1988, and for 15 years offered a mail-order catalog of all kinds of growth fantasies. The newsprint foot fetish magazine *In Step* (founded 1990 and closed in the early 2000s) had a regular column called "The Giantess Speaks" by veteran dominatrix and extremely tall, former pro-wrestler, Queen Adrena, whose private practice caters to men with this interest. *Black Giantess* (1996) featured gigantic rampaging black women, and *Giantess Show* (1995) was a photocopied magazine that provided extensive lists of giantess "sightings" and references in science fiction, television, literature, and comic books. These print-based businesses have all closed, replaced by the internet.

Online sources for giantess material have mushroomed from around five in 1997 to at least fifty significant websites. Many of these sites provide a forum for macros to share their own erotic giant/giantess stories, low-angle photographs of men or women, and morphed photo collages. People share low-budget blue-screen videos and compilations of giantess footage from pop culture sources like movies, TV, and advertising—with zero licensing rights.

While straight male giantess fantasies have by far the greatest representation in the magazines and websites, there are also sites where one can find fantasies of giant men catering to straight women and gay men. The best-known author in this genre was a man who went by the moniker Quark, whose work is part of the long and hallowed tradition of *Star Trek* slash fiction (see Chapter 11)—homoerotic stories written by fans based on characters from the popular television show. Quark's most popular story was a

Eric Stanton illustration, 1960s. Stanton Archives.
www.stanton-fetish.com

"Le Nouveau Parnasse Satyrique"
by Felicien Rops (1833-1898)

wonderfully hot and kinky homage to *Star Trek: Deep Space Nine* in which Doctor Bashir accidentally gets stuck in the holodeck, shrunk to two inches tall and sexually assaulted by Captain Sisko, Sisko's teenage son Jake, and his own normal-sized self!

CHUCKCJC, QUINTESSENTIAL MACRO

"Chuckcjc" was the nom de plume of one of the 1990s' most prolific internet giantess artists, and his fantasies and experiences were typical of many of the straight male macro types online. He was well-known among giantessophiles for the montages he created by blending cityscapes with *Sports Illustrated* swimsuit models and PG-rated sex kittens.

Chuck is proudest by far of the lengthy erotic fiction stories he writes in his spare time. The story he considers his masterwork, "Monica XL," is an ambitious multipart novella with a typical macrophile plotline. Monica is a normal-sized girl who suffers at the hands of men. Her mother is stabbed in a mugging and Monica herself is brutalized and about to be raped when a mysterious blue light comes down from the sky. Monica starts growing, eventually reaching 2,000 feet tall. (Most giantessophiles have a specific ideal height in mind, usually between 50 feet to 300 feet—Chuck is a "mega-giantess" fan, meaning that he likes giantesses 2,000 feet tall or more.) Monica's first victims are her would-be rapists, and she crushes them with her feet in an ecstatic act of revenge. "He saw the intricate stitching around the sole edges and the enormous off-white spot where the sandals were starting to wear through. Then the air rushed at him like the gale of a hurricane—blowing him back. The sole did not stop but only seemed to speed up, and its great shadow filled the window. He clenched his teeth, his jaw locked preventing a scream and then…"

Chuck's writing is like a kid's comic book because that's how he thinks about these awesome women. When Monica kills, she does it cleanly and the

violence is abstract. The story is explicitly soft focus about sex—it may be a masturbation fantasy, but there's hardly any detail. At one point, hundreds of "sex-crazed" men climb onto Monica's body to explore. "They ran along her tanned left arm…to achieve the ecstasy of her soft shoulders, magnificent towering breasts, and the firm plane of her stomach. The perverts among the crowd continued with deeper explorations…" The details are ignored.

Chuck's "Monica XL" story shifts perspectives: at one moment we're inside the giantess's head, the next we're one of those crushed, the orgasmic crescendo for many giantessophiles, but we also get to be Monica—identity is flexible and constantly changing. Chuck thinks Monica's POV is a "rush," and he enjoys expressing righteous anger through her.

Like many macrophiles, Chuck is a foot fetishist, and volunteers that his giantess fixation has

Giantess attacks Las Vegas. Collage: Chuckcjc

*"I am not just a
Goddess my little insect,
I am an avenging
Goddess, a woman of
enormous power. I
will be the judge of
mankind, and the
sentence will be extreme...
I am 100% woman...
Hear me roar!
—Monika XL,
by Chuckcjc*

something to do with his childhood love of his mother's feet. "My mother had very good control of her toes, and would use them to give us pinches on the legs." Chuck's foot fascination turned giantess-related at six. "It was the old cartoon *Superfriends*. On it there was a giantess character who could grow named Gargantua." After Gargantua, Chuck fantasized about Wonder Woman as a protective motherly figure.

Chuck's giantess fantasies turned violent and sexual in puberty. "I was very embarrassed by it, who wouldn't be? I mean, giant women? Bah! What nonsense." He was very religious, and thought he was going to go to Hell for it—perhaps he deserved to be stomped by the giantess's feet. "Slowly, in maybe junior high school I realized it wasn't going away and I started to accept it as part of me." Giantesses soon became his primary—and exclusive—masturbation fantasy fodder: "I imagined teachers as 300-foot tall towering giantesses...but soon some of my pretty classmates became giantesses in class."

When I interviewed him in 1999, Chuck hadn't had many girlfriends. "I have asked women about this indirectly... Once it was ignored, and another time the result was a very creative verbal role-play. They didn't know it was my sexual fantasy, though." Chuck described exactly what he would do if he had a willing girlfriend. He would lie on the floor and watch his partner walk around "pretending to be a cruel evil giantess with lots of foot play...she could step over me and everything just so I could get the point of view."

Photo-collage by Expander, a gay male macrophile   Mega-giantess in Brazil. Collage: Chuckcjc

ED LUNDT, KING OF THE GROWTH FANTASIES

Ed Lundt founded *Giantess* magazine in 1988 because he was convinced he could not be alone in his love of giant women. "I used the Carl Sagan technique of extrapolation. 'If you have this many planets in a galaxy, one of them must support intelligent life.'" His first ads in fetish magazines like *Gent, Juggs,* and *BUF* (fat women) only garnered four or five responses per week, and it took him over a year to make his money back on the first issue. (Ed likes giant breasts, so at first it didn't occur to him to advertise in a foot fetish magazine like *Leg Show*.) Over the subsequent 11 years, however, the size fetish phenomenon grew gigantic itself; by 1999 his mailing list included thousands of fans of all kinds, from body inflation to breast expansion, weight gain, and giantesses—all scenarios Ed himself enjoys.

When I interviewed him, Ed Lundt lived with his wife in suburban Long Island, supporting himself with his mail-order business, investments, and various jobs in the arts. They seemed to have a very strong relationship; they were physically affectionate with each other and both seemed quite comfortable discussing his unusual erotic turn-ons with a relative stranger. Ed's wife is a crafts artist. They met each other through a dating service for fat admirers, though she was nowhere near supersized herself.

Ed learned a few things about his customers over the years. He believes most giantessophiles (his preferred term) fall into two main interest areas: those who are primarily interested in the growth process itself, and those primarily interested in how the giantess causes destruction after she's grown. The growth types prefer only to see the woman grow, pop off her buttons, and rip through the seams of her clothing. Just like with the balloon fetish and body inflation, the excitement comes from the object transforming into enormity.

For Ed, the fantasy of being tiny in a world of giants has everything to do with childhood.

"The only time we experience giants in our existence is when we're little kids, and they're the adults, but when I have the fantasy now, it's not with my mother. It might be with a motherly character or someone who might treat me like a child." Yes, it's clearly a touchy subject in the scene. "Most of my customers would deny this completely, though. If you bring this up, this really hits a raw nerve. They're in total denial."

Harold Schechter, professor of American literature at Queens College, prefers to look at giantess fantasies as a symbol of something universal. "When you're confronted with a lot of these erotic images, you're entering into a very fluid, boundary-shifting, disorienting, scary, exhilarating realm of the marvelous. They're not imprisoning you in some infantile state, but allowing you access to a larger dimension of experience that other people outgrow or lose."

The vast majority of macrophiles—unlike feeders and breast expansion types—want their Mother Goddess to be menacing and frightening, not

Not Your Average Pick-up from E.L. Publications story "Overdeveloped." Artist: LoSarro

nurturing. While body inflation and weight-gain fantasies seem to evoke that idyllic moment where we were one with our mother's breast, giantess fantasies imply the threat of annihilation. Most macros want a specific part of the giantess's body to destroy them, and by far the largest subset want to be squished under her monstrous feet. For the foot-crush fan, the sexual climax of the giantess story may be either the moment of greatest pressure from her massive foot or the moment when they imagine exploding from the pressure. Ed describes the usual crush plot as a series of pops building up to the ultimate pop—quite like the mass-popping frenzy of some of the balloon fetishists' masturbation scenarios, or anyone who's ever enjoyed flattening some bubble wrap.

Many of these foot fetish types really don't want to think or hear about genitals in their giantess fantasies at all. As Ed Lundt explains, "The thing that's hardest for people to understand is that in any fetish the act that is considered the most erotic, the most sought-after, the most sexually charged, may not involve sexual intercourse or even any sex parts coming into contact."

"When you're confronted with a lot of these erotic images, you're entering into a very fluid, boundary-shifting, disorienting, scary, exhilarating realm of the marvelous. They're... allowing you access to a larger dimension of experience that other people outgrow or lose."
—Harold Schechter

Despite the common themes, Ed Lundt says no two macro fantasies are quite alike. "They can be very finicky!" Ed has gotten plenty of letters from customers complaining his stories don't contain their particular trigger item, some of which are rather obscure. One reader demanded Ed write a story with a sneezing giantess. "I can figure out a way to work one sneeze into a story, but I can't see selling many copies of a story called 'The Giantess Sneezes' to anyone except Kleenex manufacturers!" (see Sneeze Fetish Sidekink, Chapter 3). Yet another customer said he would never buy another story again because he only wanted to read about a woman between 6'4" and 7'2" spanking a man over her knee while yelling "Patch patch maw maw!"

Where BE fans of a certain age might have been triggered by Violet Beauregarde, many macrophiles' "Aha!" moment happened with *Alice's Adventures in Wonderland*. Ed says most of the children who read it just think it's a fun story. "But," he adds, "when macrogynophiles read it, their eyes pop out of their heads, and they're fascinated with it and they don't know why."

Unfortunately, *Giantess* did not survive the internet economy. Ed Lundt's stories were being copied and shared for free in chatrooms, and in 2007 he sold his entire fiction repertoire to BustArtist, the body expansion artist. Ed's last post on any of the forums was that same year, and no one in the community has

Illustration from E.L. Publications'
Always Underfoot. Artist: LoSarro.

Cut out disc →

Cut out disc →

Magic Disc Illusion ©1982 E.L. Publications

MAKE YOUR LOVER APPEAR TO GROW IN FRONT OF YOUR VERY EYES USING THIS OPTICAL TRICK DEVELOPED BY ED LUNDT!

1. Photocopy this image at 185%.

2. Get a picture (or person) that you would like to "grow."

3. Cut out the Magic Disc, including small center hole.

4. Place the Magic Disc on a phonograph turntable, with the pattern side facing up.

5. Before you start the turntable, make sure that the tone arm will not operate.

6. Adjust the turntable speed to 45 rpm.

7. Switch on the turntable (the Magic Disc may appear to wobble slightly as it spins—this will not interfere with the effectiveness of the illusion).

8. Stare steadily at the center of the Magic Disc as it spins; keep staring for at least 30 seconds.

9. Quickly turn to look at the picture (or person)—which will then appear to be growing right before your eyes!

FOR BEST RESULTS:

Stare at the Magic Disc for a full minute rather than 30 seconds (the minimum effective time).

It may help you to stare at the second stripe out from the center, rather than directly at the center.

The speed at which the Magic Disc spins will determine the speed of the illusion: 33 rpm will make for a slower, but longer-lasting effect. 78 rpm will produce a brief, but more explosive effect.

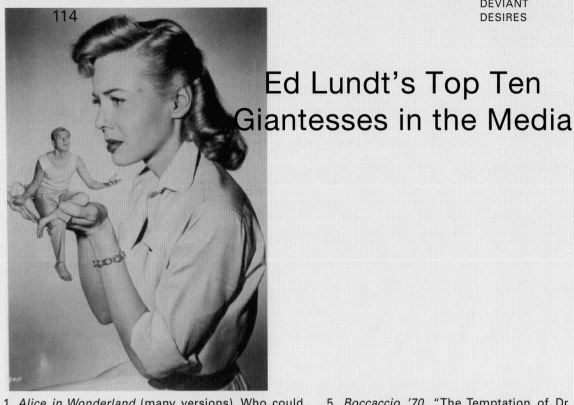

Publicity shot for *The Incredible Shrinking Man*, 1957

Ed Lundt's Top Ten Giantesses in the Media

1. *Alice in Wonderland* (many versions). Who could forget Alice's body "opening out like the largest telescope that ever was" or growing so huge that her giant limbs stuck out the windows and doors of a house? For most of us macrophiles, Alice's growth made us sexually "curiouser and curiouser."

2. *The Incredible Shrinking Man* (1957). Though not technically a giantess movie, if you're a macrophile, you can appreciate its many size comparisons. Our hapless hero shrinks smaller than his wife, smaller than a circus midget, and eventually, smaller than his wife's extremely (to him) high-heeled shoe. In other words, "Giantess, schmiantess...so long as she's taller than you!"

3. *Attack of the 50 Foot Woman* (1958). In spite of the high cheese-factor, Allison Hayes is a sight to behold as the towering giantess. Wrapped in nothing but bedsheets (strategically enlarged so as to cover her naughty bits) she regally strides into town like the empress of the toga party. Ignore the stars shining through her superimposed image... just enjoy.

4. *The 30 Foot Bride of Candy Rock* (1959). Dorothy Provine is the fiancée of a would-be inventor (Lou Costello) who accidentally makes her grow. On their honeymoon night, Artie takes a long look at her body, realizes that he is sexually inadequate for the job, and disappointedly resigns himself to sleep. In another scene, the implicitly nude giantess peeks out of a hole in a roof, while Artie stands on a ladder and gives her a shower with a fire hose—held between his legs.

5. *Boccaccio '70,* "The Temptation of Dr. Antonio" (1962). Anita Ekberg is a huge billboard image come-to-life. Her mission: to tempt and tease the puritanical Dr. Antonio. He scurries between her legs like a frightened mouse, only to be plucked up and placed on her gigantic, heaving (plastic prop) bosom. A bigger-than-life star was needed to play this colossal goddess/demon. Ms. Ekberg proves that only she could fill those size 1,200 pumps.

6. *Village of the Giants* (1965). "See them burst out of their clothes and bust up a town!" claims the movie's tagline. The "them" in question is a bunch of rowdy 60s teens (including Beau Bridges), who steal a growth formula from a brainiac kid (Ron Howard). One after the other, the teens zoom to giant size—the girls popping the buttons off their suddenly undersized blouses! Another great scene: teenage giantesses dancing, while a normal-sized boy dangles from her gigantic bosom.

7. *Honey, I Blew up the Kid* (1992). The inventor makes his wife a giantess to rescue their giant kid. The money shot is a close-up of the woman's clothed breast pressing up against the giant kid's pocket when she hugs him. What's so special about that? Inside the pocket is a full-sized convertible containing her son and his date, smothering under mom's giant boob. Pretty sick stuff, especially coming from Disney.

8. "BFGoodrich Radial Age" TV ad (1967). A man is driving down the highway, when his car is suddenly lifted off the road by a giant go-go girl wearing a metallic minidress. She pops off his tires and replaces them with BFGoodrich radials. She returns him to the ground, and proceeds to wash, iron, and vacuum the road ahead of him. Politically incorrect? You bet. But why does this schmuck drive away from such an ideal woman?

9. "Ty-D-Bowl Man" TV ad (1960s–70s). A woman finds a tiny man floating in her toilet. Paging Dr. Freud! Paging Dr. Freud! The psychological implications of this scenario boggle the mind: Is the little Ty-D-Bowl guy a mutation caused by toilet-training gone horribly, horribly wrong? Does the housewife represent his mother in this bizarre psychodrama? Some kinky suggestion of toilet slavery is going on here.

10. *Bewitched* "Samantha's Wedding Present" (1968). Endora shrinks Darrin. Ms. Montgomery is smirk-a-licious as she giggles at Darrin's humiliating little... predicament.

11. *I Dream of Jeannie* "Genie, Genie, Who's Got the Genie?" (1968). Jeannie's evil sister blinks Tony and Roger down to doll-size and imprisons them in a birdcage. Unfortunately, the special effects consist of a couple of actual toy dolls (they look like G.I. Joes) glued inside the birdcage.

12. *Schoolhouse Rock* (Grammar Rock). "Unpack Your Adjectives" (1973) A short boy laughs at a tall girl, and she grows and grows, until all we can see of her are her giant legs, feet and sandals. The boy shrinks to the size of a bug, at which point the enormous girl stomps him into oblivion with a single Birkenstock! Even though this brief sequence lasted less than 10 seconds, it "stamped" its indelible footprint into the malleable gray matter of future macrophiles everywhere.

13. *Amazing Stories* "Miscalculation" (1986). A nerdy high school kid named Beezler (Jon Cryer) accidentally spills some goopy chemicals onto a magazine (pretty obvious symbolism there!) and it transforms the cover picture of a puppy into a real live puppy. He takes the chemicals home, and starts experimenting on sexy centerfolds. He keeps getting the mixture wrong, resulting at one point in an 8-foot-tall woman. The special effects are very convincing. Spielberg's crew built an exact, scaled-down duplicate of the kid's room, so that the actress looks huge. Whoops! I just "spilled some chemicals" in my pants.

14. *Attack of the 50 Foot Woman* (1993). There are many great effects in this HBO remake starring Daryl Hannah. She bursts out of (most of) her clothing as she grows right through the ceiling; she takes a bubble bath in a swimming pool; and she stomps through town, looking for her two-timing husband (Alec Baldwin).

15. *Attack of the 60 Foot Centerfold* (1995). In this spoof of the other *Attack* movies, director Fred Olin Ray was deliberately trying to make a bad film—and unfortunately he succeeded with flying colors. There are oodles of special effects stuffed into this turkey—including a guy popping out of a giantess's cleavage—but they're consistently unimpressive. Rent, don't buy.

BFGoodrich ad from *LIFE* magazine, 1967

"It would be convenient for me to say that I do this work because I'm a feminist, that I want the woman to be big and important and I'm giving a powerful role model to the world. But that's bullshit. This is not about women. This is about men and their fantasies."
—Ed Lundt

Detail from *GrOwing Appreciation,* a graphic novel by BustArtist

heard from him since. BustArtist's investment paid off: he has been transforming these stories into high-quality comics that he's successfully marketed for sale online.

RON H. AND MS. ZENA: BLACK GIANTESSES RULE THE EARTH

Ron H.'s giantess fantasies are much more overtly sexual and political than either Ed Lundt's or Chuckcjc's. Ron tries to make his fantasies come true by acting them out with girlfriends and dominatrixes. Ron H. is African-American, and he began publishing *Black Giantess* as a labor of love in 1995 when he became frustrated with all the white giantess material. *Black Giantess* was an irregular semi-annual photocopied magazine devoted to visions of gigantic black women wreaking havoc on the urban landscape, filled with stories and comic strips contributed by friends and fellow giantess fans, as well as Ron's extraordinary handmade collages that are in many ways far more artistically interesting than many of the seamless slick photo-morphs online. Ron sold only 350 copies total of the seven issues he created.

"*Black Giantess* is a special interest, erotic, satirical work, for those into the giantess/crush/foot worship fantasy. This work is a true labor of love, which also deals with the trivialization or degradation of ideas or personages normally held to be lofty or advanced; and the empowerment of those normally consigned to an inferior or inconsequential position in our society—black women. This is a safe sex fantasy alternative to dangerous sex practices. The editor has the highest regard and respect for all women. Violence against all women across the earth must cease!"

For its few years of existence, *Black Giantess* was published out of Ron's tiny basement apartment in Fredericksburg, Virginia—an unlikely location for something so edgy. Ron is originally from Newark, New Jersey; he moved down to Virginia in 1997 to be closer to Ms. Zena, the inspiration for both *Black Giantess* and *Zena Rules* magazines (his other self-publishing effort). Ms. Zena was a part-time professional dominatrix with a specialization in foot fetish; she also sold real estate and ran a cleaning business. Ron met Ms. Zena first through correspondence and then for some foot domination sessions focusing on his worship of the giantess. Later, they developed an extraordinary family unit; Zena is a lesbian with a live-in lover and a child by a previous marriage, and Ron H. is a widower with a teenaged son. Although they did not live together, Ron and Zena raised their children together and helped each other out whenever possible. Ron created and solicited much of the art and stories for *Black Giantess*, but Ms. Zena was the living muse for the work.

POV photo from GiantessKatelyn.com

Collage by Ron H., *Black Giantess #7*

Cover of *Black Giantess #6*, collage by
Ron H.

Cover of *Black Giantess #7,* collage by
Ron H.

"Wet Nurse to Elephants." One of at least ten giantess illustrations by German artist Heinrich Kley, circa 1908

I met Ron H. and Ms. Zena in 1999 at her suburban home. At the time, Ron was 41 years old and looked like a school librarian. Although he is very tall, he moved so slowly and carefully that he managed to seem smaller. He wore tidy khakis, a button-down shirt and a soft sweater. His large soft eyes are a strikingly pale brown color. In fact, everything about him is soft, from the skin of his hands to his handshake to his voice, which sometimes got so quiet it faded from my tape recorder altogether. When he spoke, he was polite in an almost old-world style—it took some time for him to agree to call me by my first name instead of "Miss Gates." Not that he ever seemed obsequious or insincere—he was just gentlemanly. Ron worked part-time as an art therapist, but had previously been a FedEx employee and a door-

to-door salesman. Ron is also a man with a vision of how to make the world a better place; he once ran unsuccessfully for public office in New Jersey.

Ms. Zena couldn't be more different from Ron. She is short and thin and has close-cropped hair framing a round face. She talks very fast with strong gestures and is constantly moving in her seat. She is surprisingly small for a giantess fantasy facilitator, but her personality is huge and that's clearly what counts.

One of the things that makes *Black Giantess* extraordinary is its overt political content and graphic sexual detail. Ron explains that he sees his fantasy as a way of giving black women power. "The way I perceive it is that the black female has been oppressed and taken advantage of and used so much over the centuries… What would happen if she were able to get back at all of those who caused her problems? And it's a sexual thing because then she could do whatever she wanted to, as long as she gratifies herself." One of Ron's old girlfriends pointed out to him that some of his attraction to powerful female images might have to do with the fact that his father used to physically abuse his mother. "She said to me, 'Maybe it's the fact that you saw your mother being kicked around…you hoped that women if they got to a certain height could defend themselves.' I looked at it like that and I thought, 'Maybe there's something to that.'"

Black Giantess' combination of politics and sex isn't always popular—when Ron wrote a story about Thomas Jefferson's enslaved mistress Sally Hemings, some readers objected. When I comment how wonderfully satirical some of his collages are, Ron corrects me gently. "I look at my collages as very serious pornography. I wouldn't want to create a parody/slapstick thing. I've had people tell me my stuff is great comedy, but I don't see it as a joke. I don't see any playfulness in it, but other people do. I see

it as sexual first and then as political, as a way of acting out frustration."

Ron's personal giantess scenario is different from most macrophiles. For Ron, the giantess is an avenger and protector—he doesn't want to be squished in the fantasies, he wants to see the giantess kill those who deserve to die. "I know that there are a lot of people who want to be squished, but not me." Ron came to use the fantasies as a way of blowing off steam from frustrating days at his job. "And it worked. In my mind I would imagine these specific people getting destroyed by the giant woman… It's a kind of revenge." Ron feels that the giantess is not only a mother figure, but also an alter ego, a part of himself that is permitted to be angry.

When Ron first began the magazine and solicited contributions from other giantess fans, he discovered that many of their offerings were horribly stereotyped and even racist. "I did get one story in the beginning from a guy that was about a black woman that was a cannibal. Her language was something out of a Tarzan movie. I couldn't understand it. I had to send it back to them, saying, 'If I showed this to some of my friends, they'd kill me!'" The white contributors did not realize that Ron is himself black—even Ed Lundt presumed that Ron is white—and they engaged in blatantly racist tropes.

Ms. Zena remembers racial prejudice in the 50s and 60s in Washington, DC, but her grandmother always got a lot of respect from the white men, especially the doctor who ran

Collage by Ron H., *Black Giantess #7*

Collage by Ron H., *Black Giantess #7*

Still from one of Ron H.'s giantess
videos starring Ms. Zena

the local hospital. "Back then when you were black, you couldn't afford a house visit from a doctor. Your parents just whipped up whatever they could and took care of you the best they could. Dr. Hadley was always there and my grandmother would say to him, 'By the way, my neighbor down the street needs to see you too.' I noticed as a kid that he was very, very humble and I never caught him looking up at her, he was always staring at my grandmother's feet." As she got older, Zena put clues together and thought, "Damn, where did grandma get money to have all of those expensive shoes?" She thinks her grandmother was also a foot mistress. The majority of Ms. Zena's current customers are rich white men who want to worship her feet, many of whom were raised by black nannies. "I had a white slave who told me that he had a nanny that really turned him on, and that she always smelled good. He told me that his mom would sometimes be cruel and that

his nanny would scoop him up and press him against her big breasts. He felt his little wing-wong getting hard. And she relieved his stress by rubbing his back and washing him."

Race is frequently on Ms. Zena's mind in her work with clients. "I didn't like the connotation of the word slave. I had to realize it's not slavery as my ancestors went through. These people are asking for this, my ancestors didn't. I had to make a whole adjustment with that. For a long time, I would just call them my little boys, or my little flunkies." Eventually Zena got to the point where she could call a white man a slave, but calling a black man a slave was still really difficult. "If I had to call this black brother a slave, oh shit! To deal with black slaves who were turned on by having you spit in their mouth. I found that to be the most degrading thing you could ask. I had to realize that it was up to me, as a mistress, whether I wanted to do this." She once had a black client who wanted her to call him Mandingo. "He specifically wanted me to call him Mandingo and ride his back and beat on him until I broke his skin. So I got out of that."

By the time I interviewed her, Ms. Zena was no longer doing traditional pro-domme work with whips and bondage; she worked almost exclusively with foot fetishists and macrophile clients. It's less work, for one thing, and she seems to enjoy the playful aspect of it as well. One white client would ask her to stand on tiptoes above him while he knelt on the floor to create the illusion that she is a giantess. Sometimes he asks to dance with her. "Slave James would be on his knees while I'm on my tiptoes and he would try to reach up to my chin with his head." His penis would stay completely limp until he would start struggling to stretch up to Ms. Zena's chin. "He'd ask me, 'If I reach up there, could I touch my nose to your nose?' And on occasion I've bent down just a bit to get closer to see what he would do, and he just shivered. Sometimes he'd ask me to push down on his shoulders so he'd have to struggle even more. And his dick would be bouncing all over the place and dripping, it would really turn him on!"

Ron H. and other giantess fans often ask Ms. Zena to play around with small man-shaped figurines. Usually the figurine is a stand-in for the client himself. One of Ms. Zena's customers paid her to take photographs of her high-heeled shoe pressing the gas pedal of a car with a figurine trapped underneath the pedal getting squashed—a giantess-oriented version of the gas-pedal-pumping fetish. Ron likes to see women play with small figurines too, and his longest-lasting and most frequent fantasy involves the view of a black woman from behind. "You can see the soles of her feet, but you don't really see her face. She is holding this little man figure and she's jiggling it against her vagina. She could mash the little guy violently against her until he's just glue." Ron shows me one little figurine he likes Ms. Zena to use; it's a painted plaster figure of a guy with huge wide pants, wool cap and a big medallion. Ron bought it at a Woolworth's store. "You see, this guy looks like a typical knucklehead. He looks like the kind of guy who I would like to see get wiped out."

Ron's erotic fantasies were strongly influenced by a brief glimpse he had of the classic 1958 film *Attack of the 50 Foot Woman*. He remembers hearing about the film from a camp counselor he liked when he was in his early teens; he saw ads for the film and was thrilled by the concept. The concept was his erotic fantasy fodder for years before he actually saw the film on video. Ironically, once he finally got up the nerve to order it from his local video store (all the time terrified that someone would "catch" him) he was profoundly disappointed. His own imagination was far better. Nevertheless, his collages are still profoundly influenced by the look of that film, and he prefers to work in black and white to recreate that 1950s sci-fi feel.

Ron would get off on creating the giantess collages that he published in *Black Giantess*. He worked on his collages almost every night after he got home from work. "I put pictures together, get stimulated, have an orgasm, and go to sleep."

I last spoke with Ron in 2006, when he was thrilled to have his collages featured in the *KINK* exhibition at Museum of Sex.

SIZECON: A NEW GENERATION
After the demise of Ed Lundt's *Giantess* magazine and the collapse of several of the larger commercial, giantess-oriented

BLACK GIANTESS
STATEMENT OF PURPOSE

Black Giantess is a special interest, erotic, satirical work, for those into the giantess/crush/foot worship fantasy. This work is a true labor of love, which also deals with the trivialization or degradation of ideas or personages normally held to be lofty or advanced; and the empowerment of those normally consigned to an inferior or inconsequential position in our society—black women. This is a safe sex fantasy alternative to dangerous sex practices. The editor has the highest regard and respect for all women. Violence against all women across the earth must cease!

Still from one of Ron H.'s giantess videos starring Ms. Zena

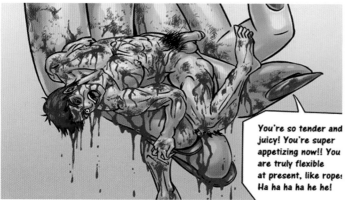

You're so tender and juicy! You're super appetizing now!! You are truly flexible at present, like ropes Ha ha ha ha he he!

Extreme tiny torture from *Her Wicked Pleasure*, GiantessKatelyn.com

websites, the macrophile community grew on its own through old-fashioned chatrooms and bulletin boards. It was an ad hoc virtual community with little or no real-life, human interaction. It might have stayed that way, but for the efforts of one young, female size-fantasy artist known as Veronica (her artwork is signed "Jitensha").

Veronica has been fascinated by giants since childhood. She would play size games with her friends, "But when I got to be about ten, I realized this was something that was different." She started keeping her obsessions to herself. "Puberty was a rough time." Even though she got a laptop at the age of 13, she was shy about sex and felt there was something "not right" about what she liked. It wasn't until she was 18, in 2006, that she found a video on YouTube and had a moment familiar to so many with niche kinks: "I wasn't alone!"

At first, when she would go into macrophile chatrooms, she was the only woman, and she got harassed. "They didn't believe there was this woman there who didn't want to be a giantess, but instead wanted to be the tiny person… God forbid you post a giant man picture!" But things have changed in the last ten years, with the addition of a wider range of giantess bodies—not just blonde swimsuit models— including older giantesses, tattooed giantesses, and gay and trans material. "The community is really different now. There are a lot more women and they are a lot more vocal." Fans of male giants can visit story archives and chatrooms on sites like Coiled Fist.

In her personal life, Veronica began to ask her partners to engage in size role-play. Her boyfriend would take on the giant role by standing over her and calling her tiny and using aggressive language while she masturbated. They are now married and in a full-time dom/sub relationship. She does house chores, and certain personal grooming, or she gets punished.

Veronica wants her male giants to be cruel and sadistic, and connects this with her Latina upbringing in Miami among macho men. When she fantasizes about female giants, though, she wants the woman to be unaware of the accidental torture: "She doesn't even realize that she's stepping on me, or sitting on me with her giant stinky crotch."

Veronica developed a devoted following in the macrophile community for her artwork and stories under the name Jitensha. She encourages people to talk about relationships and support each other in chatrooms. In April 2015, Veronica decided to invite a few of her online contacts to a meet-up in New York City. She rented a studio space in SoHo and advertised on 4Chan, Reddit, and Craigslist. More than 20 people showed up, including one other girl. People traveled from as far away as Delaware, New Jersey, Long Island, and Buffalo. "The meet-ups focused on relationships and self-care. It was a support group, not a place to exchange porn."

Scene from *Giant Hunting* by Jitensha

> *"It's like you know the funniest joke in the world and no one else gets it. Then, finally you meet other people who get the joke."*
> —Bryan

SizeCon poster by Jitensha

Bryan, who is slightly younger than Veronica, was one of those who showed up at the first meet-up. He was so nervous that he had to get drunk first. "But once I got there, there was an instant relief and a sense of connection… It's like you know the funniest joke in the world and no one else gets it. Then, finally you meet other people who get the joke."

Bryan's size fantasies started when he was about five, watching a *Tom and Jerry* cartoon. "Tom the mouse goes into the city and has to dodge all of these giant people." In terms of erotic giantess fantasies, Bryan can imagine himself as either the small person or the giant: "I'm a switch, which is not all that common." He laughs, "I never told anybody that before!" He is in a relationship with a woman who "talks size" to him.

In his professional life, Bryan had organized professional corporate meetings and he was good with money, so after the success of the first meet-ups, when Veronica proposed to him that they put on a convention for size fantasies he was enthusiastic. "Furries have their own cons. Horror fans have their own cons, why not us?"

At first, the idea of a con was not an easy sell to the community. "We got a lot of doubters. Some thought it was a prank." There had been a notorious Kickstarter called DashCon for *My Little Pony* fans that turned out to be a rip-off. They took the money and never had the event. "So it was tough getting momentum." Things took off when they decided not to focus just on giantess fans, but to also include body inflation and any fantasies that relate to size-related transformation and power dynamics. Members of the feeder and weight gain scene reached out and wanted to participate (see Chapter 8). Partnerships were made, bonds were forged.

The Kickstarter did not reach its goal, but they did raise $9,000—enough for a downsized plan. They sold tickets for $40 through Eventbrite. Anyone who paid the entrance fee could have a booth. VIP tickets included goodies such as custom artwork and videos, or meet and greets with special guests. They ended up making a few hundred dollars profit.

SizeCon 2016 was held in Midtown Manhattan on April 23 in a photo studio. They had an overflow attendance of over 125 size fans, ranging in age from 18 to 70, with about 25% women. Bryan guesses there were about 15 gay women and men and a few trans people. Exhibitors included artists, movie producers,

and actresses who would model with attendees and sign autographs. They set up a green screen area, where people could take a photo with a giant or giantess. "We even had a VR demo where people could put on headsets and experience a tiny POV in a huge world."

Even though no one under 18 was admitted to the con, Veronica and Bryan chose to keep it classy: "No giant tits in your face." There are also some fans who really just like the fantasy in a Disney-esque way and are not into it for masturbation.

JulieKat and BustArtist (see Body Expansion, Chapter 4) rented an exhibitor space for his comics. They enjoyed meeting the models, some of whom had a real interest in the kink and sometimes come into the chatrooms to talk about the fantasies. "It was a really welcoming environment. Everyone was very respectful."

For everyone I spoke to, the most meaningful part of the con were the panels, including "Size in Popular Culture," "How to Commission Artists" (the etiquette and how to be re-

alistic), a ladies panel, "Vore," and "Expansion and Inflation." The most popular panel was the one on relationships. Explained Bryan: "'How do I tell my spouse I want to be 6 inches tall? What do I do if someone finds out about it at work?' How to live moral and happy lives."

JulieKat was on the panel for female size play fans, and was delighted to see so many female faces in the crowd. "Women are showing up. Women like me, with a genuine interest. Some relationships have come out of it, too. Women are getting stronger and more confident."

As she was taking the elevator to leave, JulieKat met a cross-dresser in pearls and a June Cleaver outfit who had flown in just for the con: she was glowing, intensely relieved to find such an all-inclusive scene. "We embraced when we got off the elevator!" JulieKat and BustArtist have made plans to return.

It was a tremendous success, not only in terms of breaking even financially, but also in terms of their deeper goals. "We wanted

"Shen Shows off his Feet,"
by Jitensha

MACROPHILES
IN BRIEF

WHAT THEY CALL THEMSELVES:
macrophile, macro, tinies,
giantessophile, Gulliverian

CORE KINK:
mostly feet, but sometimes fat or
mouth

MAJOR THEMES:
growth, power play,
transformation

RELATED KINKS:
body expansion (Chapter 4),
trample and crush (Chapter 6),
weight gain (Chapter 8)

CAN BE COMBINED WITH:
inflation (Chapter 4), furry
(Chapter 11)

EROTIC EQUATION:
pressure from expanding
through clothing, pressure from
squashing tiny people

to relieve people of this burden, we wanted to get rid of that mentality that there's something wrong with them."

As this book went to press, in June 2017, Veronica and Bryan had major plans for the second annual SizeCon in July, to take place over two days at the Courtyard Marriott at LaGuardia airport, with an evening showing of the original *Attack of the 50 Foot Woman*, multiple breakout rooms, and a 360-degree live stream. They expect more than 300 attendees.

Caged tiny POV from the Male Giant Tumblr

Sidekink: Vore

Fans of vore dream about being orally engulfed by a giant, a monster, or a wild animal. Some thrill to the thought of being stuffed inside a dark mouth and swallowed whole, their bodies constricted by the digestive tract, unable to breathe. Others want to be the object of a voracious partner's desire. Some focus on biting and teeth. One vore fan I spoke with recalled the excitement and terror of his aunt telling him, "I love you so much I could just eat you up!"

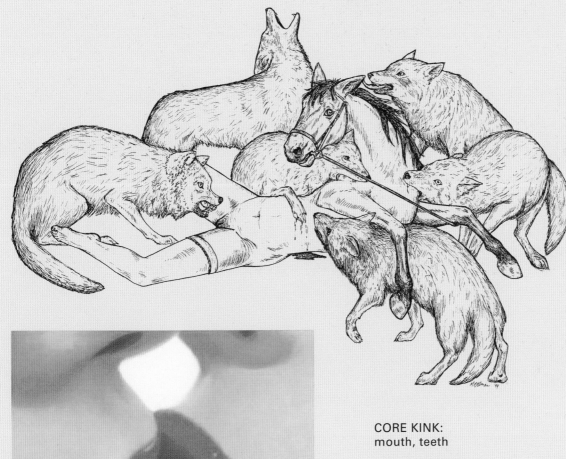

CORE KINK:
mouth, teeth

MAJOR THEMES:
oral fun, power play

MINOR THEMES:
objectification

RELATED KINKS:
feeding (Chapter 8), cannibal fetish (Chapter 10)

MAY BE COMBINED WITH:
body expansion (Chapter 4), macrophiles (Chapter 5), furry (Chapter 11)

EROTIC EQUATION:
being pressed by teeth, mouth, gullet

Janice and Pam, unknown artist

"Ponygirl eaten by wolves," by Michelle Rollman aka Piper Pony (see Chapter 2)

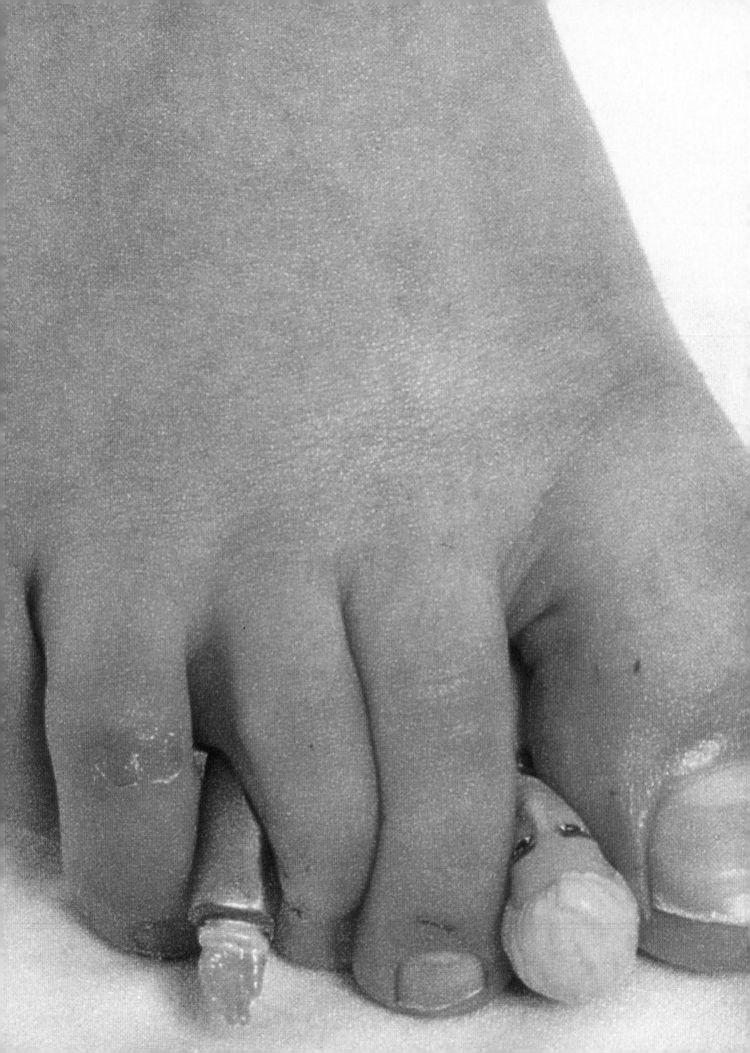

Suburbs of the Foot Fetish:
Trample and Crush

Like gas pedal pumping and some giantess fantasies, trample and crush are interrelated but distinct elaborations of the foot fetish. While many macrophiles want to keep their kink in the realm of collages and science-fiction, others want real-world feet and the visceral experience of intense physical pressure.

QUEEN ADRENA: THE TRAMPLE FETISH
In the 1990s, Queen Adrena was the premier giantess fantasy facilitator in America, specializing in trampling, smothering, and crushing clients under her huge 6'4", 300-pound body and size-11 feet. Until her retirement in 2005, Adrena was a dominatrix off and on for 25 years between bouts as professional lady wrestler Queen Kong. Some of her clients were macrophiles, and some just liked the sensation of being crushed under an immense

weight; the actions may be the same, but the storyline differs. In addition to dominating men in her attic "dungeon," Adrena also sold a whole line of videotapes devoted to trampling and giantess fantasies.

I visited Queen Adrena at her suburban Californian home in 1999, a lively place filled with all sorts of pets and people—including her psychologist husband and her nephew—running in and out the door. Adrena has a big, booming voice and a frequent laugh. She is deeply sincere yet joyful. She might be the only woman in my adult life who triggered my personal mommy switch. I understand the appeal of getting lovingly squished by her.

Adrena didn't always have confidence and joy in her big body. When she was a teenager,

Trample party at The Baroness' Fetish Retinue Party.
Photo: Mark McQueen

TALL female w big feet wanted to play in short film, must look 18-25 yrs of age - call or send resume to: P.O. Box 946, Bellflower CA 90707

everybody made fun of her extraordinary height. "The guys, they were affected by that. They would bug me by making remarks, 'Hey baby Huey! Hey, Hippo.'" Some of that teasing might have masked proto-giantessophile urges: "They wanted me to sit on them, or to have some sort of aggressive contact with them." Adrena eventually felt that giantess fantasies, foot fetish and trampling were her true calling. Adrena sees herself as a "Mother Goddess" for men who need something to worship. "I always knew that it was natural for me to be dominant, to be thought of as a goddess."

Adrena has noticed significant changes over her decades in sex work. "The first time I did it was before AIDS, and everybody wanted some kind of genital contact. They were hoping that a woman would force them to eat her pussy, or kiss her feet, or sit on him and use him," but by 1999 it was about 50% who wanted to get sexually involved and 50% just the pressure with no sex. "They just want the fetish with no particular genital contact… Many of these guys can reach their orgasm even without that."

"The more knowledge I have about the world of fetishes, the more I have developed my own fetishes."
—Queen Adrena

The internet and the increased openness to sexual experimentation led people to seek out more specialized activities: "Now they know exactly what they want to see. And they're not ashamed to admit it." In the late 90s, Adrena began to get female clients: "Female slaves just begging to smell and kiss my feet. Not as many as men, but there are definitely women who have the foot fetish." Adrena thinks all women need is a little exposure to fetishism to open up to the idea. "From my own experience, the more knowledge I have about the world of fetishes, the more I have developed my own fetishes. I know that this is what happens with women."

About half of Adrena's clients want to be trampled, walked, and stomped on in bare feet, heels, or nylons, and they seem able to withstand the weight. One of her regulars, "Facewalk," can take as much as 1,350 pounds at once. "We had six women walking on him full weight, we didn't have to hold back whatsoever." Facewalk didn't always know what he wanted; when he was a teenager he used to get in bar fights and play football so that

Queen Adrena's official photo from her "Giantess Speaks" column in *In Step*

Queen Adrena's Trampling Safety Tips

Before starting, always give the tramplee or the squashee a verbal safeword—I use "mercy." When they say mercy, that means stop immediately. If they cannot talk (because your foot is on their face, for example) have them tap you three times.

Trampling should be done on a soft surface, such as a mattress or exercise mat. Always place an extra pillow under the tramplee's neck.

Have a solid piece of furniture or a wall fixture near-by to hold on to, for balance. I have a series of chains attached to the ceiling above me and I can use them to lift myself off if necessary. A chair or stool next to you also helps.

Discuss the mental fantasy before you do anything. Ask a lot of questions about how this fantasy started. Ask about how the tramplee envisions his or her ultimate fantasy coming true. The fantasy is often more extreme than what they really want.

How much weight a tramplee can take depends entirely on their previous experience. Some have been doing this for years and have developed amazingly tough bodies. Some of the skinniest people can endure the most weight. Ask the height, weight, and shoe size of their previous trampler. Taller people may weigh more but will do less damage because the weight is distributed more evenly. Larger feet also help with weight distribution.

Trampling in heels: start out with regular square heeled shoes to get your balance and the feeling of walking on a moving sea of flesh in dangerous weapons. It's easy to slip, so be extremely careful! Apply more pressure to the balls of your feet than the heel. Some people want heel-marks on their bodies—a trophy that they wear proudly while remi-niscing about their delicious trampling torment.

Discuss in advance the specific erogenous zones they want trampled, and any health issues they might have, such as recent surgery. Popular trample zones are the chest, tummy, solar plexus, face, nose, crotch, and throat—or all of the above.

Start out standing up full weight on one foot on the tramplee's preferred area. Do it very quickly then get off. (Try not to stumble or slip—this can cause dam-age!) Ask them how it felt. Ask continuously how it feels until you feel sure the person can endure as much as they fantasize. Often a tramplee will imag-ine that they can take more than they really can. The endorphins are raging, and they do not realize they have been hurt until hours later.

Some tramplees prefer to be sat on. Do this on a bed with a pillow under their neck. Have the tramplee lie on their back near the edge of the bed, while you sit sideways on the bed. Try different positions. Sit side-saddle with your feet forward on the ground. Then lift your feet and see how they take the weight. Try sitting completely forward on their chest with thighs wrapped around their head. Try to put legs forward so the squashee will feel more weight and pressure. Couches and chairs are all fair game for sitting on your human furniture.

Facewalking: put their face to the side at first. Be very careful not to gouge the person's eyes with the heels. Always keep one foot on the chest for bal-ance, and keep most of the weight on that foot. Then use the other foot to toy with the slave's face and/or throat. Some want their nose to be caved into their skull. Go easy.

Throat walking: Many slaves enjoy being suffocated by feet on their throat. Apply a little pressure at first with the foot sideways across the throat. They will have to use a tapping signal, as they will not be able to talk.

Always stay in tune with the person beneath you! Always communicate and ask how the person is do-ing until you get to know their limits. All of these games are dangerous and require slow experimen-tation! Once you get familiar with their limits, you can sometimes keep going just a tiny bit more for a little extra fear and titillation.

Still from Adrena's *10K Facewalk* video

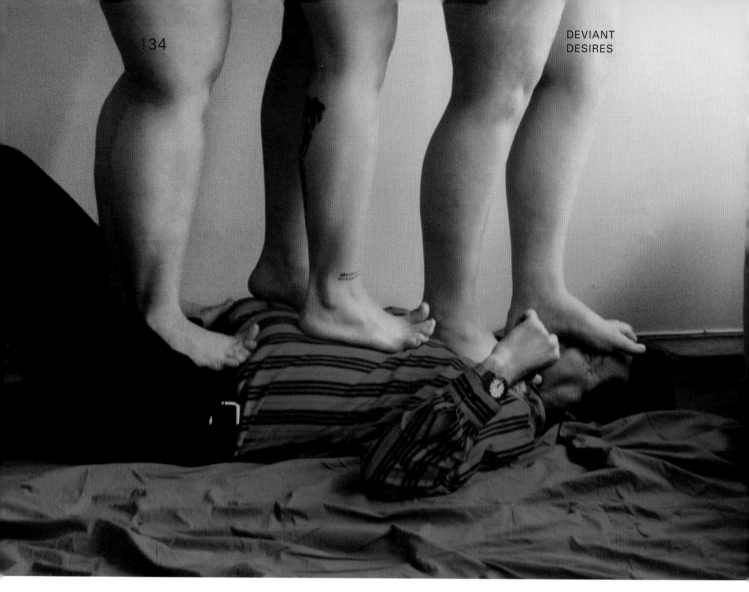

men would pile on top of him. Once he understood it was sexual, he came to Adrena. "You could walk on his face and stuff his nose into his skull."

Adrena and her husband Ken created special padded furniture so that when she stood on a man's face he wouldn't get hurt. Some of Adrena's clients needed a whole lot of weight to get the results they required. "Their bodies get stronger, so they can endure more. Facewalk has had people walking on his face for 30 years! His whole skull's all toughened up. To look at him, you wouldn't think he was any different, but if you push, it's solid rock." Of course, these activities can be dangerous. "I've broken a guy's ribs in a trampling session before. I didn't mean to." Ken thinks some of it relates to athletics and competition. "'Gee, I ran the mile in five minutes, how can I run it in four and a half?' Every time they do it, they want to set a better endurance record."

Adrena enjoyed it. "It's an act of strength and power, but it's also an act of healing. It's a great exchange."

"I like to explore the fetishes mentally, and allow them to go anywhere they want mentally, but always keep a foot in reality. One foot in reality and one foot in their face!"
—Queen Adrena

Adrena's client "Facewalk" can withstand up to 1,350 pounds on his body at one time

JEFF VILENCIA AND THE CRUSH FREAKS

I first heard about crush from another kink-ster who called this fetish too disturbing and scary for words. This in itself was fascinating enough—I always want to know what some-body with one unusual sexual obsession thinks is truly beyond the pale. At the time, in 1998, crush fetish was relatively unknown. By 2002, after the first edition of this book came out, crush had become one of the most infamous and misunderstood kinks.

Crush covers a range of activities, but essentially boils down to feet stomping on objects. In its most harmless form, crush fans want to see a man or woman stomping on cigarette butts, balloons, fruit, or even effigies of people. It makes a great add-on to an existing kink like smoking or balloons; some gas pedal pumping videos, for example, include crush segments.

In many cases the item being crushed is a stand-in for the fetishist him- or herself. Dian Hanson of *Leg Show* once showed me a wax effigy made by one of her readers. It's a tiny self-portrait made with wax, and the man affixes his own hair for realism and voodoo-like power. He sent it to her in the hopes that she would warm it up a little in a microwave and then step on it for him. "Sometimes he comes spontaneously just from seeing the effigy of himself stepped on."

Some crush, however, is not so harmless. For some fans of crush, the act of crushing just isn't visceral enough unless something *living* is feeling the pressure.

Until his forced retirement in 2002, Jeff Vilencia was the charismatic spokesperson for the crush fetish; like others, he gets sexually aroused fan-tasizing he's a tiny one-inch-long bug squished underneath the bare feet of a beautiful woman. Trampling is one real-life option he likes. Other times, Jeff chooses to make his fantasy real by lying on the floor at eye-level to a real live bug

or worm, while a woman uses her feet to crush the critter to death. He jerks off as the woman squishes the living creature, a stand-in for Jeff himself. "At the point of orgasm, in my mind all of my guts are being squished out. My eyeballs are popping out, my brain comes shooting out the top of my head, all my blood squirts everywhere, I stick to the bottom of the foot, and then get ground up into the carpeting! What a release. That imagery really gets me off! Seeing that foot coming down on me, coming into my stomach and pressing all that weight on to me till I burst! Wow!" In this perturbing reconfiguration of ritual animal sacrifice, the final murderous stomp usually brings on Jeff's orgasm—the "little death" achieved by the fate of his once-living proxy.

I first interviewed Jeff in 1998. As I drove my rental car in circles through the SoCal suburbs looking for Jeff's mother's house, I mulled over my ambivalent feelings about meeting him. I was confident I wasn't in any danger, because in his mind he's not the crusher but the crushed. The worst I imagined might be an invitation to

Still from "My Mom Crushing Toast"
by YouTuber Mistress Srinivas

Still from "Sandal Crushing House"
by Swiss YouTuber Fussabtreter1A

"At the point of orgasm, in my mind all of my guts are being squished out. My eyeballs are popping out, my brain comes shooting out the top of my head."

—*Jeff Vilencia*

CRUSH: 16mm short, 4th in series. *Casting:* **Caucasian tall girl,** 18-35 who is willing to step on and crush cockroaches with bare feet. Possible pay plus copy of video. Send photo and resume to:
**Jeff Valencia
P.O. Box 946, Bellower
CA. 90707-0946.**

play pest-exterminator-of-the-moment. I wondered whether I would stomp a cockroach for him if he asked me nicely. I've stepped on quite a few roaches in my time—after all, I'm from New York City. I wasn't as sure about worms, though that would be pretty hypocritical; I use live earthworms as bait while fishing—and that's a fairly gratuitous form of animal-torture-for-sport right there.

My biggest dilemma was whether to include Jeff Vilencia in this book at all. All of the other kinky folk are fairly harmless—they're not hurting anybody or anything but themselves. Their desires may be unusual, but the acts are consensual. I worried that some readers might just shut down and decide Jeff is evil and use that to throw all of the responsible kinksters into one big "sickos-who-should-be-put-in-jail" pile with him. I hope that you, gentle reader, are more discriminating than that. Jeff is a complex and intelligent person whose stories and opinions are worth hearing. He's no saint, but his sins compel us to look long and hard at our own sometimes inconsistent ethical universe.

When I finally arrived at Jeff Vilencia's door, I had the first of many surprises. Jeff is an attractive California surfer type—a smaller version of *Hercules'* Kevin Sorbo. He was in his late 30s, tan and athletic, with longish blond hair; he wore shorts and he had nice legs. He

Still from "Giantess Crush (ebony feet)" by YouTuber Malia Sole explained he bicycles everywhere, and refuses to take part in Southern California car culture.

Jeff brought me to his workspace in the garage behind his mother's house. As I entered, I saw racks upon racks of shelves filled with thousands of old lacquer records. Jeff has a collection of over 20,000, half of which are 78s—and they're all classical music. His favorite composer is Rachmaninoff, maestro of florid sentimentality. Jeff describes himself as an animal lover and a lover of cats. He also happens to be a vegan.

When he was gainfully employed, Jeff Vilencia made his living in film and video, and previously worked part-time as a film specialist helping to restore 1950s TV shows. The garage serves as a screening room for his own short movies on a variety of subjects, some of which are devoted to the crush fetish. Jeff began our interview by showing me the most infamous of these projects, the 16mm experimental short called *Smush*. It is unlike any other fetish film you've ever seen: he filmed it in grainy black-and-white, with professional lighting and surreally echoing sound effects, and sees it as a stylistic paean to Jean-Luc Godard. The film begins portentously with a dedication to Richard von Krafft-Ebing, author of the classic tome *Psychopathia Sexualis*.

Smush was considered serious enough art to be part of the Toronto International Film Festival in 1993, and to tour the world in festivals—including "Spike and Mike's Sick and Twisted Animation Festival"—for several years after that. The Helsinki Film Festival described the film as "sensual, teasing, disagreeable, and torturing. It fascinates, but at the same time pushes the limits of tolerance." Smush even inspired an episode of *NYPD Blue*.

Smush is quite sexy, in a twisted sort of way. The entire film is a bug's-eye view of a cute young chicana named Erika Elizondo as she pedally

FEMALES, 18-35, wanted to step on bugs barefoot for short movie

abuses two dozen live earthworms, one at a time, with bare toes, heels, and instep. While some worms are unceremoniously splatted, other times Erika teases us and draws it out, applying slow pressure or just batting them about with her toes like a cat. There's a rhythmic ritualistic quality to the film that gets quite hypnotic. She wields her big toe masterfully, at one point severing a worm in two; each half wriggles pathetically for a while before she smears them into a streak on the white butcher paper floor.

Some of the worms start to look like weird prehensile penises.

The most unforgettable scene shows one worm's insides gushing out its head like some snuff film cum shot. It's nauseating yet compelling, like a gory car accident.

The whole time there's a running monologue, as Erika tells us how much she loves to squish worms. She giggles and flips her long hair,

Jeff Vilencia. Photo: Darren Rogholt

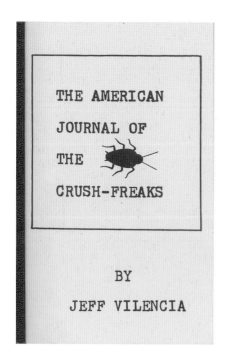

THE AMERICAN
JOURNAL OF
THE
CRUSH-FREAKS

BY

JEFF VILENCIA

WORDS AND PHRASES
TO USE ON A CRUSH FREAK

Reprinted from *The American Journal of the Crush Freaks*, Vol. One

I'm going to step on you and squish you...squish you, crush you, smash you, smush you

I'm going to squish you slowly, pressing down a little at a time, so I can feel your guts squish out

I'm going to step on you and turn you into a tiny grease spot on the ground

Parts of your tiny body will stick to the bottom of my foot as I smash you under my heel

It feels good to have you squirm around under my bare foot as I get ready to press my weight down on you and slowly squish your tiny bug-like body under the full weight of my body

I'm twisting my foot around as I grind you into the rug like a cigarette butt

looking down into the camera coquettishly and saying, "I'm going to crush you!" like Mr. Tyzik from *Kids in the Hall*. In the second half of the film she puts on some old-fashioned well-worn black pumps, and uses the pointed toe and spiked heel to skewer her victims. She tells us she borrowed the shoes from her mother and that her mother would hate what she's doing with them. What a naughty girl she is, in Mommy's shoes!

Smush is pretty good as art, surprisingly successful at bringing the viewer into the mind of a crush freak. Not a terribly pleasant place to be, I might add. There's something claustrophobic about the film; the macro lens—perfect for a macrophile—gives it a very intimate plane of focus, and the echoing soundtrack makes you feel as if you're trapped inside someone's brain. In a way, the death of the worm is similar to the popping of a looner's beloved balloon. It's not simply about feeling aggressive or bloodthirsty, but also about feelings of disgust, horror, tenderness, and even guilt and sorrow. Anticipation, anxiety, and fear all play a part in making it hot. In Erotic Equation terms, it's yet another example of physical pressure leading to explosion.

With the success of *Smush*—and his subsequent discovery that there were others out there with the same fantasy—Jeff Vilencia decided to go into the crush fetish video business. At its height in the late 1990s, Jeff's film company Squish Productions offered a catalog of over 60 videos ranging from 30 to 45 minutes long and selling for $40 to $60 a pop. Jeff produced about a dozen of these videos every year, each featuring a particular female type, "guest victim," and footwear. You could see an African-American woman in sandals squishing mealworms or a Marilyn Monroe type in mules smearing goldfish. There was a fat woman with clogs and snails, a barefoot Filipina woman with pinkies (newborn mice), a Korean woman in platforms with crickets, a Goth chick in thigh high boots and a tarantula—the list went on and on. One video description read invitingly: "Millie returns with Blood Stains of Delight! Pinkies play the part of her ex-boyfriends, bosses, school friends, neighbors, and more! You will long to be her next utterly smeared victim!"

You might think it would be difficult to find so many women willing to stomp live animals, but Jeff's casting calls yielded a steady stream of neophyte actresses willing to do almost anything for their first break in film. Jeff even got letters from professional actors' agents offering up eager young wannabes willing to stomp anything just to see their names in the credits.

S M U S H
a film by Jeff Vilencia
Starring Erika Elizondo and two dozen live earthworms' !

Festival Of Festivals Toronto International Film Festival, Canada 1993 - Helsinki Film Festival "Love and Anarchy", Helsinki Finland 1994 -
Spike & Mikes "Sick & Twisted" 1995 (World Tour!) - 2nd New York Underground Film Festival 1995! -
La Luz De Jesus "Fetish Fixation Explored in Multi-Media" Los Angeles, 1995 -
Filmmakers Alliance, Hollywood Moguls 1994! - La Fete Sauvage "Nuclear Picnic" LACE bldg Los Angeles 1993!
(c) Copyright SQUISH PRODUCTIONS Post Office Box 946, Bellflower Ca 90707-0946 (310)-867-2780
Still from film of Erikas big toe squishing a worm to death!

Jeff's most important contribution to the crush community was his short-lived publication *The American Journal of the Crush-Freaks*, through which he met and corresponded with 800 fellow crushophiles from all over the world. The 6" x 9" 160-page pseudoscientific-looking *Journal* featured Jeff's own opinions about the psychiatric profession, and the hypocrisy of a world that criticized his desires. He used sex-positive rhetoric to urge crush freaks to feel good about themselves. "In many ways we, the crush freaks, may set a new standard of looking at human sexuality. That's why I will continue to fight until it no longer has to be a battle of understanding… We are the crush-freaks and we're here to stay!" In the second volume, Jeff included detailed profiles of individual readers as "specimens" for scientific study—like little bugs wriggling under a microscope. It also featured science fiction crush stories, most of which are practically identical to the stories Ed Lundt used to sell to his giantess fans.

Show card for *SMUSH*, which showed at the Toronto International Film Festival in 1993

"If she steps down hard enough, sometimes parts of my body will stick to her foot, and she will have to wipe her sexy foot off, either smearing me on the floor, or taking some tissue and cleaning me off."
—*Jeff Vilencia*

One of the funniest items in *The American Journal of the Crush-Freaks* was Jeff's book review section, mostly featuring gardening books written by women. Vilencia systematically reproduced every sentence in the book where the female author suggests "stomping," "crushing," or "squishing" bugs—his key turn-on phrases. He carefully noted page numbers so you could look it up yourself, and he graded each book using—instead of stars—bug-crushing foot logos.

Vilencia says most crushophiles have very particular requirements, and has published their views on the superiority of crawdads over cockroaches, or high heels over clogs. Some who prefer live victims don't even identify with the creature, but just want to see a woman getting violent with something small (like Ron H.'s *Black Giantess* scenario). One man has no interest in feet, just women spraying bugs with insecticide. Another one's murder weapon of choice is dirty tennis shoes and used athletic socks.

Jeff himself prefers very large bare feet (size ten or over). As we spoke, I saw him subtly checking out my ratty, size six sneakers. So much for wondering if he might ask me to stomp a worm.

Dian Hanson has given the subject of crush some thought: "Yes, I love to step on big cockroaches, and yes, I love to step on ants, but do I condone it? Do I think it's a nice thing? No. I don't want to be the one to say, 'Yes, your sexuality is bad,' but what do you do? It's borderline. I've had readers write in wanting me to step on mice. And I once had pictures in the magazine poised over a mouse, but in the end, I wouldn't step on a mouse."

Jeff feels most people's objections to his videos are hypocritical: After all, other kinds of "unnecessary" pleasure at the death or torture of an animal happen all of the time and we don't feel quite the same kind of disgust. Hunters shoot deer not just for food, but for bloodsport and trophies. (And sometimes the deer get horribly injured and suffer for days.) I've used worms to fish, so I can't feel too morally superior to Jeff. Jeff argues the meat industry is an unnecessary animal-murdering business too, and I eat meat. Maybe the problem is really that he's choosing to do it for erotic purposes, as if sexual pleasure were any less valid a reason for killing something than food or sport.

Unfortunately, a few of Jeff's readers want to see the death and torture of higher animals. One wrote Jeff asking him to do a video with frogs, and other video producers use chicks,

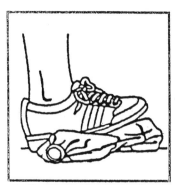

3. Step on bottles to crush.

Recycling ad reproduced in *The American Journal of the Crush-Freaks*

Crush nightmare, from *The Manly World of Lloyd Llewellyn* by Daniel Clowes (Fantagraphics Books, 1994)

Illustration by Kat from *The American Journal of the Crush-Freaks*

rats, and even other mammals. One horrifying crush video available online (NOT made by Jeff) shows a cat taped to a sheet of Plexiglas—the camera shows the view from below the clear floor as the cat gets stomped. A woman in Brooklyn wrote the *Journal* about her sexual obsession with killing scores and scores of animals every day. She went to pet shops and bought dozens of goldfish to stomp. She also went into unspeakable detail about how she crushed an injured ferret by rolling it between two wooden planks. I wish Jeff had spared me that one, or at least expressed more outrage.

Jeff may be unwilling to condemn others, but has established very firm limits on what kinds of creatures he will do in his own videos: "I don't do frogs or full grown mice." He justifies his use of pinkies because they are bred specif-

ically for the purpose of being swallowed alive by pet snakes. He figures one quick stomp from a human is probably more humane than slow suffocation by a reptile. "And there's nothing 'natural' about having a pet snake!"

Jeff has thought long and hard about the origins of his crush fantasy, and childhood fetish "acquisition" was one of his favorite topics of discussion in *The American Journal of the Crush-Freaks*. Jeff's scenario developed out of a very early childhood foot fetish combined with a desire to experience intense physical pressure. He remembers a dream from when he was very little. "In the dream, a friend and I went to a woman's house. She invited us in and put us through old washing wringers and she flattened us out and used us for rugs and walked all over us." He also remembers seeing an old Tarzan jungle movie

1950s horror comics like this one expressed the lurid fears—and sexual fantasies—of a generation of American men unsure of their feelings about women's power

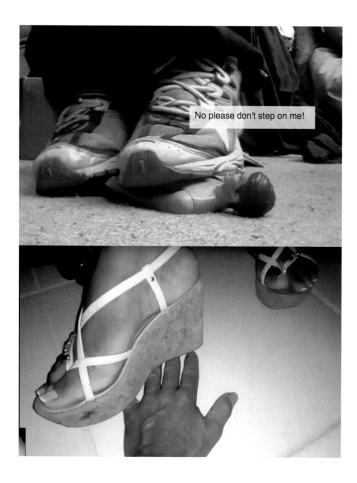

No please don't step on me!

Vilencia thinks bad sex education and lack of discussion about sexual relationships can contribute to people becoming more rigid in their kinks, moving higher up on the fetish scale. His own Sex Ed classes were terrifying and confusing; in seventh grade, the Phys Ed teacher projected almost the entire Sex Ed film without sound. "We were about 10 or 15 minutes into the picture and he finally finds the sound switch. And these old educational films had the Edward R. Murrow 'voice of God' narration on it. The first thing that comes up over the PA system, is, '...and then the boys have a wet dream!' Then the picture's over and the coach gets up and asks, 'Anybody have any questions?' and we're all looking at each other wondering, 'What the hell?' We just saw these silent drawings of penises getting erect. I remember all of the boys were trying to figure it out for weeks: 'Are we going to piss in the bed?' We had no idea. It was so poorly explained." In eighth grade, the Sex Ed teacher was a really old woman. "The first thing she said, in this stern voice, was: 'Sex causes syphilis, and you'll get the girl pregnant!' So I thought, 'Jesus! I'm going to piss in the bed, get a girl pregnant, and get VD!' And that was enough for me. I didn't want to get near a girl for years."

where an elephant steps on a tiger; he dreamed of being trampled just like the tiger. Like macrophile Ed Lundt and others of his generation, Jeff found the infamous BFGoodrich tire ad featuring a gigantic go-go girl in the 1960s to be a major inspiration. Jeff believes television's intimacy makes it more important in setting up kink triggers than film or book illustrations.

At a young age, Jeff tried to get his brothers' and sisters' friends to step on him. The goal was to have the person stand on his stomach, full body weight, without their shoes on—just like Queen Adrena's trampling clients. Jeff would ruminate over these incidents for days. "I would think about how it happened, how it felt, how heavy the other child was, how big the feet were." Jeff remembers masturbating about one particularly painful trampling he got from two older girls.

Jeff thinks things could have turned out differently if he had managed to have a positive relationship with a girl early on. The first time he had sex it was traumatic. "I was frightened, didn't know what the hell I was doing. I don't know anybody whose first sexual experience was any good or worth repeating, maybe not even the first 10! It was horrible!" At the time of our interview in 1999, Jeff had tried telling potential girlfriends about his fetish up-front, but most of them didn't go for a second date. He tried having the relationship first and then telling them about his fetish a year later—that didn't work either. Jeff had "normal" sexual relationships with women that lasted as long as two years. Some of these girlfriends even recorded crush fantasy audiotapes for Jeff, or

talked him through his fantasy while he licked their feet—but it just wasn't working. "I haven't had sex in three years. As I remember it, it's pretty messy. You sweat, your hair is fucked up, and you wake up with bad breath." And Jeff has no interest in getting married and having children. "A lot of people say 'I'd like to reproduce myself.' Well, I say, 'Are you worth reproducing? I'm not! What makes you think you are!'" One of Jeff's favorite T-shirts reads "THE GENE POOL ENDS HERE."

To Jeff, the most ethical relationships are those within the BDSM rubric, because partners are expected to communicate their needs openly. "When two SM people meet, they'll talk about what they want. They'll actually sit down with each other and say, 'I like this, what do you like? What's our safe boundary, what's our safe word?' Now how do most 'normal' heterosexuals meet? You go to a bar, you try to get the girl shit-faced so you can go home and fuck her. There's no conversation, even if you can make it home,

A woman in a Human Sexuality class once asked Jeff Vilencia, "Doesn't it get boring, the same thing, over and over?" He responded, "No. Does intercourse get boring for you?"

Still from *Death in the Afternoon,*
a Squish Productions video by Jeff Vilencia

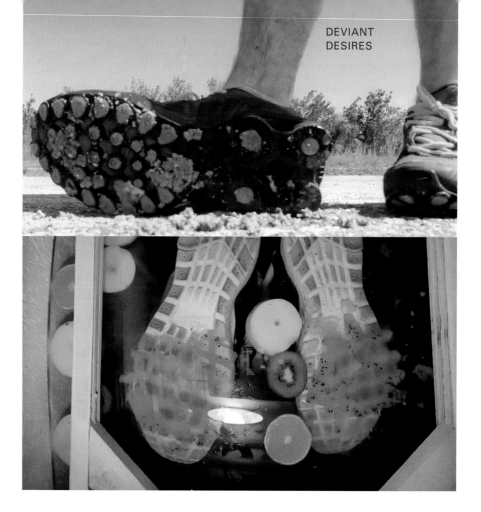

"Nike Shox Stomp Burger"
by YouTuber jeepfan7

"Fruit crush" by
YouTuber stompingnike

even if you don't pass out. You don't ask her how she feels, what she wants, what you like. There's nothing moral or decent or community-oriented about it at all!"

Cops bare sick details of animal-snuff videos

THE CRUSHING WEIGHT OF THE LAW

At the time of our original interview, Jeff was content with his self-appointed role as public spokesman for the crush freaks. He was making frequent appearances on radio talk shows, arguing his case on *The Mo Show* on Fox Television, and was a guest lecturer at Human Sexuality classes at the University of Southern California.

New York Post headline about a crush arrest made in Brooklyn

But things were changing: what used to be a small, secret underground became 1999's media scare. Exposés of the crush video phenomenon drew the attention of animal rights activists—including former child actor Mickey Rooney—and politicians. Word got out about the video featuring cat torture, and some journalists conflated all crush fetishists together; stomping on grapes was no different from sitting on a kitten. Jeff protested that the cat video was an outlier. "I love cats, I would never harm a cat! Of course people would be upset seeing something like that!" According to Jeff, People for the Ethical Treatment of Animals named him as the person who turned the porn industry on to crush.

On Oct 20, 1999, California Republican representative Elton Gallegly introduced a bill in Congress to impose a prison term of up to five years for the sale of videotapes depicting animal torture and killings. Gallegly claimed that crush videos were a multimillion-dollar business—a rather outrageous exaggeration—and emphasized their sexual purpose. Just as they say that marijuana leads to harder drugs, Gallegly claimed that crush is a "gateway fetish." The bill passed into federal law with allowances for videos with "serious religious, political, scientific, educational, journalistic, historical, or artistic value."

By 2000, at least two of Jeff's colleagues had been arrested for animal abuse after policewomen posed as crush actresses in sting operations. Jeff claims one acquaintance was entrapped by an undercover cop who convinced him to do a rat-stomping video he would not otherwise have done. The man received a sentence of three years in jail. One woman who crushed three mice for a video was arrested in August 1999, and sent to jail because she could not come up with the $45,000 bail. The videographer was not charged.

At one point, Jeff was doing two call-in radio talk shows a day trying to make it clear that not all crush freaks wanted to see cats and larger mammals suffer. He reasoned that videos showing hunting and dogfights are legal, so singling out crush freaks—just because it's sexual—seems unfair. Then, he says, the *Globe* and *Enquirer* published his name and photograph next to descriptions of the cat torture video. People started calling his mother and screaming at her. Jobs fell through and no one wanted to hire him. His brother, an animal lover, wouldn't speak to him. Jeff says he tried to hire a company that promised to fix his reputation, to prove that he had never made a crush video with anything bigger than a fetal mouse, but they wanted $10,000 to do it. Jeff Vilencia's life was "pretty much ruined."

On April 20, 2010, the Supreme Court of the United States, in an 8-1 ruling written by Chief Justice John Roberts, overturned Gallegly's law on the ground that the law violated the First Amendment right to freedom of speech, and created a "criminal prohibition of alarming breadth." David Horowitz, executive director of the Media Coalition, told the *Houston Chronicle* that this was the right thing to do: if the First Amendment were rewritten "every time an unpopular or distasteful subject was at issue, we wouldn't have any free speech left."

In December 2010 then-President Barack Obama responded to the Supreme Court decision by signing a federal law that specifically banned so-called "crush videos"—depictions of small animals being tortured to death by humans. Videos of hunting and dogfights, however, were spared.

"Dear Jeff Vilencia: Do not send us any more of your cruel, disgusting shit. You are a sick asshole. The next time you send anything to us, I am going to report you. People like you should be put behind bars."
—Letter to Jeff from a former customer

Promotional still from *Death in the Afternoon*, a video by Jeff Vilencia

A crush freak's car?
Photo: Katharine Gates

In 2014, Jeff Vilencia tried to revive his business by sending out a flyer to his old mailing list. Many wrote back, incensed to receive the solicitation. It was a bad business gamble and Jeff lost a lot of money.

In 2016, the first prison sentences under the new statute were issued to Brent Justice and Ashley Richards, a couple who made videos horribly torturing several different animals, including a puppy.

On the upside, Jeff now has a serious girlfriend. She occasionally steps on him too.

CRUSH IN BRIEF

TERMINOLOGY:
crush

CORE KINK:
foot

MAJOR THEMES:
power play

RELATED KINKS:
gas pedal pumping (Chapter 1),
trample

EROTIC EQUATION:
pressure from weight

From a crush fantasy
photoset in *Footsy*

Sidekink: Car Crush
(Unsafe at any speed)

ARE YOU READY to meet your Maker?

Some fans of intense physical pressure may go to extreme lengths to get the sensations they crave, going beyond the limits of safety or sanity. Associated Press reported on September 15, 1999, that Brian Loudermilk of Okeechobee, Florida, a 28-year-old father of three, died several hours after he was discovered pinned beneath the tires of his own truck in the driveway of his home.

Police were baffled by the scene. "Investigators said they didn't know how Loudermilk got under the tire. He was found in a 2-foot to 3-foot deep hole that fit his body. A pillow was found at the scene, as well as a wooden board that overlapped his body." The left rear wheel of the 1994 Honda Passport rested on the board on Loudermilk's waist.

It should be noted that there do exist endurance performers who engage in these types of acts to public acclaim, and appear to take steps to ensure their survival. Nevertheless, car crush should be rated "unsafe at any speed."

TERMINOLOGY:
car crush

CORE KINK:
cars? pressure itself?

MAJOR THEMES:
power play

RELATED KINKS:
gas pedal pumping (Chapter 1), crush

EROTIC EQUATION:
pressure from extreme weight

SmashmanSF specialized in getting frat boys and college athletes to stomp or drive over him

Wet and Messy Fun: Getting Down and Dirty

Cake sitting. Photo: Jo Duck for an ad campaign for Bompas & Parr, a trendy British caterer

I discovered the weird world of wet and messy (WAM) way back in 1992 as I was browsing the racks of Baltimore's Atomic Books. I wandered past rows and rows of homemade zines with covers that were either confrontational—someone glaring at the viewer, bored—or violent, dark, or Satanic. Even the sex magazines! Then I saw *Splosh!*, the magazine of the messy fun fetish. The cover model was a cheerful girl next door in frilly lingerie, but you couldn't see much of the outfit because she was practically covered from head to waist in baked beans, like Ann-Margret in the film *Tommy*. She looked surprised and thrilled, not humiliated or degraded.

I sought signs of cruelty or even irony—I would have been familiar with those. I found none. Instead, I found pictorials of women in evening wear slowly submerging themselves in bathtubs of melted chocolate, prim ladies at fancy restaurants letting go and having a food fight, brides in bridal gowns falling into swimming pools.

The letters column was filled with grateful notes from messy fun fans who thought they were the only one who liked to masturbate wearing thigh-high rubber boots sitting in a bathtub of raw eggs. Others described their jerk-off rituals sitting in cheesecake or submerging themselves in clay fully clothed and cross-dressed. Some described sploshing as foreplay—beds carefully covered in plastic sheeting and special clog-free drains installed in their showers. There were indignant critiques, complaining there weren't enough photos matching a specific fantasy, like women in prom gowns getting pies thrown in their faces. And they were very serious about it. From its inception

Satin dress and petticoats, with cake, custard, and raspberry jam. Photo: *Splosh!*

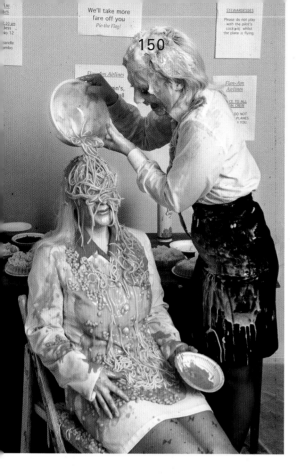

in 1989 to its last issue in 2013, *Splosh!* represented a very potent sexual obsession for its readers.

Of course, erotic food play is nothing new. The Book of Genesis is a story of the eating of fruit leading to lust and shame. Erotic eating—where lovers suggestively suck lollipops or swallow oysters to suggest fellatio or cunnilingus—is a highlight of the 1963 film *Tom Jones*. Many couples have fooled around with edible underwear or dripped honey on each other to lick it off as foreplay. But messy fun isn't about oral sex. Lots of food may be involved, but hardly any of it gets consumed. For *Splosh!* readers, clothes had to be ruined, propriety abandoned. It didn't have to be food, either: there were women head to toe in wallpaper paste, even cans of poster paint. The mess itself is the erotic goal.

Splosh! may have been a fetish magazine for people who get off on getting dirty, but it was astonishingly clean. There were no four-letter words, no spread shots, and the only sexual contact between models might be a (relatively) dry kiss. The women looked approachable and fun; they were proud to be messy. Conventional pornography engages shame, but *Splosh!* was unremittingly shameless.

Perhaps the most surprising aspect of the fetish is that it's so focused on slapstick humor. You could find jokes in *Screw* or *Hustler*, but they're generally nasty and mean. It's rare to find people with fetishes willing to laugh about it, because no matter how funny their sexual practice may be—and that's both funny "ha ha" and funny "peculiar"—it's serious to them. They don't want to be laughed at. *Splosh!*, on the other hand, had terrible puns, dumb jokes, and stupid merriment. Every issue featured corny pictorials: food fights at office parties, clumsy waitresses spilling platters on customers, uptight people and orderly situations getting madly out of hand, like the Marx Brothers or Three Stooges as porn.

"Once Upon a Slime" is a comedy skit from a *Splosh!* video: "Listen to posh Auntie Mandy and her big-titted tormentor Karen as they tell the story of 'Nuddy and the Big Ones,' with visual aids for the very young, ensuring our snooty storyteller gets completely covered in baked beans, spaghetti, syrup, eggs, and plenty of pies." If it weren't for the vaguely erotic look of open-mouthed shock and pleasure on her slime-covered face, you might think the video was for kids.

"WAM" seems to be a new phenomenon. The very first messy fetish groups to go public appeared within the gay male community in the mid to late 1980s. The Texas Mudmen in the USA

Sloppy waitress skit, a popular plotline for *Splosh!* pictorials. Photo: *Splosh!*

Splosh! magazine covers

(later called Sludgemaster) and a British group called S.L.O.S.H.
(The Society for Lovers of Slapstick Happenings, still going strong)
organized special events where gay guys could muck around in
mud or slather each other with soapsuds. Unsurprising it emerged
right as HIV and AIDS awareness hit, when getting slippery with
strangers offered a fun, safe alternative to bodily fluids.

The late 1980s and early 1990s saw a growth in messy fetish materials. A Texan by the name of Rob Blaine began creating messy
fetish videos in 1991. Rob put his Messy Fun, Inc. catalog online
in 1995, and by 1999 had 7,800 customers. An English company
called WSM (Wetlook + Slapstick + Mudlarking) began making
hetero-oriented messy videos. *Splosh!*, the first magazine devoted
exclusively to messy fun, was published in England quarterly from
1989 until its founder's death in 2013. *Splosh!* produced messy
videos and coordinated special events called "Splosh Days" where
readers could get together for a weekend of messy misbehavior.

Messy fun made its real splash in the mainstream in 1994 when
director John Waters enthused about *Splosh!* to Jay Leno on *The
Tonight Show.* Waters also promoted messy fun in—of all places—
People magazine. In 2015, Goliath Books published fetish photographer and video maker Charles Gatewood's *Messy Girls*, 368 pages
of pretty girls smeared in every substance imaginable. Charles told
me, "Messy stuff is the next big thing!"

Curious what makes the messy fetish tick, I visited the *Splosh!*
video studios in a tiny basement in London in 1998. *Splosh!* was
edited and produced by mess enthusiast Bill Shipton and his
business partner, Hayley—a woman so reclusive and unwilling to
give interviews or be photographed I began to think she was a
figment of Shipton's imagination (or a brilliant marketing ploy).
Shipton himself turned out to be a great entertainer and quite a
visual feast. He bore an uncanny natural resemblance to Bozo the
Clown: his hair went up in all directions, he had a funny round
paunch and his nose was large, misshapen and very red. In spite
of his potentially frightening appearance (I am phobic about
clowns) Bill put me at ease. His conversation was peppered with
bad puns and laughter.

Bill explained most *Splosh!* readers have a specific substance they
want to get messy with, what the scenario should be, and how they
want the mess applied. Sploshing breaks down into three quite
distinct substance subgroups—wetlook (water), mudlarking (mud
and clay), and mess (anything and everything else).

2016 newsletter of the Society for Lovers of
Slapstick Happenings, UK (note superhero
costume, see Chapter 11)

Bill Shipton's Twitter profile pic, 2012

Wetlook is probably the easiest to understand: we know how damp clothing clings to the body, and we're familiar with spring break wet T-shirt competitions. But Bill Shipton's readers had no interest in wet T-shirts. "Oddly enough, it's got to be perfect, glam clothing—something you wouldn't expect to get wet, the more expensive the better. They want people in proper nice shoes, and they've got to have handbags and jewelry and God knows what else."

One *Splosh!* reader who called himself "The Persuader" would manage to coax strange women online into taking baths in their business suits, preferably navy blue ones. The women apparently enjoyed the dare and would come back from their bathrooms—still dripping—to email him descriptions of their adventure. One of his most successful techniques was a question and answer game; women who got the answers wrong would have to pour a glass of water on their suits and tell him about how it felt. Another reader specifically wanted to see women in wet saris—a common stand-in for sex in Bollywood—and sent Bill his personal "Top Ten List of Best Rain Scenes in Indian Films."

The various clothing factions got cranky if *Splosh!* pictorials failed to meet their specific requirements. "There's one guy, he's been writing to us since issue one, going: 'Yes, it was all right. But you can't call it a proper sexy wet and messy mag if it's got no petticoats in it!'" Ruining fancy clothes also has the appeal of extravagance. Bill explained: "There is a tremendous pleasure in blowing a lot of money on something that gives you silly gratification." There was even a newsletter called *Wet Pumpers* for people aroused

Wetlook series. Photo: David Wilkey, *Splosh!*   Fancy leather in oily bathtub. Photo: Rob Blaine

by women's high-heeled shoes getting soaked. Clearly, there's an overlap here between messy fun and the shoe fetish, but Bill felt it's more than that: "Shoes are things you don't get messy as a kid."

While some wetlook types want to see gradual submersion in water, others like the effect of surprise. The setup is critical in these pictorials—several panels of the woman teetering on the edge before the final splash. The woman's facial expression has to be silent-movie-style hamming of the most obvious kind. Bill Shipton elaborated: "It has to be pantomime shock rather than real shock and it has to be followed quite closely by a shot where she looks like she thinks, 'Well, that was actually quite fun.'" As a special request, *Leg Show* once did a pictorial of a woman falling into a swimming pool. "Then the reader wrote in," explained erstwhile publisher Dian Hanson, "incensed that we had it all wrong, she was supposed to fall in backwards, not sideways. Can't you GET IT RIGHT?"

For Bill, it was "about pricking pomposity. It's about taking terribly stiff starched people and totally destroying the situation. And that, I think, is a very, very healthy thing." He explained, "One of our readers says that what she gets out of it is just this feeling of abandonment. For one moment, for the period of time you're doing it, you don't care. You're told from the age of three on, don't scuff your shoes, don't play with your food. And suddenly for a few minutes, you can chuck all that away." In terms of the Erotic Equation, WAM generates excitement by exploiting the tension between sensuality and propriety.

But at its core, it's sensory play. Foodstuffs like custard and melted chocolate just feel good on the skin. Bill describes a whole subset of his readers who like to pour mess inside their clothing so it squishes around and presses up against the body, like stuffing a chocolate bar down your underpants and wearing it through the entire day. One *Splosh!* reader likes to go to a supermarket wearing ladies' tights under his trousers. "He buys custard, goes to the toilet and fills up the tights with it, and then drives home."

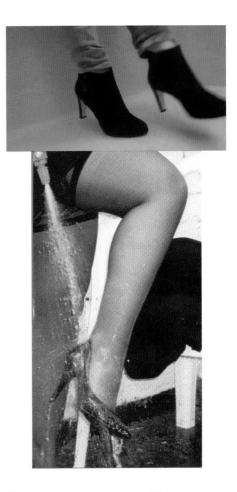

Erotic cross-dressing is common in WAM. Rather than an expression of trans identity, Bill Shipton believes it is a way for some men to conjure a female partner to play with—and "partly the abandonment [of rules], 'I'm throwing away all of the strictures at the same time.'"

For the people who call themselves mudlarkers, the messy play substance must be mud and nothing else will do. Most of us

Falling into a pool. Photo:
Leg Show

Still from a YouTube video,
"Suede boots in a pool"

Wet pumps for the benefit of the
messy shoe fetishists. Photo: *Splosh!*

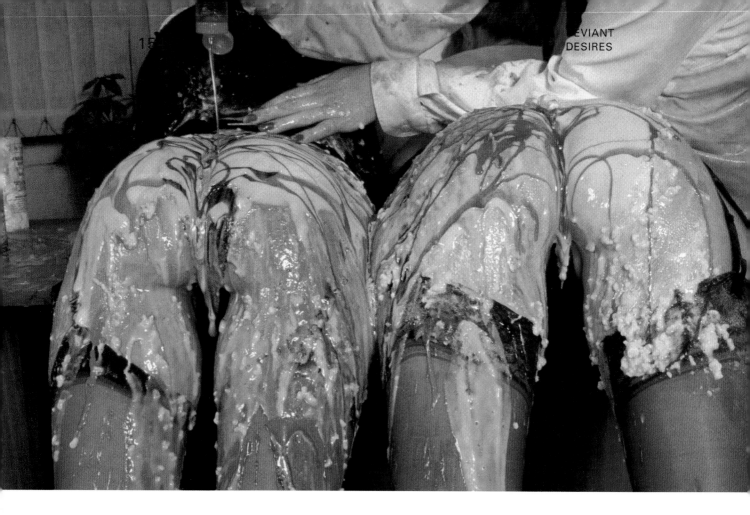

"For normal day wear I put on size 14, but if I feel like slopping around the house with a large tin of apricots in syrup and two tins of Ambrosia rice pudding dropped down my drawers, then I wear a pair of voluminous satin bloomers size 24!"
—Mike of Seaford, *Splosh!* #22

Rice pudding, custard cream, green cake icing, and sticky strawberry sauce. Photo: *Splosh!*

remember loving to play in mud and clay as children, and WAM fans understand this primal appeal. Some *Splosh!* readers' mudplay practices included artificial mud pits using powdered clay from the craft supply store and a kiddie-pool in the basement. Other US and Australian mudlarkers are fortunate in having access to naturally occurring mud: Texan Rob Blaine used to share GPS coordinates with detailed reviews of safety, privacy, and sensual qualities: "Super-smooth mud with very little scratchy grain. Nudity OK, but please only share with trusted wammers."

Quite a few mudlarkers combine their play with a rubber fetish. A whole group of British ladies like to jump in mud puddles with their rubber mackintoshes on. One of Bill's favorite stories came from a Canadian reader who enjoyed submerging himself in mud wearing a girl's rubber ice skating outfit.

Splosh! published a letter from one mudlarker exploring his earliest childhood associations: "Why is it that the only real childhood memory I have is the red rubber sheet on my cot? The feel, the smell, the two small holes—I can see them now as I talk. I think it's because my parents were not the most demonstrative people in the world and so I got my pleasure from things rather than people. Textures and smells were very important to me and still are."

Bill and Hayley's Tips and Tricks for Messy Fun

The simplest thing to start with is the giant cans of chocolate pudding you can get at Costco or the Price Club. You can do it in the shower or bathtub or on the bed—put down plastic or a bed-wetter sheet first.

When trying it the first time, always warm up your materials a bit. There's nothing more miserable than being sploshed with something cold and clammy.

Some jams and jellies contain dyes that will color hair and clothing. *Splosh!* learned the hard way: "We once used some black currant jam. Everyone's hair turned bright blue. We all had to run to the hairdressers and have our hair dyed back again."

Flour-and-water based materials like batter harden rapidly. Any part that happens to have a bit of hair (like, for example, the pubic area) will get uncomfortably stuck. "It's probably the most painful depilatory in the entire world!"

If you're going to wear high-heeled shoes in the mud, put an elastic band around them so they don't come off in the suction.

Shave completely before using liquid latex, as you will pull your hair out when trying to get it off.

If you like cracking eggs on your head or body, you can soften the eggshells by leaving the eggs in a bowl of vinegar overnight.

Wallpaper paste is fun, but make sure you buy a non-toxic brand. Some contain fungicides which can be harmful to your health.

Clay fans recommend Aardvark powder available at ceramics supply stores. Mix with water in your kiddie pool (on the ground floor—this can get heavy!)

Do not have sexual intercourse while covered in some materials, as they may cause vaginitis or worse. Paint, raw eggs, and some other potentially toxic substances should be cleaned off before penetration. Other materials can be douched out after sex. When in doubt, always ask your doctor.

Goldilocks taking a porridge bath.
Photo: *Splosh!*

Unknown business man in the bath

Paint pour by Messy Fun, Inc.
Photo: Rob Blaine

Texas mudman. Photo: Scott Baker,
Sludgemaster

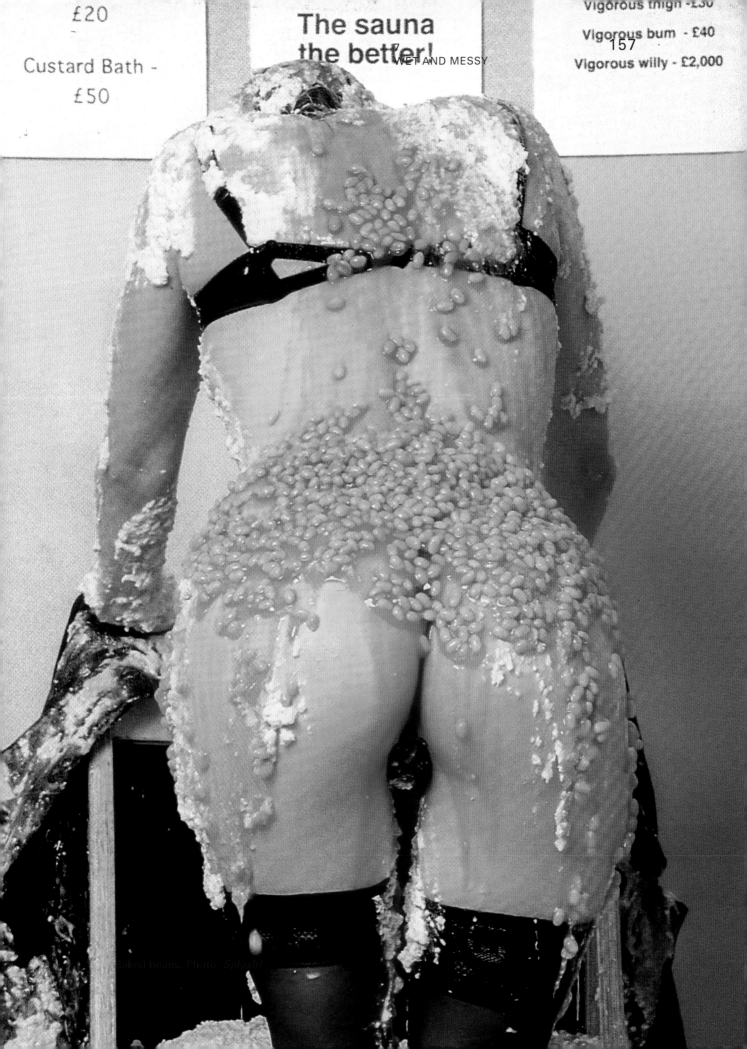

£20

Custard Bath -
£50

The sauna
the better!

Vigorous thigh -£30

Vigorous bum - £40

Vigorous willy - £2,000

Baked beans. Photo: *Splosh!*

Rubber, like mud, is a touchy-feely fetish. When you're in rubber and submerge in water or mud, the rubber presses against your body in a tight embrace, a kind of clammy bondage. Another rubber fetish mudlarker liked wearing a full rubber scuba outfit in the mud because "he liked the idea of being very, very messy, and then instantly very clean."

It's all about navigating risk and safety. The spot where risk-taking becomes pleasure is different for each of us. One mudlarking *Splosh!* reader had a powerful childhood memory of almost drowning. Submerging himself in mud, he safely recreated his trauma.

When I asked Bill Shipton whether sploshing has to do with infantile shit-smearing, he replied: "It has that element, but (sploshers) wouldn't want to go anywhere near that. They want it to be nice."

On the other hand, the Houston-based gay male sploshing group Sludgemaster (active in the late 1990s, now defunct) regularly used shit and piss in their messy play, as well as snot, spit, and sewage. They enjoyed industrial-strength mess like machine oil and engine grease, too—it was all part of a macho-man, construction-worker and biker aesthetic (whereas straight messers seem to prefer substances with more domestic associations). Scott Baker, Sludgemaster's founder, didn't see much of a difference. "Since the beginning, I never really generalized or drew lines for our fetishes. I present them all together. What's totally offensive to some is perfectly acceptable to others. To me, slop is slop—and slop is erotic in any form." Scott felt that those who enjoy hardcore mess each have their own particular take on what makes it hot. For some, it's a form of humiliation; for a few, it's the ultimate taboo, and for others, it's a form of intimacy. Unlike videos sold by *Splosh!* and Messy Fun, Sludgemaster's videos almost always showed overt sex acts between real messy fetishists.

Gas masks, rubber, and mud.
Photo: Scott Baker, Sludgemaster

Industrial grease. (Toxic!)
Photo: Scott Baker, Sludgemaster

QUICKSAND AND STUCK

The uniquely suctiony qualities of mud and the thrill of danger
are the turn-ons for the small subset of the mudlarking crowd that
enjoys fantasies of people drowning in quicksand. About half of
the quicksand types find their sexual thrills from imagining themselves getting slowly sucked under the surface, while others jerk
off thinking about someone else sinking in the stuff. Some like to
fantasize about rescuing the person at the last minute, and others
really just don't care what happens to the victim, as long as they're
being pulled inexorably into the grasping liquid. The extraordinary
irony of the whole thing is that quicksand fantasies are based on
completely impossible scenes from Hollywood films like *Tarzan*
and *Indiana Jones*. True quicksand—a combination of sand and
flowing water—behaves nothing like the pop-culture version in
the movies. It's actually quite safe.

Jiminy Thicket, creator of the Quicksand FAQ, told me his story
over a sushi lunch in San Francisco. Jiminy began drawing pictures
of women sinking in mud when he was still a kid. He enjoys the
idea of being gripped and held tightly by a silken texture—one
that evokes the damp suction of intercourse. He plays in his own
fake quicksand pool at home, and he can suspend his disbelief
about the reality of quicksand long enough to feel the necessary

*"It's...a very effective
way of creating some
of the experiences
you get through sex...
It's the feeling of
something next to you
on your skin. It's a
feeling of liquids and
pressure."*
—Bill Shipton

Quicksand scene from a video
by Messy Fun, Inc. Photo: Rob Blaine

adrenaline rush that becomes sexual arousal.
He also enjoys breath control and containment,
for the same reasons any SM player might wear
a rubber hood. Oxygen deprivation or
suffocation—as folks who risk death by hanging themselves during masturbation sessions
know—can heighten arousal and make orgasms
more extreme. Jiminy also loves watching other
people sink in quicksand: "What sounds escape
from a helpless individual, struggling violently
against a pool of rising muck? Aren't they the
same desperate grunts and moans that come in
the moments of intense passion?"

I found a mesmerizing video on YouTube—a
full 10 minutes of a man in jeans and thigh-
high rubber waders half-sunk in deep mud. He
struggled to pull himself out of the mud, yanking
and tugging, wiggling and flopping. The audio
featured no sounds but the sucking noises, rem-
iniscent of well-lubricated sexual intercourse, at
full blast. At one point, the mud crested the tops
of the waders and filled them, and you could
hear the man's sigh of satisfaction.

PIEPLAY

For a subset of sploshers, there's really only
one scenario that interests them: people getting hit in the face with pies. Mike Brown,
aka Pieface Mike, started showing up in San
Francisco Bay area nightclubs in 1990 with a
suitcase full of pies and an assistant carrying a
camera and paper towels. Mike's most important prop was the business card he would hand
to attractive women. It read, "Good evening
miss, would you like to smash, rub, and place
a pie in my face?" At the apex of his career,
Mike brought his "pie-formances" to the
International Fetish Ball and even hired himself
out as entertainment at bachelorette parties.
Mike calculates that as many as 1,200 women
pied him over a period of five or six years.

I first met Mike at an Alternative Press Expo
in about 1996. With his shiny bald head and
shapeless black cassock that stretched all the
way from his neck to the floor, he cut a memorable Uncle Fester-like figure. When I heard
about his kink and told him that I would be
honored to pie him right then and there, his
eyes got really wide, and he trembled all over.
In 1998 I made the trek to visit Mike at his

Mudplay photo by Candy Custard

Pieface Mike's calling card

Major Themes:
Taboo

The erotic imagination manipulates the power of taboo to maximize the intensity of sexual play. In terms of the Erotic Equation, pressing up against the resistance of taboos is a way to generate excitement. Breaking rules is exhilarating. Fear of discovery (and even anticipation of punishment) can heighten the thrill.

Especially in cultures with puritanical leanings where sensual pleasure of any kind is viewed with suspicion, breaking rules—even ones that have nothing to do with sex—can acquire a specifically erotic charge. You'll find kinks for swearing, smoking while pregnant, eating while fat, unshaven female armpits, and even wearing white shoes before Memorial Day.

Tourists in the world of kink often assume that the allure of the forbidden is the primary engine behind non-conformist eroticisms. Yet a closer look

always reveals something more primal is going on. In messy play, the core attraction is actually the sensory pleasure—naughtiness gets laid over top of something fundamentally joyous.

Shit-eating is the most condemned, misrepresented and misunderstood kink. Even within the BDSM community, known for its tolerance, scat play is taboo, and coprophages are the Untouchables of the kink scene.

I interviewed a shit-eater a few years ago. We ate at a fancy restaurant in midtown Manhattan. He was a stunningly handsome, tall, Nordic type in a tailored business suit. When I asked him if he was drawn to shit-eating because it is the most taboo, he looked at me blankly. "I want to do it because I want to be of *service* to a woman. I want to offer myself to her in the most intimate way possible."

Cover of *Playing with Taboo*, by Mollena Williams. Greenery Press

Diaper fetishist from *The Play Pen*, an adult baby magazine

Looks like scat, but isn't. Treacle from *Splosh!*

Pieface Mike and friend

childhood home in a suburban ranch house outside San Francisco. Mike traces his passion for pies to his early love of the Three Stooges—an obsession he shares with most American pie fans. When he was little, he was forced to play a recurring chase game called Kissing Cooties, in which some boys got kisses while others had their faces smeared with cream. He didn't get kisses. "The thought of those nasty, freckle-faced girls mischievously pushing sweet cream into my nose, eyes, and mouth while they laughed and made fun of me made me melt with real humiliation and yet fearful fascination."

Mike began masturbating while throwing pies in his own face in his teens. "I was taking pies in the shower with me and I was experimenting with that, to enhance my own orgasms."

Mike believes that he is unusual among pie fans; most of the other ones only want to see women getting pied and don't want to get pied themselves. And he knows of quite a few pie-sexuals whose interests are definitely more hostile and violent than his own—one has even gone out and pied women on the street without permission. Mike strongly disapproves of this, and puts the political pranksters who pie celebrities in the same non-consensual league. (He also hates them because he thinks they've stolen his shtick.)

Months after our interview Mike revealed to me that on the day I visited him he purchased seven pies; he had placed them carefully on the bed in a back room of the house—just in case I brought up the idea of pieing him. But he was too shy and anxious to get up the nerve to ask me. Yet another missed opportunity.

Mike disappeared from the scene in around 2002.

CANDY CUSTARD

Candy Custard, a British splosher, is one of the fresh faces of WAM. She always loved getting stuck in mud as a child, but she didn't connect it to her erotic life until her late teens. In around 2002 she saw Bill Shipton and some of his messy girls profiled on a sex show on Channel 5 in Britain. Two of the models were getting messy with beans while another was sitting on a huge cake. "I blushed even though I was alone, and in that moment had a huge realization." After her marriage ended in 2006, Candy contacted Bill and offered to model for *Splosh!* She was extremely popular: not only was she a pretty model, but it was her kink too.

Since Bill Shipton's death in 2013, Candy has hosted private messy sessions at her home. Clients contact her with their requests,

sometimes writing elaborate scripts for roleplay and other times wanting Candy to ad-lib. One of her favorite sessions was what she calls the "Asploshalypse," involving 150 cakes, custards, and tins of pudding, plus 20 buckets of porridge and the deepest inflatable pool she could find.

About 70% of Candy's male clients want to dress up as women, and they bring their own outfits to wear—mackintoshes, Lycra, zentai, wedding dresses, multiple layers of winter weather gear—while submerging in her custom-built deep mud pit. "Some like to fill Ugg boots with custard. Some like to fill a swimsuit with porridge or sit on a cake wearing Speedos, or even naked." Others prefer to stay clean them-selves: they pull the cord of the gunge tank so that Candy is the messy victim.

Domination also features heavily in requests. Most want her to dominate them for the duration. Public humiliation is another special request. For one client she set up an elaborate day-long adventure in which she destroyed his clothing with slimy gunk, then forced him to change into a garish pink and yellow spandex outfit and walk, covered in goo, to the train station and home.

Candy met her boyfriend at a "Splunch" (a meet-up for wammers) arranged through chat-rooms, and is very happy to have found some-one who shares her interest. But her dream is to have someone else deal with the aftermath: "I'd love to swan into a fully prepared food fight scenario, dolled up to the nines, have some reason to set off a tit for tat mutual messing, have my fun, and then swan off again leaving the devastation behind. To add excite-ment to that even further, I'd like to do it in a huge hotel suite and be rich and extravagant enough to pay them handsomely to clean it up and replace everything. In the meantime, I'll settle for someone else lining the walls and floors with plastic!"

Pieplay photo by Rob Blaine, Messy Fun, Inc.

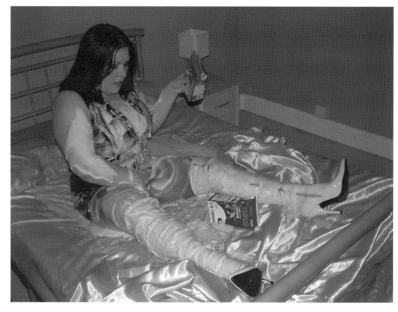

WAM IN BRIEF

TERMINOLOGY:
wam, mudlarking, wetlook, splosh

CORE KINK:
goo, mud

SUBKINKS:
wetlook, mudlarking, splosh,
pieplay

MAJOR THEMES:
taboo, sometimes power play

SUBTHEMES:
embarrassment, peril (in the case
of quicksand)

RELATED KINKS:
scat (shit play), piss play, clowns,
adult babies

EROTIC EQUATION:
pressing against rules of
propriety, weight of mud, or food
on clothing

Sploshing truly hit the mainstream in October 2016 when trendy UK confectioner Bompas & Parr promoted "Cake Holes," a cake-sitting photo series beautifully realized by fashion photographer Jo Duck. They'd found out about WAM when someone asked them to cater a sploshing party. A little bit of research and they realized this was a unique use of their products…and a marketing opportunity. "When a freshly chilled cake first touches your behind, you can't help but let off a range of squeamish noises," Bompas said. "Also, the surprisingly satisfying sound of a bum squashing a meringue is one sound I never thought I would come across, nor will I ever forget."

Candy Custard   Candy Custard in her playroom

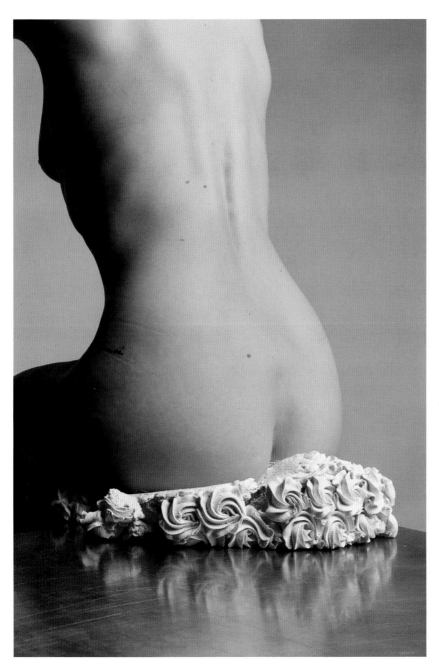

"*To me, the most arousing sight of all is a shapely girl's naked bottom being slowly lowered into a large quantity of something dark and messy, then watching it surging up around her cheeks like a tidal wave as they push it aside.*"
—Splosh! *#22*

From the "Cake Holes" series by Jo Duck for
Bompas & Parr

Ducky DooLittle as Knockers the
Clown. Photo: Charles Gatewood

Sidekink: Clowns

TERMINOLOGY:
clown, sometimes klown

MAJOR THEMES:
taboo, sometimes power play

SUBTHEMES:
embarrassment

EROTIC EQUATION:
pressing against social rules of propriety

To both those who fear them and those who love them, clowns represent the rule-breaking, anarchic id. Their costumes hide their identities and transform them into the trickster archetype, which in some ancient cultures was a figure with a gigantic phallus. Traditional clown acts include many kinks we know: pie throwing, tickling, water spraying, cramming into tight spaces, slapping, spanking, age play, and gender play.

Kinky folk, like artist and educator Ducky DooLittle, dress up as clowns during erotic performances to explicitly abandon propriety. They are crass, dirty, and unashamed. One male prodom, who went by the name Ouchy the Clown, made use of coulrophobia (fear of clowns) to enhance his clients' excitement.

Ouchy the Clown. Photo:
Glenncampbellphoto.com

Sugar Weasel, a male escort whose clientele ranges from "recent divorcées, bachelorettes, punk rock chicks, and married women looking to fuck a grown man in make-up who acts like an idiot"

For the Love of Fat: Feeders and Gainers

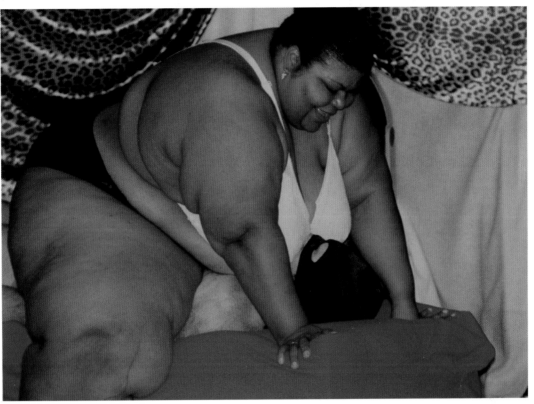

Heather Boyle Nymeyer with admirer.
Photo: BigCutieEllie of BigCuties.com

Modern Western culture has a hate/hate relationship with fat. We exalt clinically underweight fashion models. We spend billions annually on mostly ineffectual weight loss methods and risky surgeries. We'll do almost anything to force our diverse bodies to conform to an impossible ideal, while affluent nations nevertheless grow more and more obese. We may no longer be able to crack racist or sexist jokes in polite company, but fat people are still fodder for laughs.

In this pervasive climate of fat-phobia, fat admirers (FAs)—men and women who prefer fat partners—are rebels. Fat admiration is not about people "settling" for fat partners. According to various polls and surveys, about 10-15% of us would prefer fat sexual partners. Yet many would be too embarrassed to be seen in public for fear of ridicule; FAs might even marry someone with

a socially acceptable body, yet secretly yearn for more flesh. Those FAs who have the nerve to be out of the closet are often active in the fight against oppression of fat people, radicalized by the social, cultural, and political oppression of fat.

Of course, a preference for fat partners shouldn't be considered a kink or a fetish, any more than a preference for male or female partners. But there is no doubt that fat itself can be a core fetish material. It's a touchy-feely substance, as sensual as leather or rubber. While many find fat sexually repulsive, many FAs have a directly sexual response to fat, separate from the person the fat is attached to. Cellulite, double chins, and folds of fat over knees and elbows arouse them.

Just as foot fetishists might want to imagine themselves crushed under a giant foot, some

Mistress Magick, one of Queen Adrena's girls, smushing an FA customer. Photo: Queen Adrena

*"Fat is comforting.
It's warm. It's
soft. It's cuddly. If
our society did not
revile fat, I think
people would just
rush to it."*
—Dian Hanson

FAs crave the sensation of being crushed under a massive fat body. Just as latex fans might find it orgasmic to see their balloons or inflatable costumes grow even larger, some fat fans want to see their fat partners gain more and more weight, challenging the confines of clothes or pushing the limits of a scale. And some fat people thrill to the feel of their own skin, the sensation of being one giant sex organ, and the taboo joys of uninhibited eating and weight gain.

The sexual attraction to fat is innate; we shouldn't consider it deviant at all. Smut publisher Dian Hanson is a slender woman who has dated several fat men. To Dian, an erotic preference for fat makes sense. "It's comforting. It's warm. It's soft. It's cuddly. If our society did not revile fat, I think people would just rush to it." Wherever it is on the body—whatever that body's gender—fat is like a big squishy breast or ass. The late cultural critic Leslie Fiedler suggested that supersized fat people are appeal-

ing because they remind us of when we were being pressed against the gigantic breast of our mother, "whose bulk—to our 8-pound, 21-inch selves—must have seemed as mountainous as any 600-pound Fat Lady to our adult selves."

The eroticizing of fat does not exist in a cultural vacuum. Fat phobia stems from Puritanical notions that fat people are too sensual, too fleshy, and too unregulated. Fat is viewed as somehow sinful, and calorie restriction as some kind of universal moral imperative. We enforce these rules overtly through insults and covertly through "concern trolling" (constantly harping on fat people's supposed bad health).

We can admire those who torture themselves with regimens, but fat people threaten us with their public displays of orality and appetite. We can't imagine someone might choose to be fat, so we label fat people food addicts to assert our conviction that they are out of control.

Illustration: Ned Sonntag

Leslie Fiedler pointed out that hatred of fat is directly related to sexual repression. "In cultures, or classes within cultures, whose codes are notably repressive and strict, fatness has…tended to be feared; but in more permissive and relaxed communities and castes, it is respected and honored." Lurking beneath fat-phobia may be a hatred of non-white cultures, of the lower classes, of women and of sexuality.

Fat phobia in the United States seems to be a predominantly white, middle-class phenomenon. The National Association to Advance Fat Acceptance (NAAFA) was founded in 1969 as a working-class organization fighting fat discrimination in the workplace and the stereotype of fat people as lower-class, lazy, and uneducated. The fat acceptance community is far more diverse in terms of cultural background than many other political movements. Latin, Arabic, African, and Asian cultures have long celebrated and revered fat people. Japan has its cult of sumo wrestlers and black American culture produces notoriously big rap stars—who often brag that their sexual appetites are as massive as for food.

By contrast, fat-philia derives at least some of its erotic punch from the same cultural baggage; rejection of those sex-negative body-shaming rules can be liberating. Fat's symbolic connection to femininity, sensuality, and physical appetites adds another layer of excitement onto the core kink material. In the days of the circus sideshow, the Fat Lady often had to turn away suitors, for as Leslie Fiedler explained, her supersized body represented "Eros without guilt or limit or satiety or exhaustion." And for fat people who experience a daily assault of fat-phobic verbal assaults, fat-shaming advertisements, concern trolling, tiny airplane seats, and the like, finding a partner who truly desires their body exactly as it is (or even bigger) can be a life-changing experience.

There's a long history of erotica devoted to the joys of ample flesh. Before the health crazes of the 1980s, porn models were much juicier. The 1970s—that heyday of shameless libertinism—was also the apex of fat pornography. At one point during the decade there were at least eight fat-oriented smut rags going at once. *BUF* (Big Up Front) ran from 1975 to its last issue in 2009. *Plumpers and Big Women* ran from 1993–2010. Yet I find disturbing the shoddy presentation of those hardcore FA magazines, which make the models look cheap. It seems as if the photography reflects some of the same cultural shame and prejudice. Perhaps men who bought *BUF* and *P&BW* were so in the closet that they needed their porn to make them feel shame and to help them hate the fat women of their desires.

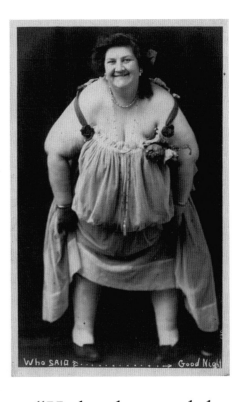

"He loved to watch her move and jiggle. Her huge belly was just past her knees. Her breasts hung to her ever-larger belly button, which was 9" deep. He loved to enter her there and climax on her belly."
—from "BBW Bordello," an erotic story by Supersize Betsy

Sideshow fat ladies had to turn away marriage proposals. Vintage card from Showhistory.com

Dimensions (1984–2000), on the other hand, was a non-pornographic, sex-positive magazine for heterosexual FAs that combined a political agenda with an overtly erotic one. *Dimensions'* readership was fairly evenly matched between women and men, mixing personal ads, discussions of cultural bias, and medical advice on staying fit and fat, with R-rated pictorials of happy 300-pound women in bathing suits. *Dimensions* also promoted a "500 club" celebrating the sensuality and desirability of women over 500 pounds. The magazine was named after both meanings of the word: dimensions as in measurements, and dimensions as in other realities, other worlds. It always had a strong sci-fi/fantasy component. One FA explained, "We're trying to create an alternate universe where the largeness is a preferred thing."

Fat admiration isn't limited to straight men. Gay male fat admirers call themselves chasers, and many chubbies and chasers belong to an organization called Girth & Mirth, which has chapters all over the US and Europe promoting social events. Magazines for chubbies and chasers included *Heavy Duty* and *Bulk Male*. The 21st century has seen a surge in chubby gay pornography, a trend that overlaps, and follows in the footsteps of, the 20th-century phenomenon of "bears"—big, hairy guys.

Dan Austen is gay trans man who has often found himself the object of attention from chasers. He once asked a lover what the appeal was: "It was a very childlike, nurturing thing. He liked a big man because it was a motherly image, it made him feel secure—it went right back to childhood. And it's not necessarily neurotic, it's about childhood needs and desires being realized in adulthood."

Female fat admirers (FFAs) have become a major part of the community in the new millennium. Ginger, a lifelong FFA, finds fat sexually exciting in exactly the same way some FA men do—it's not simply a preference for big teddy-bear men and roly-poly daddies. "I am a genuine fat admirer. I am attracted to the same things as male

FAs: cellulite, rolls, double chins, round faces, huge bellies, etc. I am attracted to the way fat moves, how it jiggles and sways… I am also turned on by other themes and fantasies familiar to my fellow FAs, like outgrown clothing and progressive weight gain. So to say that I merely prefer big men is not enough. My sexuality is identified with my preference."

Ned Sonntag is a fat admirer with a lifelong erotic fascination for women over 400 pounds. He is a professional artist beloved by FAs for his illustrations for *Dimensions* magazine. Ned is a small, now elderly, man, who usually wears a white fedora hat. He's quite shy, and his voice is very quiet, though with a nasal Midwestern accent and a wry sense of humor. Dian Hanson told me Ned is so entranced by very fat women that he can see one walking down the street and enter a fugue state. He doesn't know where he is or what he's doing—his voice trails off, and sometimes he just turns around and follows her for a little while with his mouth open and drool forming at the edges of his lips. Ned was married for decades to the actress and playwright Katy Dierlam Sonntag, who before her death in 2012, weighed over 450 pounds, and once did a stint as Fat Lady Helon Melon at the Coney Island Sideshow performing her theatrical monologue about fat-phobia.

Ned Sonntag traces his fascination with fat to his childhood in obesity-prone Indiana. He remembers being transfixed at 10 by a fat neighbor at a family barbecue. "There was some rock 'n roll song on the transistor radio, and she had these shorts on. She was just tapping her thumb against her thighs to the rhythm, very unselfconsciously, and these ripples of oceanic flesh were"—and here he sighed—"rippling back and forth across her ample thighs." When Ned and his family moved to Florida, he found himself identifying with fat people as fellow rejects and outsiders.

Fat women were the subjects of Ned's earliest doodlings. In ninth grade, he began drawing pictures of big, beautiful women in elegant evening gowns and pearls to counteract the stereotype of fat women as poor, white trash. When he moved to New York in 1974 to attend Pratt, he was a starving, skinny little artist in love with gigantic women. "In Brooklyn, around the art school, there were all these great Russian Jewish ladies. They were very large and they had outrageous hips and all different body shapes. I was much happier!" Ned went to his first NAA-FA dance on Valentine's Day 1976. In 1979, he met his future wife Katy at a Klaus Nomi show.

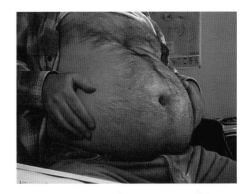

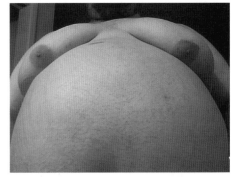

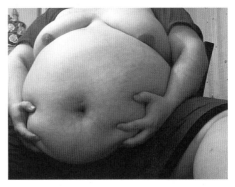

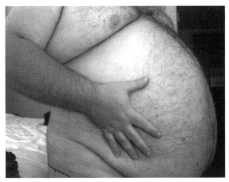

Belly sampler from gainer profiles on sites like Bellybuilders.com, a male gaining site, and fantasyfeeder.com, which has both women and men

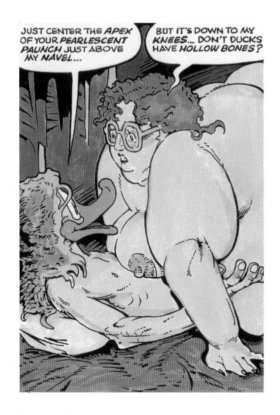

JUST CENTER THE *APEX* OF YOUR *PEARLESCENT PAUNCH* JUST ABOVE MY *NAVEL*...

BUT IT'S DOWN TO MY *KNEES*... DON'T DUCKS HAVE *HOLLOW BONES*?

Illustrations: Ned Sonntag

For Ned, sex with his wife was an experience of total submersion in fat. He explained his love of his wife's body: "There's more skin. There are acres of creamy flesh. As part of penetration, you bump up against the large belly region which kind of flows up against your chest, bonks up under your chin. You're floating around in an ocean of female flesh!"

In the gay male chaser scene, a major erotic trigger is "gut flopping", where the fat partner lifts up and drops his belly onto his partner, making a huge slapping noise. Sensual belly rubs are also a major turn-on in the gay male chaser and gainer crowds.

Although fat bodies may be abstract fertility symbols, many FAs are very fixated on precise weights and measures. Ned Sonntag explains: "What did you weigh back then? What do you weigh now? What are your dimensions? It's all measurements and numbers. Quantifying everything." Gay male chasers can be just as fixated on numbers as the straight guys. Dan Austen was astonished at how his chubby chaser lover could literally get off on taking his measurements. "He would take a tape measure and measure my waist and he would be getting a raging hard-on just looking at the numbers! He would see '44 inches' and he'd get really excited. He'd talk about my weight measurements. He'd say 'Ooooh, 245…245…' over and over."

Like many FAs, Ned Sonntag found watching his wife eat to be very erotic. Videos of women eating huge meals and talking about how much weight they think they've gained are easy to find on YouTube. The term "stuffing" is used for videos featuring excessive eating but which do not emphasize the end result of weight gain. In one, fetish model Melissa devours a gigantic meatball sub, then lights up a cigarette and proclaims her total satisfaction as if she's just had an orgasm.

For those who eroticize weight gain, switching the before and after photos of a diet advertise-

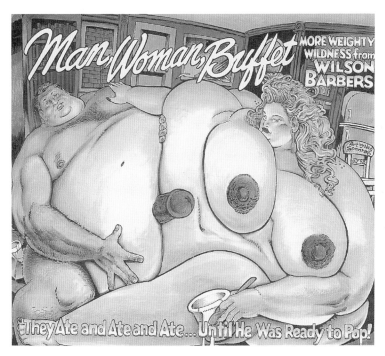

"I'm an appetite outlaw with wild, wild ways and a baaad attitude."
—Katy Dierlam Sonntag

ment can be pure pornography. They can meet and chat on websites like FeedMe and Fantasy-Feeder where they can talk about people popping out of their clothing, just the way giantess fans do. In fact, many weight gain stories show up on body inflation websites, and many BE types are themselves fat admirers. Just as with the body inflation fantasies, many people—both male and female—sexualize the fantasy of their own bodies growing bigger and bigger. "When a woman gains weight and you're an FA, that is an extremely ecstatic experience," explains Ed Lundt, erstwhile King of the Growth Fantasies. "It pushes all of your neural hot-buttons in a way that nothing else does."

While most fat admirers prefer to keep their weight-gain scenarios in the realm of fantasy, some FAs, FFAs, and chubby chasers engage in consensual feeding sessions with the goal of measurable weight gain. Men who want to feed women are called "feeders" and the women who enjoy growing call themselves "feedees." Gay men who feed their lovers or who get together in mutual feeding sessions call themselves gainers

and encouragers. You can sometimes find personal ads reading: "Chubby seeks same for weekend of Gaining and Encouraging." Dan Austen says, "They see the whole body as a sexual organ, so the bigger it is, the better. If you could increase the size of your penis, why wouldn't you increase the size of your body?" One gay male gainer once described the pleasure of growing: "If there's one thing that makes me truly happy, it's the feeling of a full gut. Every day I wake up excited to stuff myself and push my limits."

The sexiest scenario for a feeder or feedee might involve measuring, weighing, and photographing the body before and after a feeding session. They might keep a video and photographic record of the growth so that they can watch it happen over time. Some feeders and feedees fantasize about gaining weight to the point of immobility—which usually happens at around 450–480 pounds—and beyond. A common target weight, at least in fantasy, is 1,000 pounds.

Gaining and encouraging has grown significantly in the gay male community in the last ten years.

"Man, Woman, Buffet," Ned Sonntag illustration for *JUGGS* magazine, fiction by Wilson Barbers

Heather Boyle Nymeyer

"Ballpark Figure Salon" by Ned Sonntag,
originally published in *Puritan* magazine

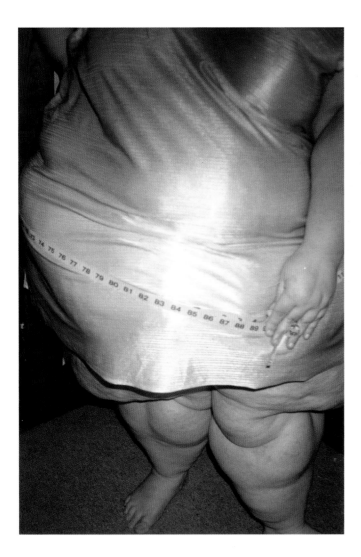

26 yo, cute gainer, 5'10", 305#, dark blonde/blue, seeks much fatter (450+), older (30-450) man to encourage me to greatness. I want to weight over 500# before I'm 30. I like, but don't require, tattooed Marlboro Men who wear denim, flannel and baseball caps, drive old pickup with fat tires, most of all, have massive, soft, low-slung bellies hangin' over their 60" belts.

AZ—Hi. looking for a young woman (25-35) who wants to go from chubby to plump, plump to fat, fat to fatter, and fatter to obese. This handsome, romantic and loyal feeder will help you reach each milestone and be there through thin and thick, spiritually, emotionally and physically. So—stop the diet yo-yo, eat everything you want, and get as fat as you can with the adoring support of a "good man".

The website Grommr, which describes itself as, "A social and dating site for gainers, bloaters, encouragers and admirers," now has almost 100,000 members who share side-view selfies of their bellies popping out of their pants. Members can arrange to meet up for sex or feeding or both. Gainer Camp in Seattle was a series of weeklong gatherings of gainers and encouragers where the kitchen was always open, the living room littered with cases of soda, pizza boxes, and Krispy Kreme bags. "This isn't a sex camp or a social camp or a vacation opportunity," the website explains. "This is a serious event for gainers who want to spend a week focusing on gaining with a group of like-minded individuals." In addition to eating and local excursions, the men also had a health workshop led by a man who calls himself BigFatJeeebus, creator of the Gainer Health Support Network. "You can be healthy and obese if you make the right choices!" The Gainer Camp from 2013 proudly claimed 60 pounds of weight gain between only five men.

There can be a very dark side to feeding, if both parties are not careful and realistic about monitoring the weight gain. This is not so different from the potential dark side of any SM play—both parties have to take responsibility for knowing and understanding risk and setting limits. In Grommr's FAQ, the question "Isn't gaining unhealthy?" gets a response, "Sure, so is driving a car, living in North Philadelphia, rock climbing, and taking Tylenol." Although size acceptance advocates such as the Health at Every Size movement contend that there is no simple causal connection between weight and ill health and that the multi-billion-dollar diet industry is behind much of the effort to convince us otherwise, some feeders and gainers feel it's prudent to establish limits and stick to them.

Feeding is an extremely controversial issue in the fat acceptance community. NAAFA strongly frowns on feeding, and many fat women and FAs will not even discuss it. Many in the anti-feeder crowd see feeder behavior as insidious and

Taking measurements can be a form of foreplay for fans of weight gain.
Photo: Bountiful Productions

Personal ad from *Heavy Duty* magazine

Personal ad from *Dimensions* magazine

Top Ten Weight Gain Media Sightings

(with contributions by Wilson Barbers and Conrad Blickenstorfer)

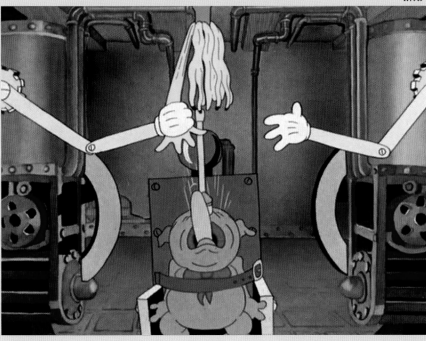

Still from "Pigs Is Pigs," a 1937 Warner Brothers cartoon

1. *Death Becomes Her* (1992). Goldie Hawn's fattening is the first in a series of physical grotesqueries that culminates in a *Tales from the Crypt*–style ending. Too negative for some.

2. *The Man with Two Brains* (1983). Kathleen Turner's weight gain is the final punchline of the film, and the fat character is treated positively.

3. *La Grande Bouffe* (1973). French film about extreme eating, although the subject is treated quite darkly—like the Mr. Creosote sequence in Monty Python's 1983 *The Meaning of Life*.

4. *Li'l Abner,* "Stupefyin' Jones" by Al Capp (c. 1978). The town fattens the local beauty so that their men would no longer go after her. Capp did several weight gain sequences in his strip, but Ms. Jones is the one the FAs remember.

5. *MAD* "A MAD Look at Fat." The December 1988 issue of the magazine includes a Dave Berg look at dieting.

6. "Betty Boop and Little Jimmy" (1936). Our heroine grows to super-size simply by laughing. "If you're thin/Don't worry over that/Just begin to laugh/and you'll grow fat!" This cartoon reigns high in most fantasizers' memory.

7. "Pigs Is Pigs" (1937). An early Friz Freleng-directed Warner Brothers cartoon featuring a feeding machine used by a mad scientist on a young, gluttonous pig.

8. "The Fat Boy of Steel," *Adventure Comics* #298 (1962). All of the people in Superboy's home town—girlfriend Lana Lang included—grow fat thanks to some radioactive milk.

9. "The Fattest Girl in Metropolis," *Lois Lane* #5 (1958). Lois is transformed into a matronly femme by a mysterious growth ray.

10. *The Cook* (1965). Harry Kressing's cult novel. A chef uses his cooking mastery to transform a blonde heiress into a mega-sized glutton so large that she can't get around without the help of servants. He marries this fantastic beauty and the novel ends, hinting of even greater growth in the years ahead.

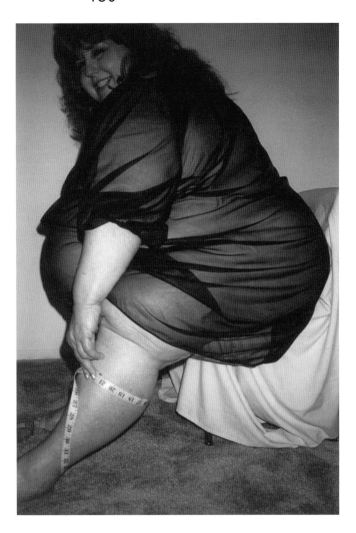

Ambrosia, a popular model for Bountiful Productions,
documented her weight gain over a period of years.
Photo: Bountiful Productions

which to this day prominently features a banner reading, "This site is 100% weight gain fetish free!" includes an editorial by a writer named Yohannon, who accuses feeders of the kind of manipulations common to abusive relationships. A woman who is new to the movement and unsure of her self-esteem and personal weight limits may not be able to say no. If she refuses to gain weight, the feeder may use guilt tactics or threaten to leave her. At this point she may be too ill to take care of herself. Yohannon points out that one woman named Trish who used to be in the *Dimensions* "500 Club" gained so much weight that she died from related causes, so he offers his essay as the memorial she never got in the magazine.

Despite Yohannon's construction of feedee women as victims, there definitely exist women whose primary erotic fantasy is to be fed and to gain massive amounts of weight. They are adults making adult decisions. Like experienced SM players, they maintain an awareness of the line between fantasy and reality and they play safely. Even though outsiders presume that the feeder is the one who is taking the dominant role, in practice, the feedee experiences the feeding sessions as a kind of worship. Food is brought to them, they are massaged and served and pleasured—their sensual enjoyment is the object of the activity.

HEATHER BOYLE NYMEYER
Heather Boyle Nymeyer has wanted to be fat ever since she was a child. "I was always amazed by women who were fat. I wanted to hug them." Not only that, she wanted to know what it felt like to be in that fat body, "and I wanted to be even fatter than her." When she was little, she often wanted to play games that involved stuffing her clothes, but her peers' reactions made it clear that this was something she would have to keep to herself.

Heather's erotic fantasies involve her own body covering a king-sized bed. "I want to ooze over the edge!" She wants to take up space; she

predatory. They presume that this activity is not fully consensual and that the woman is being taken advantage of in an area where she may be somewhat weak. To suggest that fat people might choose to get even fatter threatens some fat activists' claims that fatness is never a matter of choice and therefore should be treated as a disability. On the other hand, suggesting that feedees are not fully responsible for their own actions plays into some fat-phobic arguments that fat people are "food addicts." They can't help themselves, they're not in control of their desires—they are, somehow, infantile. Feedees counter, "You have no right to tell me what I can or cannot do with my body in the bedroom or out."

Feeding provokes vehement flame wars on the internet. The Rotunda, a fat activist website,

wants to engage in pure, hedonistic gluttony. Eating becomes erotic only when she consumes more than is comfortable. "It's so exciting, knowing that it's all going to turn into fat." She loves wearing clothes that are too tight, or having experiences where she doesn't fit into the space. Recently she had an MRI and didn't fit into the enclosed space. "It was torture, I have claustrophobia!" but for the next three days, she masturbated to the memory.

Up until she weighed 450 pounds her growth journey was solitary. At first, she set goals and limits for herself: "If I get to 300 pounds, I'll be fat enough." Then she went to 350. She came to a series of crossroads and made choices. "I decided not to have children when I couldn't get on the floor to play with them." At a certain point, she realized that there

was no end. At 600 pounds and now using a scooter to get around, she has no plans to stop. "I know my body is not a prime machine, but I'm healthy enough." If she had a choice between living an extra five years and going on a severe diet, she would choose a shorter more pleasurable life. "It can be very dark," she says. "I choose to be fat over health issues. I have good labs and a good heart." She's lucky enough to have found a doctor who understands it's pointless to scold her about her weight. "His cholesterol is worse than mine!" And she dismisses as a myth the idea that being fat causes diabetes. "It might exacerbate it, but it doesn't cause it."

Heather is in a poly relationship. She has one male partner with whom she plays feeding games in bed, but her husband has no particular interest

Belly appreciation by DeviantArt
user Prisonsuit Rabbitman

Heather Boyle Nymeyer and friend.
Photo: BigCutieEllie of BigCuties.com

SUPERSIZE BETSY

Supersize Betsy was one of the first female feedees who was totally open about her fantasy of being fed and gaining weight. She was a popular model for FA magazines and for two videotapes about the feeding fantasy. When I interviewed her in 1999, she was supporting herself as a professional writer and author of weight gain, FA, and feeder fiction.

Betsy was unhappily married for 12 years to a man who wanted her to be thin; he was rich and she was trying her best to be a trophy wife, but it didn't work. Diets and medication were making her sick. Then, a couple of years before her marriage broke up, Betsy saw an episode on fat admiration on one of the daytime talk shows. "That kind of started me thinking, 'I'm going to go find someone who wants me as I am, or at least as I'm supposed to be.'" The first thing she did after her divorce was to join NAAFA. "It still took me about a year to get my head out of that consciousness where you think you still need to lose weight and where there's something wrong with you the way you are."

At the time of our interview, Betsy weighed 420 pounds, but only about 15 of those pounds were put on through erotic feeding and gaining. In 1993, Betsy did a video for *Bellybusters*, the pro-weight-gain newsletter. It was done in black and white and it's just called *Betsy*. In that video she mostly ate. "I was in lingerie and I ate a large coconut cake and several quarts of half-and-half, which is a favorite of mine. I actually prefer cream for that purpose because it has more calories for the same amount of liquid." Solid food is not as pleasant for these sessions, she has found. "It weighs me down and makes me feel bad—it isn't as erotic as the liquid which fills you out but doesn't make you feel like you can't move the way a really heavy meal does."

After the eating, she took off her lingerie and modeled her nude body. She never spread her legs or had sex for any of the photos or

in her weight gain. "He respects my choices for my body." People assume that feeders are some kind of predator, but "that's bullshit. These fantasies are mine." She's aware that she might sound like a crazy person, "but I know I'm sound. I'm no crazier than the next person."

Heather concedes that she's an extreme case. By far the majority of feeders and feedees just keep it all in the realm of fantasy. "I know from the outside it looks like people are feeding themselves to death, but that just isn't true." She tells her friends that if she dies in bed choking on a Ho Ho, "You let everyone know I died in my very best way. Celebrate that I lived my life unapologetically."

videos—she believed it was less interesting to her viewers than the eating anyway: "They are more turned on by seeing me massage my belly than they would be by a spread shot, or any form of sex. And they're really turned on by my eating or seeing me weighed." At the end of the video there was a masturbation scene, but the rolls of fat on her belly covered that area, so nothing was exposed. "The real sensuality is in the conversation that's going on between myself and the cameraman, where he's saying, 'Oh, you'd really like to be fatter.' We just talk about it, and it gets very intense."

For Betsy, as for the gay male gainers, her belly is a major erogenous zone. The skin is sensitive as it expands, and gets tighter. A major turn-on for the video viewers is belly rubs, and she says that all of them, "down to the very last one, have some kind of fantasy of me sitting on top of them or laying on top of them or just enveloping them. To them, it's like being smothered in chocolate syrup. It's not a death wish or suffocation thing—it's more about being able to feel this femininity surrounding you completely."

In that first video, Betsy weighed only about 320 pounds, but on subsequent shoots she weighed in at 344, 410, and 420 pounds, so her fans had a chance to see her progressive growth. "They love to weigh and measure you, and I enjoy that too. Keeping a record

Still from feeding video starring
Heather Boyle Nymeyer

Heather Boyle Nymeyer's profile pic

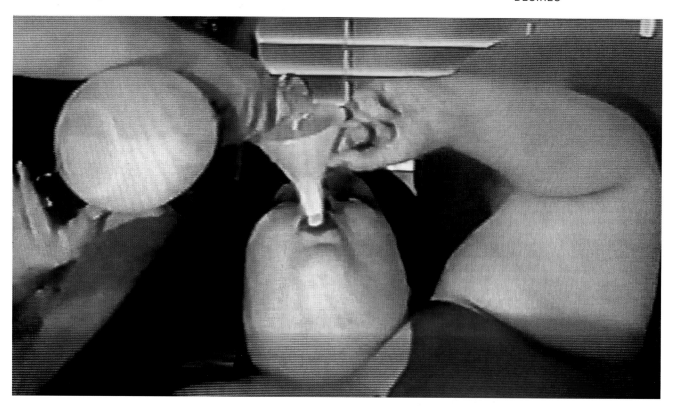

"Being a feeder or a feedee is not really a choice, any more than one's sexual orientation is a choice. Personally, I think it's time to try and be happy!"
—Supersize Betsy

of it and documenting it is important." The ideal feeder/feedee dream is to start with someone who is relatively small and grow them to enormous proportions, keeping a photographic record of the whole process.

Her second video, "The Feeding Fantasies of Betsy," was for *Dimensions* magazine, and included an interview with Ruby from *Dimensions* about what it's like to be a feedee, and some of her fantasies. "[Ruby] prepares this enormous meal for me, and there's about 20 minutes spent on me eating it in this black lace ensemble. About halfway through, my tummy overlaps my waistband. There's a scene of me being weighed at 410, and my tummy being measured at 84 inches, showing where it expanded right then after the feeding."

After the meal, Betsy massaged and moved her tummy around, dancing and letting it all hang out. "There's also a short scene where Ruby funnel feeds me on the couch. She places a funnel in my mouth, which I'm actually holding, and then she pours a quart of half-and-half into it. You kind of swallow, and you try to keep up with the other person's pouring."

Force-feeding was one of Betsy's major fantasies from an early age, even before it was sexual. It's not unusual for feeders and feedees to have begun thinking these things as children. "Most of us have seen an old cartoon called 'Pigs Is Pigs.' It's a *Merrie Melodies*

Still from "The Feeding Fantasies of Betsy"
video produced by *Dimensions* magazine

cartoon from 1937, which showed this little pig getting strapped down in a chair by a mad scientist and being force-fed by a machine and growing fatter and fatter." Betsy remembered wanting to be strapped down and have that done to her. "Feeders, too, remember that was the first time they had a glimpse that someone else had thought of strapping someone down in a chair and making them grow fatter."

At the end of the cartoon the scientist lets the piggy go, and the piggy has to waddle out the door. "That's one of the most erotic scenes for me. The waddling of this enormous piggy. He's just about to leave and he sees that there's this other piece of pie on the table and he eats it and he explodes! Then he wakes up and it was a nightmare."

Betsy's favorite masturbatory fantasy was a man being so turned on by her growing body that he has a huge erection. "Sometimes I visualize him climaxing either on or in my body—like between the folds of fat on my tummy or sometimes even in my belly button, which is currently four inches deep." She also loved to imagine herself getting weighed—"even if I was too large to move I would conjure up a special bed with a built-in scale."

Betsy also explored feeding in partner play. Several months before our interview, she had gone for the weekend to the house of a friend who loved to cook her fattening food. Though it wasn't ostensibly a sexual game, for Betsy it was extremely exciting. "The night when I got home after the weekend I had a wet dream. I actually climaxed in my sleep thinking about the whole experience."

Betsy became such a celebrity in the feeder community that she would often receive gift certificates for cookies, donuts, and ice cream from her admirers all over the world. "I actually prefer prime rib and baked potatoes! I like sweets, but I can't eat them the way they'd like me to. I can't sit there for an hour and just eat

candy nonstop the way I could a big steak with Bearnaise sauce. I can eat several of those!"

To Betsy, feeding and gaining absolutely had to be a part of a negotiated, consensual arrangement: "It would be terrible if a woman was forced to gain weight against her will." In any case, all the feeders Betsy knew were gentlemen in every sense of the word. "They just want to grow this huge woman that they can get lost in, you know? And they have fantasies about her lying on top of them and just smothering them with her flesh. They're more submissive than anything else."

Betsy got lots of offers from men who wanted to fatten her for a night or a weekend, but at 420 she knew she was getting close to limits she set. There are consequences to weight gain: "Especially at my current weight, I realize that my mobility is an issue. I may only have about 80 pounds that I can put on. I wouldn't want to put it on casually. I'm sort of saving myself for the right man."

In her fantasies, Betsy wanted to be the fattest woman on earth. "In reality, there are things that I like to do that involve getting out of bed!

Weight gain to immobility is the fantasy for some gainers. Illustration: Ned Sonntag

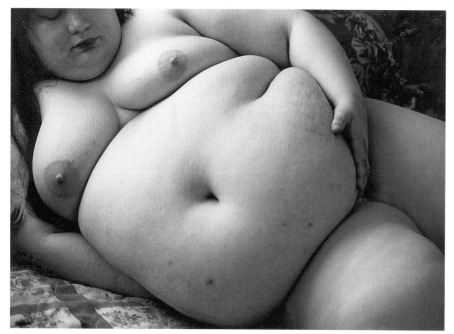

FEEDERS AND GAINERS
IN BRIEF

TERMINOLOGY:
FA, feeder, gainer, encourager

CORE KINK:
fat

MAJOR THEMES:
transformation

SUBTHEMES:
(sometimes) object
transformation

RELATED KINKS:
preggo, mpreg, body expansion
(Chapter 4), stuffing

There are other problems that come with the size, like skin-fold rashes. You'd have to be with somebody that's willing to care for you 24 hours a day." At the time of our interview Betsy had been looking for six years but hadn't found a man who really wanted to take her to immobility. "They may fantasize about it, but they don't really want to do it." She also had back problems which her last hundred pounds exacerbated. "I love being large. It's who I am. The only thing I would change is that I would find a way to fix my lower back problem, which stems from a childhood injury; it has nothing to do with my weight. Except that it got worse that last hundred pounds. If only I could control that pain and still be fat."

UPDATE

In the Fall of 1999, Betsy met the man of her dreams— a handsome, intelligent chemist from Germany who shared her erotic feeding fantasies. In the first two weeks after their engagement, Betsy gained 10 pounds. Within months, Betsy moved to Germany and got married. A friend of Betsy's told me that a German doctor convinced her to go on a paleo diet, which likely hastened her death in 2012.

Betsy and her 4″ deep belly button

Balloon, body inflation and weight gain combined in "The Fat Boy of Steel"
Adventure Comics #298, 1962

Sidekink: Smoking

"Us Tareyton smokers would rather fight than switch!"

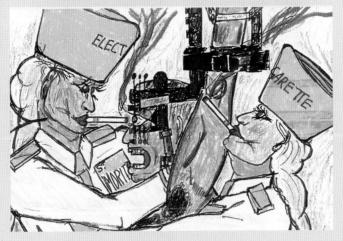

Smoking fans want to watch their partner casually and masterfully inhale deeply from a cigar or cigarette. They enjoy the sight of the cheeks suctioning inwards, and eroticize French inhales, snap inhales and other oral skills, such as dangling the cigarette off a lip. Nose exhales or smoke rings can be eroticized. There are websites devoted exclusively to clips from films of actors smoking.

As with erotic eating, part of the excitement comes from seeing a partner indulge in a guilty pleasure without regard for rules. One reader in *Smoke Signals* magazine explained, "When we see a woman do something 'naughty,' we know that she may be more willing to do something else considered 'naughty.'" For some, the ultimate excitement might come from seeing a pregnant woman smoking, as a sign of true rebellion.

While in the early part of the last century, women who smoked in public were viewed as "loose" and likely prostitutes, Virginia Slims' 1968 "You've Come a Long Way, Baby" advertising campaign presented female smoking as a sign of female liberation and power. Ads aimed at men featured cowboys and other hyper-masculine icons, bringing home its appeal to a gay male audience.

Cigarettes can be a tool for BDSM play. Some smoking fans want the their partner to blow smoke in their faces as a form of domination. "Dark side" smoking fans may wish to be burned by the cigarette.

TERMINOLOGY:
smoking, darkside

CORE KINK:
mouth

MAJOR THEMES:
power play, taboo

MINOR THEMES:
oral fun

SUBFETISHES:
specific brands, cigars, young or pregnant smoking

MAY BE COMBINED WITH:
crush (Chapter 6), balloon popping (Chapter 3), preggo

EROTIC EQUATION:
suction of the mouth

The Tareyton ad campaign of the 1960s appealed to fans of both smoking and impact play

Masterful smoking from a photo set by shesmokes.com

Detail from a fan letter sent to Dian Hanson showing cigarette torture, courtesy Dian Hanson

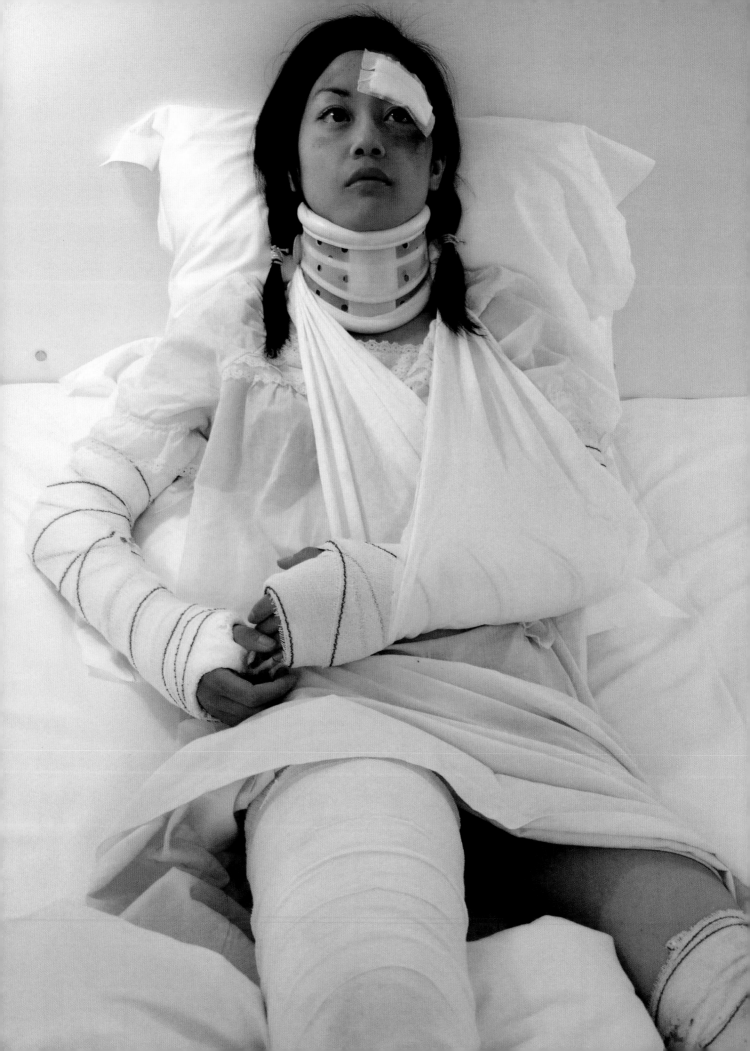

Medical Play:
Let's Play Doctor

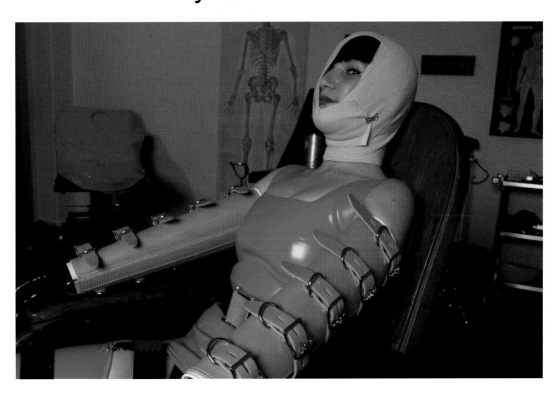

Japanese Hospital, 2016.
Photo: Romain Slocombe

For those fascinated by intimate power and pain games, yet unmoved by the trappings of traditional BDSM, medical play provides a whole new set of toys and scenarios. Impact play (whippings and paddlings) isn't for everyone. And with old-style BDSM play, there's also that politically tricky master-and-slave matter to reckon with, the baggage of institutional power and punishment, dramas few privileged first-worlders have experienced in real life.

Perhaps because of this, kinky folk are increasingly branching out into other power narratives that connect with their actual lived experience. Ponyplay works within the more affectionate realm of animal domestication; most of us have loved pets, especially in childhood. Medical play clicks with those whose terror and excitement at being examined and poked intimately by a total stranger connects with the reason "playing doctor" is the first sex game most children ever explore: the combination of total helplessness, anticipation of pain, bodily penetration, and the knowledge "it's for your own good," while the doctor is "just taking care of you" and "has to," provides a whole spectrum of emotional and physical triggers for erotic excitement.

ROMAIN SLOCOMBE
Romain Slocombe, a Parisian artist and novelist, translated his personal kink for medical bondage into a body of viscerally terrifying yet decorously attractive paintings and photographs. When I first picked up one of his books in the late 1980s, I could not tell if it was an art catalog, a medical brochure on the treatment of accident victims, or a new kind of SM pornography. In a way, it's all three.

Medical play scene at MedicalToys.com

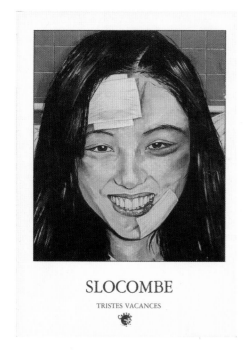

SLOCOMBE

TRISTES VACANCES

Slocombe's palm-sized booklet *Tristes Vacances* (*Sad Vacations*, 1986) begins with a newspaper story, a description of a highway accident involving a busload of Japanese schoolgirls on vacation in France. This is followed by a very precise medical description of their injuries. Then the color plates of his paintings—a girl sits on the floor looking at us sadly, almost accusingly. She is half-undressed, perhaps still wearing the clothes she had on during the crash. A masculine hand intrudes forcefully into the frame to hold the girl's bandaged arm aloft. It's hard to know whether he does this to better reveal her injuries or to prevent her from covering up her breasts. In another picture, a girl poses on a stool like a 1950s pin-up, smiling coyly at us. She wears an improbable clothing combination—an expensive white fur wrap and a white cast on her outstretched arm.

In *City of the Broken Dolls* (1997), Slocombe switches to photography. They're the sort of snapshots a lawyer might take for a personal injury lawsuit or a hospital might use to document a treatment record—their artlessness is the most jarring thing about them. It helps the viewer suspend disbelief. Each picture is accompanied by a cursory diagnosis: domestic accident: explosion of gas stove; attempted suicide: jumped from the 2nd floor; railroad accident: train derailment. The injuries are domestic and industrial—nothing so intimate or erotic as personal assault. Some women are immobilized in full traction, their white panties made accessible to our gaze. Whenever underwear is visible in these pictures, it's always the same white color as the bandages. The injuries are more hidden than shown, hinted at but concealed; we don't see the supposed gaping wounds or literal gashes on these women.

Slocombe's bandages are a medical version of traditional Japanese erotic rope bondage, *kinbaku*, though Westerners tend to use the related term *shibari*. The prospect of containment, immobilization, and helplessness arouse both the wrapper and the wrappee. Slocombe prefers to tie his models up in ordinary, ugly, prosaic hospital supplies. It's not hi-tech equipment or exotic stuff, either. They're the sort of bandages you might see on the street put to a nasty new sexual use. The thrill comes from the stark realism of the situations, and believability of the injuries. Romain Slocombe finds most conventional SM scenes boring because they're too staged and artificial. You wouldn't see a woman tied up on a medieval wheel in real life, but you certainly might see one in traction in the hospital.

In Slocombe's world, the violence is always off-screen. The trauma is clearly over, but its aura lingers. Slocombe explains to me that

Cover of *Tristes Vacances* by Romain Slocombe

"Hematoma of left jaw with fracture of left supraorbital ridge." Painting: Romain Slocombe from *Tristes Vacances*

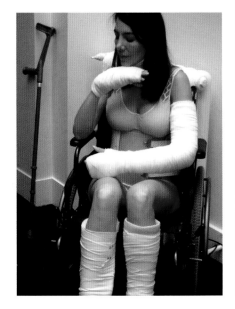

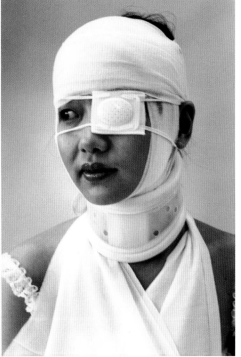

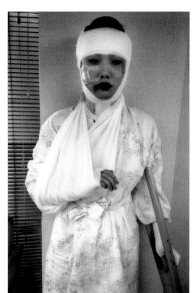

his own sexual excitement comes from fear—especially fear at the loss of beauty. "There is also a slightly sadistic thrill in seeing someone one loves and one finds beautiful and whom one desires—seeing her in this difficult situation, injured in hospital, or suffering. It's very ambivalent." These are damsels in exquisite distress. The girls are safe and healthy now; they are being cared for and fussed over. They can even smile and be flirtatious. The invisible cataclysm, a crisis of bodily integrity too upsetting to witness, is cured through the medical equipment. These talismans of safety, containment, and protection—the bandages, slings, eye patches, and casts—are the true erotic focus.

Even though he has since moved on to writing celebrated noir fiction, Romain Slocombe remains an art celebrity in Japan. His brutal yet sentimental aesthetic appeals to both women and men there. After one Tokyo TV appearance, young girls lined up asking to model for him. Slocombe has found that his models get quite aroused by being immobilized and bound in this way. Some remember enjoying the special attention they got as little girls whenever they wore bandages.

Slocombe remembers being terrified of car accidents as a child. At the same time, he felt that people who had been in an accident had a special erotic aura around them. Sometimes he would wrap a napkin around his own head and pretend that he was hurt. He recalls seeing a print ad showing a cartoonish car wreck. "The young mother and the young boy are both crying, saying, 'Oh, my arm is broken, my leg is broken!' and the father, who isn't injured, says, 'Oh, my God, my family injured, my car broken, fortunately I have an insurance policy!' It was an advertisement for an insurance company! And it had for me the same sort of thrill that I got when thinking about bandages."

LAURAL WOOD AND MEDICAL TOYS

Laural Wood is a lifestyle dominant whose erotic obsession with stainless steel and latex blossomed in the late 1990s into a $200K-a-year business in medical play supplies and rentable playrooms for the kinky set. At the height of her business, Medical Toys had 10,000 square feet of inventory and playrooms in Eureka, California, where people could come and rent out space for group activities. Since then, she has moved her warehouse to

"Girl in wheelchair with arm in cast, neck brace, body brace, and short leg casts," 2016

"Girl in eye patch," 2004

"Japanese hospital #26," 2016

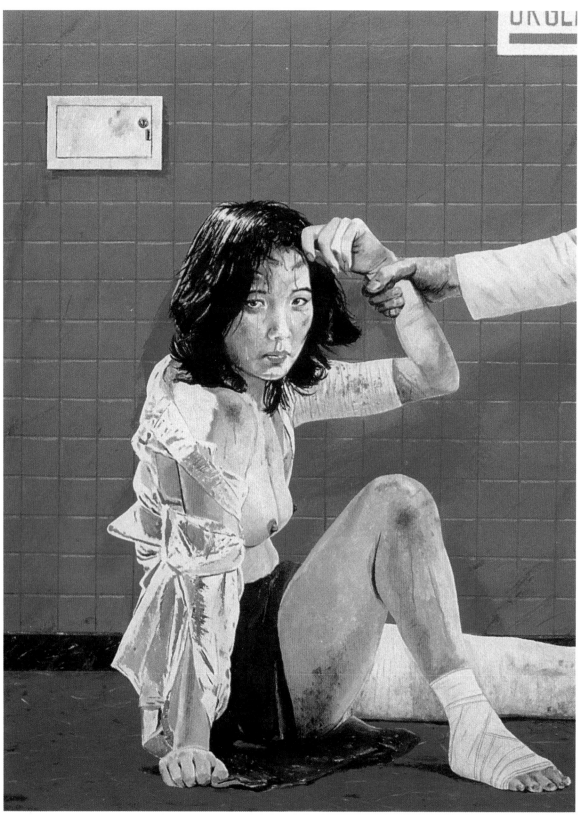

"Traffic accident: schoolgirl run over by car," from *Kowasareta Ningyo*. Photo: Romain Slocombe

"Fracture without displacement of left tibia—deep cut in left bicep," painting by Romain Slocombe from *Tristes Vacances*

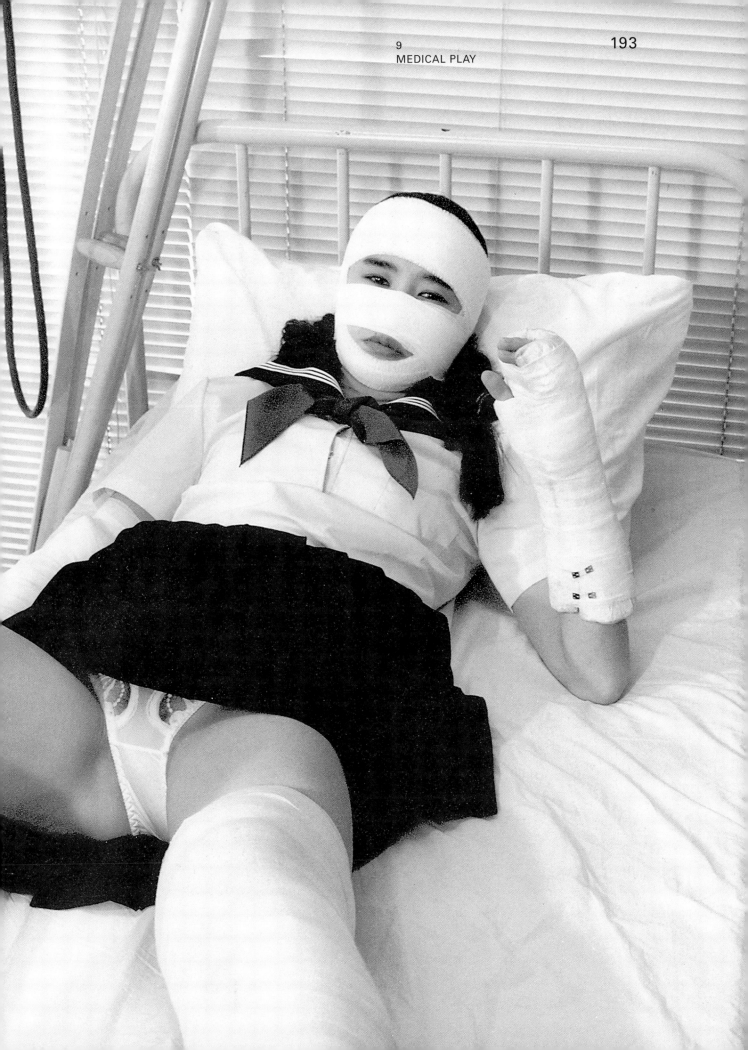

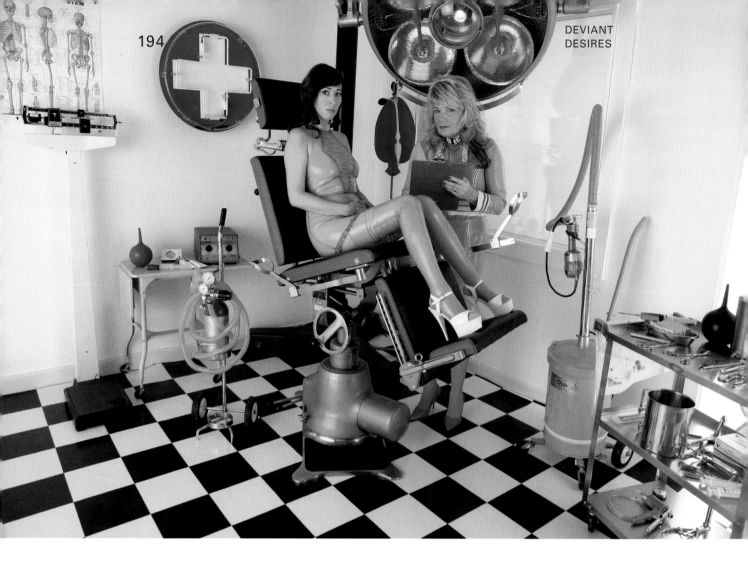

Nurse Laural Wood with patient Kumi
at the MedicalToys.com playroom

*"BDSM is childhood
joyous play plus
adult sexual privilege
plus cool toys."
—Midori, BDSM
educator, author
and performance artist*

Florida and no longer hosts events. I first met Laural in 2006 when
she set up a medical playspace for my *KINK* exhibition at Museum of
Sex in New York, and I spoke with her again by phone in 2016.

In 1992, Laural had been involved in BDSM for several years when
she went to Europe and saw something new: fetish fashion latex
nurse outfits and beautifully choreographed club scenes with medical play. Maybe it was because her mother was in medicine; maybe
it was because she found it at once more aesthetically appealing
and more intimate than anything else BDSM offered, but she had
found her niche. Laural thinks the experience of the doctor-
patient relationship is inherently sexual: "You're spreading your
legs, he's penetrating you. He's collecting your bodily fluids."

Her first toy purchase was a Wartenberg pinwheel. "I didn't know
what it was. I thought it was a torture device and had to go to a
medical library to find out what it was (this was before the internet)." Turns out it is a tool still in use by doctors for nerve reflex-
ing, but used on an unsuspecting bottom in the right situation it
awakens and sensitizes skin. The fact that it looks terrifying is an

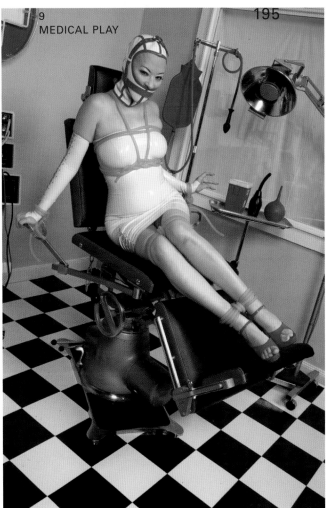

extra plus, and variations include one styled after a medieval morning star weapon. As the website exhorts, "They are just great for taking along with you in your purse or attaché or the glove box in the car for those unexpected play times on the road!" Laural's first website in 1997 was named after the scary-looking tool.

Laural found that it was difficult to source the toys she wanted to play with; medical supply companies were leery of selling specula, TENs electrical devices, and sounds (metal rods that are inserted into the urethra after surgery) to a non-professional. So she launched MedicalToys. com in 1999 as a mail-order business with advertisements in *Bizarre* magazine. Her first year she made $20K in gross sales. The next year it was $200K. Laural attributes the recent surge in medical play popularity to the spate of medical TV shows that appeared in the mid-to-late 2000s.

The MedicalToys website has never been a slick sales machine. Laural is so concerned with education and safety that most product pages are filled with paragraphs of safety instructions, disclaimers, warnings, and tips. There are lengthy essays on the history of vibrators and how to clean insertable toys. "Business advisors have told me that the site is too information-ish, that we have to clean it up and make it slicker, but I want all of that information right there and up front. We want them to know what to do with it before they buy it." For a while, Laural wrote a medical play column for Hustler's *Taboo* magazine to educate people on safe and fun play.

One obvious toy is the speculum, for gynecological exams. But in addition to vaginal specula, you can also get anal specula and even nasal specula. The Barr Rectal Speculum is a real medical device that with ratcheting levels can

Anna Rose in latex and oxygen gear.
Photo: MedicalToys.com

Kumi in medical latex scene.
Photo: MedicalToys.com

"I love stainless steel. It's so shiny and heavy and bright and NEFARIOUS!"
—Laural Wood

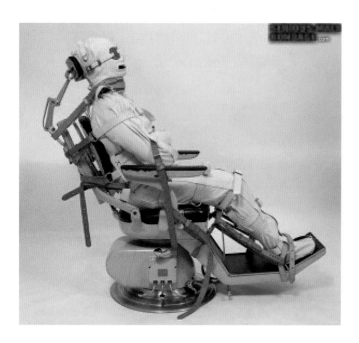

Institutional bondage from gay male extreme bondage site Ruffstuff.com

force the anus to 3" in diameter "much to the chagrin of your quivering patient!" Of course, anyone with a core attraction to latex gloves and latex wrappings can get hot from the unique odors and textures of toys in that material, but for Laural, there's nothing like stainless steel. It's not the usual touchy-feely or smelly fetish material, but its very brutality is what elicits the excitement. "It's so shiny and heavy and bright and NEFARIOUS!"

Perennial popular sellers include casts, bandages, and various items for mummification. You can get traditional straitjackets and sensory deprivation hoods in off-white canvas and tan leather straps for a realistic psych ward scene, or you can go for a fashion-aesthetic black leather or latex.

She sells full-leg braces; a person strapped into these is unable to walk or bend their legs. "Just like all of the other authentic products on this page, these particular restrictive devices are the actual leg braces used for incarceration of 'alleged' criminals!" The authenticity is part of the thrill. Vetwrap is a self-adhesive bandage tape that comes in many colors, and you can completely cover someone head-to-toe in the stuff. One of the more memorable scenes at her play space was when a 6'5", 400-pound man came in to be completely encased in a full-body cast. "We started at 10 a.m. and went until 8 p.m. putting on the cast. He stayed in it until about 4 a.m."

Romain Slocombe is an inspiration for many medical scenes. Laural recalls a time four couples from Seattle, San Francisco, and Colorado met up at her playrooms for a multi-day scene inspired by Slocombe's *City of the Broken Dolls*. "We had a fantastic time!" They stayed in a local hotel and every morning they would come in and play in a different room, taking turns being the broken doll that needs to be fixed. "They tried out everything we had: cupping, pumping, electro-stim. They were ingenious. It's all about playing and exploring."

Laural plays 95% of the time as the nurse, but 5% of the time she wants the experience of someone paying attention to her. "I think it's healthy to switch every now and then. I learn what things feel like, where a boundary might be that I didn't realize." She's had many offers to do pro-domme work, but that doesn't interest her. She likes being the instigator and facilitator.

Laural's favorite activity is putting someone into a hood or other sensory deprivation so that they have no idea what's coming next. "You can rub the Wartenberg Wheel along their arm and they actually think they're being pierced, but it's just intense nerve stim." The sense of terror and anticipation from hearing some weird new snapping or clanking noise is part of the repertoire of a skilled top: "This will only hurt a bit!" She's

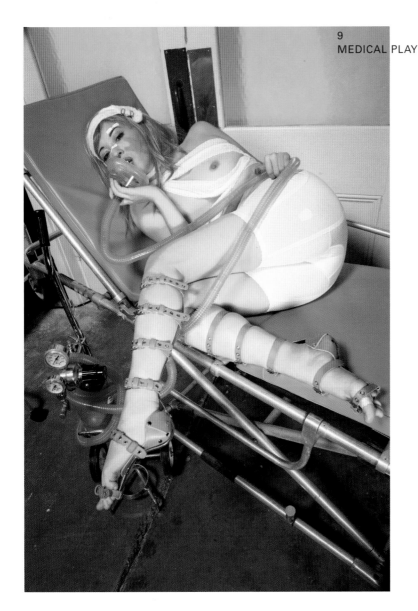

"I think it's healthy to switch every now and then. I learn what things feel like, where a boundary might be that I didn't realize."
—Laural Wood

always trying to get people to try something new. "What's the worst that can happen? If you don't like it, you don't have to do it again."

If many of these activities sound excruciating, they are. Those who play with pain know it can trigger the release of endorphins, the brain's natural opiates, and some heavy-duty pain players may just have the pleasure and pain parts of their brains wired a little more closely together than the rest of us do. But it's not just about pain: it's about caretaking and vulnerability. Many kinks get their energy from mining the rich emotional territory within the continuum between hurt and comfort. The bodily invasions of the medical clinic or the tender intimacies of the baby's changing table are merely

literal representations of our need to cross each other's emotional boundaries, our need to be deeply touched.

Even though you'll see only women in the photos, it's usually men who want to be the center of the scene, at the mercy of a hurting/comforting nurse. Laural found that many of her clients and customers are men who were in the armed services, and the first time they had ever been naked in front of a woman was during their physical examination. CBT—cock and ball torture—is the #1 area of interest for these customers. Chastity devices, scrotum squeezers, and sounds (a stainless steel rod inserted into the urethra) are top sellers. Originally designed for patients with syphilitic scarring that would block

Kumi, in an homage to Romain Slocombe's
City of the Broken Dolls. Photo: MedicalToys.com

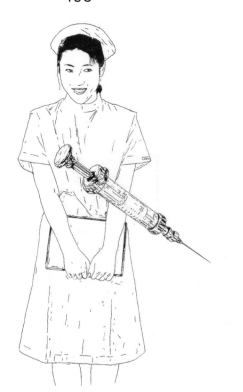

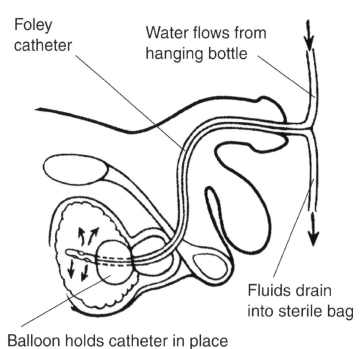

Foley
catheter

Water flows from
hanging bottle

Fluids drain
into sterile bag

Balloon holds catheter in place

off the urethra and make it difficult or impossible to urinate, the sounds would be inserted in increasing diameters to open up the tissue. You can get ones with a beaded surface, or ones that vibrate, as well as ones that deliver small electric shocks, like those attached to a TENS, a tactile electro-neural stimulator used in therapy from acupuncture to chiropractic.

The largest sounds on the website has a diameter of .70 inches, but I have heard of men stretching their urethra so wide as to be able to be fucked in it. Laural has found that there are some body modification fans who use sounds for the effect, competing with each other to see how large they can get their urethras. "Some get a little obsessed!" But for Laural and other medical play people, the scene is far more important than the end result.

Catheters are also popular. Laural describes a scene: "I love it when I'm slowly threading the catheter into his urethra. His legs are spread, I'm entering his most intimate places. He's anxious, it's uncomfortable." When the catheter pops through the orifice between bladder and urethra, urine sudden-

ly gushes out. Catheters can be fixed to prevent the "patient" from urinating, causing pleasurable discomfort, and the release can be orgasmic. Catheters can also be fixed to a tube and gag so that the urine passes back into the bottom's own mouth, for those with urophilic tendencies.

A popular item for beginners is the ultraviolet wand, an antique quack medicine device kept in business by fetishists and spas. It lights up with a brilliant neon-purple glow and when it touches your skin you get little zaps of electricity. "We like the ones with the big rheostat dial. It's much more intimidating than the ones you get during a massage."

Cupping and pumping use heat and suction to bring blood to the surface of any body part. In addition to the obvious penis pumping supplies, you can pump nipples and clitorises. It's exciting to see you or your partner's clitoris swell to more than twice its ordinary size, and the engorgement hugely increases sensitivity.

Shaving supplies are available for those who enjoy the thrill of having extremely sharp blades

Nurse Okuda, drawing by
Romain Slocombe, 2016

Side-view diagram of male urinary tract with
Foley catheter in place to drain urine. NIDDK

How to Clean Insertable Sex Toys

by Laural Wood

THINGS YOU'LL NEED:

Soap, warm water, and clean dry cloth
Rubbing alcohol
Hydrogen peroxide (not recommended for any
metal toys!)

1. Wash all insertable toys before and after use.
Warm water, soap, and a soft cloth can be used
on almost all types of toys, including those with
batteries and electrical parts as long as you do not
immerse or soak! After washing the toys, dry them
with a lint-free cloth or let them air dry well. Then
store in clean, sealed containers or Ziploc bags.
Storage is as important a part of keeping your toys
clean as the actual cleaning process.

2. To sanitize silicone toys, you can either put them
in a pot of boiling water and soap solution (use
only a small amount of soap or else you will have
a soap "lava flow") on the stove for approximately
two to three minutes. The other method is to run
them through the dishwasher cycle, but do not use
any soap with the wash cycle and do not let them
run through the hot air dry cycle. Be sure to stop
the dishwasher after it finishes the washing cycle,
then remove the toys and let them air dry. This
cleaning method works for silicone toys and other plastic, glass, rubber, or latex materials toys,
as long as they do not have batteries or electrical
parts. Follow with wipes of alcohol swabs.

3. Take extra care with some of the newer "Cyber-
skin" toys made of ultra-soft, ultra-pliable elas-
tomer material, which are very delicate, so they
need special care when cleaning. Hand-wash with
warm (not hot) water and a gentle soap, then allow
them to air dry.

4. For anything made of leather, they need to be
washed with a foaming cleanser and scrubbed
down with a brush, then rubbed down with hydrogen peroxide, allowed to air dry, and afterward
gone over with saddle soap and leather condition-
er. This kind of care is very important with leather
toys and items, as they can become stiff and brit-
tle, then become hard to use.

TIPS & WARNINGS:

Using condoms on all of your toys during
use will help to keep them clean, and will
stop them from gathering bacteria and
other germs.

If a toy comes in contact with blood, you
must wash it with warm water and soap,
then follow by washing it down with a
solution made up of nine parts water and
one part bleach. Be sure to thoroughly
rinse off the bleach solution afterwards
and allow to air dry.

Never submerge, boil, or run a battery-
operated or electrically-operated insertable toy through the dishwasher. Immersion in water will ruin these types of toys.

Sex toys in dishwasher.
Photo: MedicalToys.com

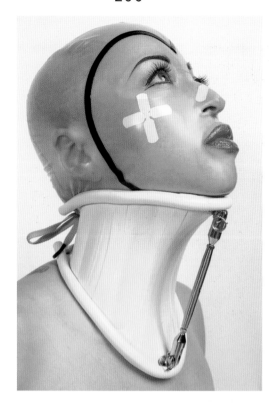

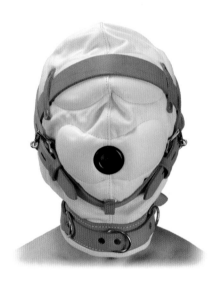

near their nether regions. A shaved pussy or scrotum is much more sensitive. Shaving is also a common practice in age play, as adult babies must be hair-free.

Some medical play gets its inspiration from the terror of sitting in a dentist's chair. Mouth spreaders force the mouth open. "Evil Doctors and Nasty Nurses love the looks and function of this rather merciless mechanism! And when you are ready (or they are drooling and gurgling for mercy) just squeeze the tabs and remove it!" Some players get off on seeing their partner drooling helplessly. I know one pro-domme in New York known as Nurse Wolf who specializes in dental play. One of her clients continually begs her to pull his teeth, but so far she has demurred.

Enemas are a major form of anal play; klismaphiles (or enemaniacs) can purchase bags that hold as many as 2 gallons of liquid. For some, an enema is just a way to clean out the rectum before anal sex, but for many it is an end in itself. Tops may like to force the bottom to hold in all of the liquid and enjoy watching the bottom squirm with discomfort. Enema tips can be combined with butt plug nozzles for extra sphincter stimulation.

Both catheter and enema play force us to break down one of the earliest bodily prohibitions, toilet training, which taught us that the pleasurable things our bodies do are shameful and must be controlled. Releasing urine and feces in front of another adult can be an extremely liberating and intimate experience.

In recent years, Laural has noticed a crossover between medical play and other kinks. For example, some visitors want to play veterinarian to a partner who is either a human puppy or a furry. They can pretend to get "fixed." Others mix medical play with adult baby play. It's all about finding that thrilling tension between hurt and comfort.

It's not only healthy people who want to explore their anxiety over bodily integrity, though. Some of her visitors have significant past medical history, such as missing limbs or severe scoliosis. (Some of the amputee visitors even had cult followings of their own in the world of amputee devotees—people who are aroused by partners missing limbs.) For these people, eroticizing can be a way of dealing with the pain they had as children. As Laural says, "We have to turn it around for ourselves, get past what happened and have fun with it. Let go of the idea that pain is getting you down."

Medical neck brace repurposed for bondage. Photo: MedicalToys.com

Institutional bondage. Photo: MedicalToys.com

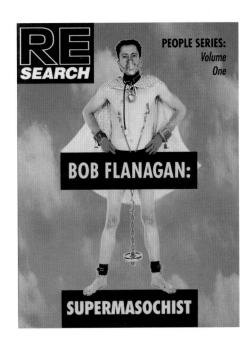

Bob Flanagan: Supermasochist, RE/Search publications

This reminds me of performance artist Bob Flanagan, subject of the 1993 RE/Search book *Bob Flanagan: Supermasochist*. Bob was diagnosed with cystic fibrosis as a child and was given only 7 years to live, and both of his sisters died from CF as children. Throughout his life, Bob was subjected to brutal treatments to clear his lungs, and suffocation and needles were his constant companions. Instead of giving up, he and his wife Sheree Rose transformed Bob's torture into pleasure, his death into erotic art. He invented new ways to turn catheters, sharps, hospital gowns and pressure cuffs into sex toys. In one infamous performance, he hammered a nail through his own penis while singing "If I Had a Hammer." Bob lived well past his diagnosis and died in 1996 at the ripe old age of 43, longevity he attributed to his use of BDSM to master his own body.

There are some kinds of play that Laural refuses to participate in and she will not sell the equipment, either. Customers request eye specula like those seen in the movie *A Clockwork Orange*, but they are not safe and she does not carry them. She also will have nothing to do with saline injection, which if done wrong can go very badly.

SALINE INJECTION PLAY

Efrain Gonzales has been documenting the New York BDSM scene since the 1970s and you'll find him, his camera, and his septum piercing at pretty much any leather event in New York. Efrain now offers tours of New York's BDSM history, illustrated by his photographs of the Hellfire Club, the Folsom Street East, The Eulenspiegel Society, and the newly defunct National Leather Association.

A few years back, Efrain went to a play party in a fancy home in the suburban enclave of Frederick, Maryland. At one point, the host brought out a bunch of bags of saline solution and needle, "Who wants to play?" Efrain volunteered. They laid him out on the pool table and proceeded to pump two quarts of saline solution into his scrotum. Efrain claims it did not hurt, "I was walking around the place with these two gigantic balls hanging between my legs! I was the center of attention!" he smiles gleefully, remembering all of the attention he received. "The next day I woke up and the saline had migrated to my foreskin." His meatus (urethral hole) was swollen shut and he had a terrible time urinating. "The drive home was kind of fun too."

Whitehead gag. Photo: MedicalToys.com

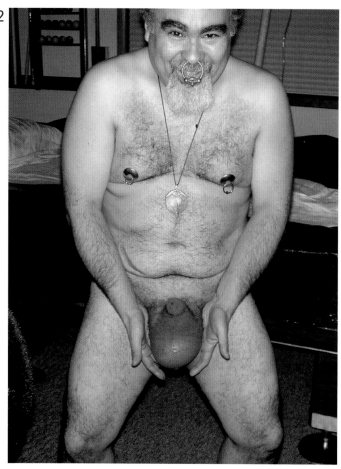

MEDICAL PLAY IN BRIEF

CORE KINK:
PVC, rubber, stainless steel

MAJOR THEMES:
power play

SUBKINKS:
dental play, braces and bandages,
vet play

EROTIC EQUATION:
pressure from bondage, pushing
against skin, and bodily limits

Laural and other medical players feel that what makes
medical play enjoyable is the conscious and conscientious
pushing of one's own boundaries. It's a pressure-release valve
for our anxieties over bodily integrity. She also thinks that
lack of self-awareness of a medical fetish may be to blame
for some women's overuse of plastic surgery. "They want
the attention of a handsome doctor, they want him to cut
into them. But wouldn't it be better if they were aware and
didn't actually have to undergo these procedures? What if
they just did some safe, sane, and consensual medical play
instead?"

Efrain Gonzalez's saline-inflated scrotum.
Photo: Efrain Gonzalez

Sidekink:
Adult Babies

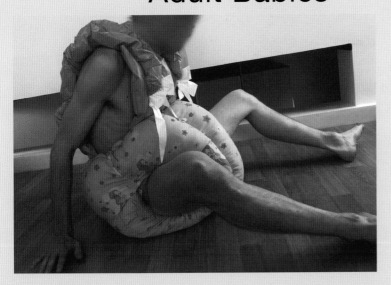

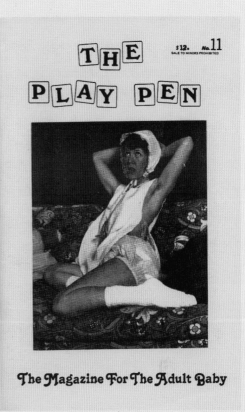

The Magazine For The Adult Baby

Adult Babies (ABs) experience joy in returning to a state of infantile bliss, a time when the pleasures of life included being fed, comforted, diapered, and loved. ABs yearn for caretaking, but may also seek out punishment. Most ABs enjoy wearing diapers and some wet or "mess" them in order to feel the warm damp sensation in their groins. Some also enjoy forms of bondage and penetration that are true to the baby experience, including being strapped into chairs, "forced" to use pacifiers, and having their temperatures taken rectally. Sexual release, if and when it happens, is usually achieved manually.

Chrissy S. is a playful two-year-old going through toilet training and sometimes messing by accident. She is the baby girl persona of a 61-year-old New Jersey husband and father who has been collecting 1950s–1960s infant paraphernalia for the last 40 years. Chrissy owns thousands of vinyl bibs, hundreds of high chairs, pacifiers, frilly dresses, and rubber pants. Twenty years ago, Chrissy attended her first AB weekend gathering at a hotel where she was able to live as a baby for three days. "Nannies" or "babysitters" were available to feed and change her and put her to bed.

In a sense, all taboo-breaking sex fantasies probably represent some sort of rebellion against toilet train-ing, because that was the period we were first taught to deny our polymorphous sensuality and bodily pleasures. During toilet training, the adult world tried to make us conform to the idea that mess and disor-der is "dirty" and taboo and dangerous.

TERMINOLOGY:
age play, ABs, littles

CORE KINK:
PVC, sometimes rubber

MAJOR THEMES:
love, taboo

SUBTHEMES:
hurt/comfort, dirty/clean, embarrassment

SUBKINKS:
Daddy Dominant/Little Girl (DDLG), Adult Baby Diaper Lover (ABDL)

RELATED KINKS:
medical play, school days

SOMETIMES COMBINED WITH:
dominance and submission, plush, lactation, messy fun, shaving, spanking

The Play Pen, ABDL magazine, mid-1990s, from the collection of Chrissy

Diaper selfie, unknown DeviantArt user

Eat Me!
Cannibal Play Feeds a Need

Swisspiggy, a user at CannibalPlanet.earth, looking to have his meat inspected by femcan Lana

Meatgirl by MukisKitchen.com

A quarter century has passed since I first heard the tale of the Turkey Man, who had a pro-domme truss him up and "cook" him like a Thanksgiving meal. His was the story that pro-pelled me on my lifelong journey to explore the edges of the erotic imagination. Back then I thought he was unique, but over the years I heard about similar kink scenarios. Nurse Wolf—a different, brilliantly nasty New York dominatrix—has a client who phones her for a bedtime story about Hansel and Gretel; he imagines himself the child victim who gets fattened up and cooked by the witch. They discuss recipe options while he masturbates. She has another client, an elderly gentleman, who comes specifically to watch her strip another woman naked and paint dotted black lines over her body to outline and label the cuts of meat—short loin, brisket, chuck—while they discuss cooking and eating methods.

If Turkey Man got online now and did an in-ternet search for related fetishes, he would find himself immersed in a vast web of interlinked pervert communities. Pieces of his kink show up everywhere: Since his ritual involves being shut up in a small, hot, womb-like space, he might hook up with the many folks who find erotic ecstasy in containment and immobilization. If being transformed into an inanimate object is part of his thrill, he might find kinship with the people who enjoy being used as pieces of furni-ture. If human-into-animal metamorphosis is the turn-on, he could frolic with ponyplayers and furries. Turkey Man might discover an affini-ty with erotic feeding, or follow links to vore chatrooms and tap into an impressive archive of homemade illustrations and fantasy stories about humans and animals eating each other alive.

Turkey Man's scenario seemed quirky, but hardly threatening. After all, he just wanted to pretend to be the center of a holiday meal. Then, in 2001, a German computer programmer named Armin Meiwes killed, butchered, and ate a man he met in an online chat room for cannibal fetishists. Meiwes had met others who wanted to act out the fantasy with him but they backed out. Only Bernd Brandes really intended to go through with it. He gave his videotaped consent to the act, even requesting his own penis as a last meal before bleeding out. Since the arrangement was consensual, the German judge sentenced Meiwes to only eight and a half years in prison.

Cannibalism has existed around the globe and throughout history, but in the 21st century it has become an erotic lifestyle. For tribal peoples, ritual anthropophagy was a way for the living to incorporate the powers of the dead. Christians symbolically consume the flesh and blood of Jesus as a means to experience divine communion. In 2017, people can log into chatrooms like PulpToon or Dolcettgirls and discuss their intense fantasy to eat and be eaten for the purpose of sexual pleasure. And it appears that for 99.99% of these self-described "cann fetishists," it's a just a fantasy; their erotic imaginations enlist oral

eroticism and thrills of taboo and peril into a dark and compelling role-playing game that they have no interest in acting out for real.

Shortly before Thanksgiving in 2005, I took a plane to Los Angeles to witness a pornographic photo shoot created by, for, and starring cannibal fetishists who met each other online in such a chatroom. Instead of roasting turkey with my family, I sat in a white-bread suburb of Los Angeles, observing the preparation of the main course of the holiday feast: a woman. First, two female chefs stripped her naked. They pulled her arms back tightly and placed her face-down on very large metal platter. They spread her legs wide, exposing her shiny hairless pussy and anus, and used thick ropes to bind her ankles and wrists together at her thighs. They poured oil and honey over her body until she glistened. They thrust a corncob into her vagina, and shoved a red apple into her mouth. Then, with some considerable effort, they lifted and maneuvered the entire platter into a realistic white prop convection oven resting on a sturdy table.

After a series of photos of the roast inside the oven, with closeups of the model's surprised yet excited facial expression, the chefs removed her and prepared for the pornographic money shot. The photographer switched the lighting gels so that the roast's skin took on an orange, roasted look. They poured on more oil and some pepper, then poked a cartoonishly large meat thermometer into her ass. The needle on the prop's dial pointed to "well-done pork." Dinner was served!

The photo shoot was for Muki's Kitchen, a commercial cannibal porn website that sells hundreds of such photo portfolios a month. Since opening in 1999, Muki's Kitchen has produced 155 photo portfolios, all serving up the same goofy plotline: A woman is captured, stripped, trussed, stuffed, and "cooked." Mr. Muki, himself a woman-eater—the term for the top in this scenario—is the Kitchen's sole photographer, set builder, and webmaster. (Mr. Muki is his professional pseudonym: He leads an unassuming life supported partially by the website and partially by his wife, a corporate executive. Anonymity was a condition to the agreement that allowed my access.)

"When I was a child I made the connection that my naked body looked like the chicken my mother was cooking."
—Mr. Muki

"Every cannibal has a favorite recipe," Mr. Muki says. The most popular is the spit roast, a woman skewered through the vagina and out the mouth—a visual effect achieved through the use of cardboard tubes painted to resemble metal. There's also the face-down suckling pig, the parturition-style turkey girl (Mr. Muki's favorite), and finally the old cartoon-gag cliché, the jungle cannibal stew pot. These, often campy, pictures are actually more about EC Comics–style peril and food preparation than cannibalism: you don't see much carving or eating, and definitely no blood.

I sat with Mr. Muki while the models cleaned up and he smoked a postprandial pipe. When I interviewed him in 2005 he was 45, with a short beard, nerdy glasses, and a gray mullet. Mr. Muki explained that his own fantasy started when he was very young. "When I was a child I made the connection that my naked body looked like the chicken my mother was cooking," a fact he found both disturbing and fascinating. In third grade, his teacher read excerpts from *Robinson Crusoe*; the idea of being captured by cannibals and stripped naked grabbed his attention. "I had this recurring fantasy that I had to pick lots and lots of fruit and that if I didn't pick enough fruit, they would cook and eat me using the fruit as flavoring. I'd imagine myself panicked and picking fruit, but at the same time excited that I might fail and get eaten."

His role in his adult fantasies is more diffuse. "I totally identify with the woman and her helplessness. At the same time I look at her body and see her as good enough to eat!" Because he finds

Meatboy selfie, DeviantArt

Promo shot from 1960s "roughie" porn film
Boiled Alive, published in *BIZARRE*, March 1968.
Collection of Gurgurant

ADULTS ONLY $6.95

CANNIBAL TIMES

VOLUME 1   SPRING 1994   NUMBER 2

Aimez Vous Les Femmes?

"I know the reality of cannibalism would never live up to the fantasy... I think boobies are just great, but there's nothing edible in a boob."
—Mr. Muki

naked men unappealing, he has no interest in seeing photographs of male meat. He has made photosets of meatboys, but has found them not only to be less fun to do, they are also not as successful financially—unless the model pays for it. Plus, the meatboys in the cann fetish scene can be a vocal and difficult minority. "They kept complaining that I didn't cook the guy exactly the way they wanted to be cooked."

When Mr. Muki got older, he heard about cannibal serial killer Jeffrey Dahmer and it terrified him. "Back then, I worried that this fantasy meant I wanted to be like him." Now he's not concerned, though. "I know the reality of cannibalism would never live up to the fantasy," he said. "If you really were going to eat somebody you'd have to behead them. You'd have to clean them out," he explained. "You'd have to skin them, because humans have sweat glands—they're not like chickens! But sex is all about skin!" He continued, "I think boobies are just great, but there's nothing edible in a boob. It's glands and fat. So that goes! This is getting pretty unattractive." Mr. Muki prefers his fantasy fantastic, not as it would be in reality. "I want it to be presented beautifully, like a Hollywood picture."

What made the photo shoot I witnessed unusual is that the main course was not simply another porn model from L.A.—she is a bona fide "meatgirl," a woman who wants to be make-believe eaten. Meghan Vaughan was then a 31-year-old artist living in Cincinnati who flew to L.A. to act out her fantasy of being served

From "A Matter of Taste", a fiction piece in
ADAM magazine, 1960. Collection: Gurgurant

Cannibal Times,
an unpublished zine from 1995

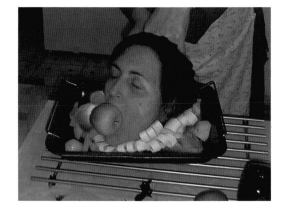

on a platter. She's among the half-dozen women who have since come out online as meatgirls, and while Mr. Muki claims that as many as 15 percent of his customers are female, Meghan was the first to pose for the cannibal public. To Muki's woman-eater customers she was a dream come true, that exceedingly rare woman who actually gets off on fulfilling the fantasy they're obsessed with.

Meghan joined me in the courtyard after her shower and lit up a cigarette. She had Bettie Page black bangs with pigtails, while wearing an all-black art student version of hillbilly chic. "I was chubby in high school and none of the guys wanted to look at me," she said. Neither masturbation nor sex worked for her until her 20s. She explored BDSM, but it wasn't until she saw the Muki's Kitchen website that it all clicked. "Bondage, submission, gagging, humiliation, exhibitionism, objectification—it was all there!" She immediately offered to star in a Muki portfolio based on her own hillbilly cannibal comic book, *Little Red Roundbottom*.

Since that first shoot, Meghan has become something of a cann fetish celebrity, and the photo shoots promoted sales of her art on

the CannToon (now PulpToon) website. "For me, it's all about being the centerpiece, the center of attention," she says. "It's the same attention you give the turkey on Thanksgiving. Everybody is just obsessed with that turkey. 'Ooooooh, the turkey the turkey the turkey.' 'When is the turkey going to be done?' It's so exciting!" Was the photo shoot a turn-on for her, and not just a job? "I'm too focused to get turned on during the shoot, but when I get home? As a man would put it, it gives me something to fill the spank bank with!"

While Mr. and Mrs. Muki's home sex life involves simple light bondage and lots of oral sex ("Cannibals give good head!" Mr. Muki proclaimed proudly), Meghan's meatgirl lifestyle is a more elaborate affair. Her home dungeon—a small room in her house where she, her partner (now husband), and friends play—has a home-made rotisserie and an electric fireplace that crackles realistically. "When I get home tomorrow, I'll ask my partner to hog-tie me the same way we did in the shoot, because it will be the hottest position for a while. When I'm trussed up like that, I like to have a lot of ass play. I even squeal like a pig!" Meghan is never actually dead in her fantasies. "It's like being drugged

Betty Pig, a Scottish woman who built an oversized oven in her house to act out her fantasies. Photo courtesy Gurgurant

Femcan artwork by Karla79de, from CannibalPlanet.earth

yet still aware," she says. "Like when your body is paralyzed but your mind is still awake. I like to think I'm inanimate, without a conscience. There's a feeling of transcendence when I'm being transformed."

Even though individual photos in the Muki's Kitchen portfolios can come across as scary, cruel, or demeaning, Mr. Muki makes sure the models are obviously alive and happy to do it. "I want my customers not to feel like freaks to have these fantasies," Mr. Muki said, "and humor is what keeps it feeling fun and sane." To help both male and female customers feel comfortable, Mr. Muki also pretends that the Kitchen is a mom-and-pop operation, although Mrs. Muki's only real task is to keep an eye on the tone of the website.

That evening the Mukis, Meghan, and I drove to Bahooka, a historic tiki-themed restaurant in Rosemead, in eastern Los Angeles, to meet a few more cannibals: Gurgurant, a collector of jungle cannibal gag cartoons and lifelong fan of the stew-pot girl fantasy; Canntoon, an ambitious 20-something promoting his own cannibal website; and Andy, a TV producer so terrified of being identified he avoided me completely.

Photo from a PETA protest in Madrid. "Don't they know how much these images turn us on?" asks Gurgurant

Most of these people had never met each other in person before, and it took several rounds of rum-based zombies to bring the conversation to their favorite topic. They laughed about the anti-meat ads produced by PETA—photos of naked models shrink-wrapped into huge supermarket meat trays. Gurgurant asked, "Do they know how much those turn us on?" It was a congenial evening, with plenty of cracks about "long pig" and juicy thighs. These cann fans weren't scary in the least.

Gurgurant's cannibal fascination started at an early age. When other kids played doctor, he played cannibal witch doctor. He remembers a 1950s French cartoon where a giant catches a group of boy scouts and shrinks them down in a machine so that he can eat them in a sandwich. The machine had tubes that undulated and gyrated rhythmically, in an almost sexual manner. "A giant thinking I would be a tasty snack was very arousing to me and made me want to touch myself." He role-played with girlfriends over the years, but he feels his greatest accomplishment was writing and directing *Jungle Drums*, "the only true cannibal fetish fantasy video ever made."

Recently, I spoke with Agatha Delicious, the admin for the PulpToon website and forums, to get her take on the kink. PulpToon is a membership site "devoted to creating fun and kinky new comics in the spirit of the classic 'pulp' magazines of yesteryear." They feature new, fully-illustrated comics every week "in an ongoing unlimited orgy of sexy peril and naughty misadventure." And the art can be really good: there's one Marvel-quality series called "Revenge of the Third Reich" where Zombie Nazis kidnap a girl and bring her to their secret moon base to hook her naked body up to some nefarious machine that will somehow bring Hitler back to life. The conceit is that the comic has been rediscovered, so it's suitably aged and damaged-looking.

The intro splash screen on PulpToon explains: "This is a FUN form of fetish art and is meant

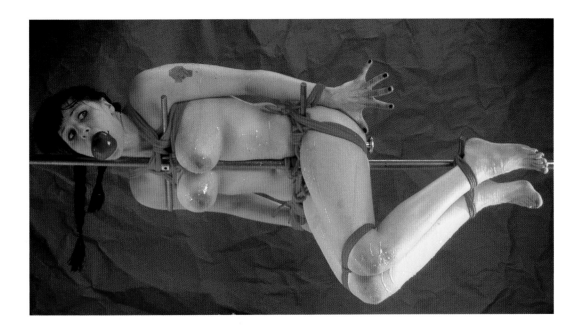

to be creative and sexy as well as delightfully strange. All stories and deceptions are STRICTLY based on fantasy." This is a more explicit version of the lurid EC Comics of my childhood. Precisely the material Fredric Wertham's *Seduction of the Innocent* warned conformist, 1950s America would make their children into cold-hearted killers. Although you can get stories, videos, photos, and comics with themes like "Aliens!" "Mad Doctors!" "Witches!" with saucy vixens and over-the-top betrayals, cannibal scenes remain by far their most popular items.

Agatha has had a lifelong fascination with predator and prey, especially if the two can have a relationship. Agatha's favorite masturbatory fantasies include being captured and enslaved by ogres who threaten to eat her if she fails to be a good servant. "I want to imagine being used for sex or for food, but I don't want real pain. It stays in the fairy-tale realm." What does it for her is the threat of being turned into the object of a dominant creature's appetite.

Up until she was about 21, Agatha thought she would get married and do the usual kids and career stuff, but in 1999, when she got out of the military, she discovered Muki's Kitchen and some cann fetish chatrooms. She realized she didn't have to be normal; she could make stories and art and movies about her own fantasies—and make a living at it.

Agatha tries to make videos and paintings that will sell, but it's always a struggle between her aesthetic vision and her low budget.

"I like to think I'm inanimate, without a conscience. There's a feeling of transcendence when I'm being transformed."
—Megh

Meghan from a Muki's Kitchen photo shoot. Photo: MukisKitchen.com

Jungle Drums poster (1994), from "the only true cannibal fetish fantasy video ever made," directed by Gurgurant

"I want my customers not to feel like freaks to have these fantasies, and humor is what keeps it feeling fun and sane."
—Mr. Muki

She's a bit disappointed her best-selling videos are the ones with two pretty, blonde, tattoo-free models and no fancy extras. "The guys don't care about all that effort I put into props. They just want to see a particular look on the chef's face, a particular look on the entrée's face."

Like Agatha and Meghan, Mr. Muki and Gurgurant share a preference for the gentler side of cannibalism. "Some cannibals complain that Muki's is too 'Muki-esque,'" Mr. Muki said. "They mean this fluffy, soft, fantasy cannibalism without any of the messy stuff, the blood and the guts. So be it!" While Mr. Muki and Megh agree that the fantasy scenarios they have in their heads might include beheadings and actual eating, the details remain bloodless and cartoonish. They have absolutely no interest in realism.

For Meghan, Williams-Sonoma catalogs inspire masturbatory fantasies of being skewered on the latest Cuisinart rotisserie. She looks to Bed Bath & Beyond, and Bobby Flay's *Boy Meets Grill* on the Food Network, for sex-play ideas. She said,

"Someday I'd like to be photographed for *Better Homes and Gardens* as this beautiful spread on a festive holiday table."

There do exist websites that cater to the darkest aspects of the cannibal fantasy. They're not camp, and there is no humor. Unlike Muki's Kitchen, Dolcettgirls (named after a reclusive Canadian artist) and Necrobabes (since closed) use more "cinema vérité" visual styles that suggest documentary rather than fantasy. There's some nudity, but the real effort is put into the acts of torture, hanging and asphyxiation being the top methods. The main difference between Necrobabes and a slasher flick is that the movies have better effects. (It's a belief in the porn world that the way to avoid prosecution is to choose between sex and violence—Muki's chose sex, the others chose violence.) While Mr. Muki makes only what he himself wants to see, Necrobabes did market research and produced what would sell.

It comes as no surprise then, while other sites tease that "it's more real than you think," the

A canntoon British humor postcard by Bamforth, from Gurgurant's collection

Cookbook for Cannibals (1990), a zine produced by RK Enterprises, with chef "Sal Monella"

Gurgurant's Top 10 Cannibal Scenes in Pop Culture

1. *Aimez-vous les Femmes?* aka *A Taste for Women* (1964), a French art film about a cannibal cult in a vegetarian restaurant. The serving scene near the end, where the cooked heroine is served to the hungry cult, is the *pièce de résistance*.

2. *Raw Force* (1982), a kung fu movie that does a lot to eroticize the subject. The scene in the monk's temple, where the captive women are being roasted and eaten by the cannibal monks, is a cann-fetish treat.

3. *Gentlemen Marry Brunettes* (1955), a comedy movie with some pretty fetishy scenes. Jane Russell and Jeanne Crain are put into a big pot by cannibals and one of them, wearing a chef's hat, puts a sign by the pot that reads, "Menu, Chicks."

4. *Baghdad Café* (1987) has a brief, and often edited out, scene in which the German tourist imagines herself being boiled in a pot by black cannibals.

5. *Slumber Party '57* (1976), a drive-in movie T&A film that contains a naked-girl-in-a-pot scene.

6. The Greek film-noir movie *Efialtis* (*Nightmare,* 1961) has a scene at night club where a nude blonde woman is being cooked in a pot by a tribe of dancing cannibals.

7. *Africa Screams* (1949) is one of my favorite mainstream jungle comedies. The way the chief smacks his lips and fawns over Lou Costello has fed many a fantasy where I have replaced Lou with someone more decidedly female and tasty. Honorable mention to the Hope and Crosby *Road to Zanzibar* in the same vein.

8. *King Solomon's Mines* (1985). Sharon Stone (with Richard Chamberlain) meet a cannibal out "grocery shopping" and he thinks Sharon is a nice ripe tomato. Later on, the same tribe drops them into a giant cooking pot full of vegetables to boil up for a nice stew.

9. *I'll Be Glad When You're Dead, You Rascal You* (1932), featuring Betty Boop in an animated music video to the song performed by Louis Armstrong. Betty gets abducted by pygmy cannibals while on safari in Africa. They tie her to a tree and get her ready for the pot. Honorable Mention to Harvey cartoon *Chew Chew Baby*, one of the very few (possibly only?) cartoons where the cannibal actually eats people.

10. *Island Girl (1993),* an obscure black comedy about a foreign exchange student in the US from a South Pacific island where her tribe are cannibals. She misunderstands some of American culture, such as what a hot tub is for. Some of her "enemies" end up on the menu until she learns that it's all a big misunderstanding.

Still from *The Cook, The Thief, His Wife & Her Lover,* a 1989 Peter Greenaway film with a cannibal conclusion

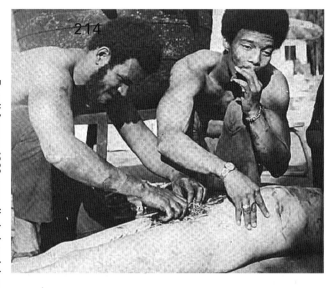

214

Mukis insist that rumors of genuine cannibalism are invoked to ramp up sexually desirable anxiety. Gurgurant argues that almost every person who claims to want to go through with it is just a poseur. "When you read through these boards there will always be some meatboy who will say, 'I'm looking to do this for real,'" he says. "Most of the community just ignores them." They're enjoying the pretense, but—like the men Armin Meiwes let go in earlier encounters in Germany—they run when the butcher knife comes out. "We all wondered, 'Gee, was he one of the ones we just ignored?'" Gurgurant said. Subsequently, any post on Canntoon or PulpToon message boards not clearly using the language of fantasy was deleted.

Mr. Muki is absolutely clear that doing any of this in reality is not acceptable, "I think Meiwes got off too lightly. The fact his victim consented to being killed is proof he was not mentally capable of consenting to anything!" He also pointed out that Brandes was so detached from

reality that he expected eating his own penis to be a transcendent gourmet experience. In *Cannibal: The True Story Behind the Maneater of Rotenburg*, author Lois Jones recounts Brandes' final, bitter disappointing moments: his penis was just a bunch of hard gristle and fat.

Meghan, on the other hand, was more sympathetic to the dead meatboy: "If that's what they want to do with their bodies and with their lives, why shouldn't they?" Nevertheless, she would never think of offering herself up as an actual meal. "Then I wouldn't be able to do it over again, would I?"

Cann fetish enjoyed 10 years of relative calm until the New York "Cannibal Cop" case thrust the community back into the limelight. In 2013, a New York police officer named Gilberto Valle was turned in by his wife after she used spyware to find out what he was doing online. She discovered that in online chats with other men he spun plots to pay them to kidnap, torture, rape, kill, and eat her, several of her friends, and a local teenager. Valle showed the men pictures of the victims he described. He accessed a crime database illegally to get information on them.

Valle had met his wife on OkCupid. His court-appointed psychiatrist said that Gilberto's shyness about women was "something I hadn't seen since the 50s." His wife, Kathleen Cooke Mangan (whose name, my editor pointed out, contains "lean," "cook," and the key letters from the French verb "manger," *to eat*), was his first sexual partner.

Turns out Gilberto Valle was one of Mr. Muki's customers. "The defense lawyers called me up, wanting to get copies of all of the images he downloaded," says Mr. Muki. *The New York Post* reproduced one of the Muki's Kitchen pictures on its cover. Unlike with the Meiwes case, though, Mr. Muki comes down strongly on the side of Valle's defense. "What, are we prosecuting people for thought crimes now?" According to a paralegal on Valle's defense team, Valle's own Dark Fetish

Network profile explicitly stated, "I like to push the envelope but no matter what I say it's all fantasy." In one chat he wrote, "I just have a world in my mind. In this world I am kidnapping women and selling them to people interested in buying them." When one chat buddy asked for his real life information, he refused.

Mr. Muki doesn't believe Valle ever had any intention of going through with it, pointing out that many of the details in Valle's emails on the forum were 100% fantasy. "Valle claimed to have a house in the country with a barbecue pit where they could do the cooking, but that was fantasy. He never walked into a hardware store to buy rope." Famed court-ordered psychiatrist Park Dietz interviewed Valle for 18 hours and found no evidence of pathologies, "which is very rare" and called him, "the nicest guy you'd ever meet."

Mr. Muki concedes that Valle was compulsive in his surfing of cann fetish websites, and that he

liked to make it seem real for himself and others to add to the excitement, but that he never had any intention of going through with the acts. His only crime was misuse of the police database. And, rather than fueling a criminal spree, fantasy chatrooms and pornography can provide a safety valve for such urges.

The jury took 16 hours to find Valle guilty in 2013 on all counts, and he served 21 months, 7 of that in solitary "for his own safety." Then, in 2014, Federal Judge Paul Gardephe overturned the jury verdict, saying "Despite the highly disturbing nature of Valle's deviant and depraved sexual interests, his chats and emails about these interests are not sufficient—standing alone—to make out the elements of conspiracy to commit kidnapping." The US Court of Appeals, 2nd Circuit, agreed in 2015. Saying they were loath "to give the government the power to punish us for our thoughts and not our actions," a majority of a divided three-judge panel wrote that "fantasizing about committing a crime, even a

Rotisserie device, MukisKitchen.com.
The model is not actually being skewered—
it's a clever piece of fakery

"I think Meiwes got off too lightly. The fact his victim consented to being killed is proof he was not mentally capable of consenting to anything!"
—Mr. Muki

CANNIBAL PLAY IN BRIEF

TERMINOLOGY:
femcan, meatgirl, womaneater, meatboy

CORE KINK:
skin?

MAJOR THEMES:
power play, taboo, transformation

MINOR THEMES:
objectification, predicament

RELATED KINKS:
vore

SOMETIMES COMBINED WITH:
piggyplay

EROTIC EQUATION:
pressure of bondage

crime of violence against a real person whom you know, is not a crime." Though some have speculated it might go to the US Supreme Court, as of now there appears to be no notice of appeal, so Gilberto can be presumed to have won unless the feds later change their minds. In the beginning of 2017, Valle released a memoir entitled *RAW DEAL: The Untold Story of NYPD's "Cannibal Cop."*

Cann fetish pushes the edge of even the BDSM community's tolerance. Last year, a BDSM artist put on a performance where she had herself tied up. She arranged for her top to slice off an extremely thin layer of her skin and cook it on a camp stove set up for that purpose. He then ritualistically fed her own skin to her. The outcry was immediate and severe, and the performer was roundly condemned by many. It seems that extreme body modification may be acceptable, but the deep taboo against cannibalism is still beyond the pale.

Photo montage by boymeat
on CannibalPlanet.earth

Sidekink:
Human Furniture

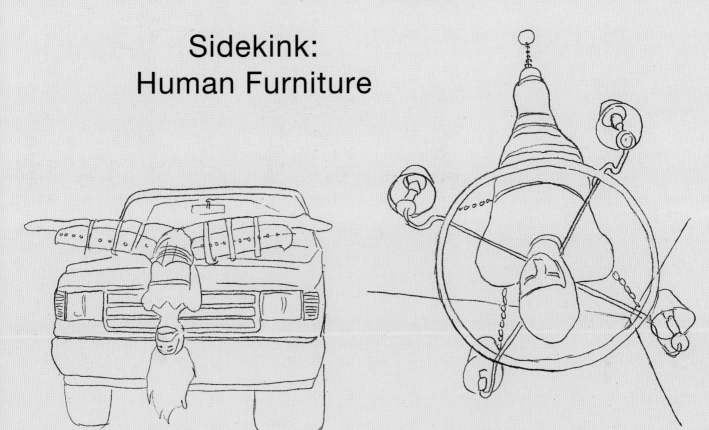

For those who desire to explore extreme bondage, objectification, and service, human furniture play pushes all of the right buttons. The most famous creator of human furniture is a reclusive man going by the name Gord. His House of Gord website showcases his masterfully creepy erotic artworks: using full-body Lycra, rope, straps, metal welding, and various ingenious devices, Gord transforms willing and eager women into chandeliers, treadmills, dining tables, garden fountains, hood ornaments, office chairs, display stands, sprinklers, rocking chairs, swing sets, and wheelchairs. Unfortunately, Gord declined to allow us to reproduce his photographs in this book.

TERMINOLOGY:
human furniture, forniphilia

CORE KINK:
in Gord's case, Lycra; bondage

MAJOR THEMES:
power play, transformation

MINOR THEMES:
service, objectification, predicament

RELATED KINKS:
cannibal fetish, ponyplay (Chapter 2)

EROTIC EQUATION:
pressure of bondage

Drawing based on a hood
ornament by House of Gord

Drawing based on human
chandelier by House of Gord

© Robert Hill 93

The Sexy Fandoms:
Slash Fiction, Furries, Robots,
and Superheroes

Wolf in Sheep's Clothing, a forced feminization/furry fantasy by Robert Hill. Collection of Katharine Gates.

Comic book, fantasy, and science fiction fans have taken their place in the world of kink, bringing with them a massive library of pop culture narratives. Characters from *Star Trek*, Disney films, *Harry Potter,* and the X-Men are some of the main protagonists of their libidinal dreams. These horny nerds aren't simply passive consumers of sanitized, prepackaged corporate product. They are actively making their fantasies come true by creating their own costumes, writing their own erotic stories, and performing in collaborative spectacles of pop culture carnality and fluid sexual identities.

SLASH FICTION

I love slash fiction: pornography featuring male TV and film characters having gay sex. Ever since the late 1970s, a group of mostly female, heterosexual *Star Trek* fans have been writing their own smutty stories featuring Kirk's rotund bottom and Mr. Spock's green Vulcan penis. In the beginning, these stories would be called "K/S" for Kirk/Spock—the slash between the letters indicated homoerotic content and gives this genre its name. One of the first stories had a plot device familiar to any trekker: Kirk and Spock beam down to a planet, the transporter breaks and they're stuck while Scotty tries to recrystallize the dilithium. Spock goes into Pon Farr, the violently sexual seven-year itch suffered by the otherwise prudish Vulcans. If he doesn't get any nookie he'll die. Kirk bravely offers to submit to Spock's sexual needs in order to save his friend's life. Afterwards, they both realize they craved that all along.

I started collecting slash fiction in 1989, after attending a lecture by Film and Women's Studies Professor Constance Penley. Along with several other woman academics, Penley sees slash fiction

Spidey in bondage, a superhero fetish scene by German creator socccerbondage

A SAMPLING OF K/S
STORY ELEMENTS

Kirk realizes his first mate's sexual attraction for him when he accidentally discovers a human-shaped dildo in Spock's bedroom. Kirk promptly orders himself a Vulcan-shaped dildo (bright green with two ridges) from a mail-order catalog

McCoy figures out that Kirk and Spock are lovers when the ship's supply of anal lube runs out

Kirk tries to find Spock's mysterious Vulcan prostate, with embarrassing results. Dr. McCoy catches the captain and his science officer *in flagrante delicto* playing "nurse and patient" in sickbay with his new hi-tech anal speculum

Spock goes into Pon Farr while on an away mission. Lieutenant Uhura and Nurse Chapel offer to sacrifice themselves to save Spock's life and have a catfight over who will finally get into the Vulcan's pants. Kirk has to jump into the fray and explain it's his job. By this time, Spock's cock has gotten so engorged that Kirk needs McCoy's help to guide it into his battered behind. In the closing scene, Kirk's ass is bloody and he's walking funny, but he's deeply satisfied

as an example of women's creative strategies for dealing with the sometimes oppressive gender and erotic conformism in popular culture. In *NASA/TREK: Popular Science and Sex in America,* Penley describes this process as a form of appropriation. "These products mimic and mock those of the industry they are 'borrowing' from while offering pleasures found lacking in their originals." These women are demanding sexual thrills from a narrative that was always weighted towards adolescent boys. Other academics have pointed out that the love between Kirk and Spock represents an idealized "love between equals"—a power parity that heterosexual women can rarely achieve in a patriarchal society. The stories offer a better universe, informed by the socially tolerant Vulcan philosophy of IDIC (or Infinite Diversity in Infinite Combinations), a universe where sexual diversity is both expected and valued.

There is something liberating in women making Kirk and Spock perform for them sexually, and seeing these women aggressively manipulate the products of a gigantic corporation like Paramount in ways that make copyright lawyers apoplectic. In her book *Enterprising Women,* trekker and Professor of Folklore Karen Bacon-Smith argues that slash fiction is a kind of revolutionary feminist text. The stories are transgressive because they represent women owning their desires, making stuff that makes them hot, and doing this in the face of both legal and cultural opposition. Paramount has in the past attempted to suppress K/S slash, seeing it as a real ideological and financial threat to their empire—to the slash women, this only makes it more dangerous and exhilarating. Over the decades, a whole non-profit underground industry of sexy trekkers has formed around publishing stories and music videos, giving away prizes, having special mini-conventions within the established Trek conventions, and throwing fund-raisers for pediatric AIDS research.

Kirk/Spock slash illustration, origin unknown

I recommend searching the web for K/S music videos, where selections of scenes from the original series are carefully edited to reveal the homoerotic subtext. The best of these is a skillfully edited mash-up of BDSM-tinged scenes between Kirk and Spock over the throbbing soundtrack of Nine Inch Nails' "Closer."

My well-thumbed K/S collection reflects the breadth of these women's imaginations. The stories are extraordinarily well-written, with convincing plots and believable dialogue. They have to be, for me to suspend my disbelief that a womanizing control freak like James Kirk would ever let Spock fuck him.

A few authors see Mr. Spock's logical mind and lean, powerful body as masculine compared to Kirk's labile emotionalism and soft roundness. Most find masculine and feminine qualities in both characters, and the stories become meditations on gender fluidity. In a few stories, conflict is created when Kirk resists the telepathic mind meld during sex. It's the ultimate intimacy (mind melds seem to inspire the hottest writing), but it also represents loss of control to the authority-minded captain.

Some authors develop more SM-inflected scenarios. One story has the anti-Kirk—from the evil Terran Empire featured in the original series episode "Mirror, Mirror"—violently raping Spock. One K/S subgenre, called "hurt-comfort," requires Spock and/or Kirk to undergo severe sadistic torture at the hands of Romulans before they can open up and learn to take care of each other.

What mystifies many people about slash fiction is why women would want to fantasize about two male bodies, but plenty of straight women find gay male porn orgasmic. A woman can imagine herself in the scene without getting distracted by a rival female body. Some of the thrill also comes from the possibility of fantasizing about having a differently sexed body—being inside the mysterious *other*, being able to transform and morph through many genders, sexualities, and identities.

While slash started with K/S, you can now find pretty much any combination of characters, as long as the original characters were not gay. You can read stories about Luke Skywalker and Han Solo, Fox Mulder and Director Skinner, Wolverine and Cyclops. These days, slash fanfic is often tagged by combining names, like "Snarry" for Snape and Harry. While gay male slash far outnumbers lesbian scenarios, some female slash does exist—written by both women and men. X/G stories, about Xena and Gabrielle from *Xena: Warrior Princess*, don't quite have the shock value of K/S,

Stills from a K/S music video by T Jonesey and Killa, which asks, "What if they hadn't made it to Vulcan on time?"

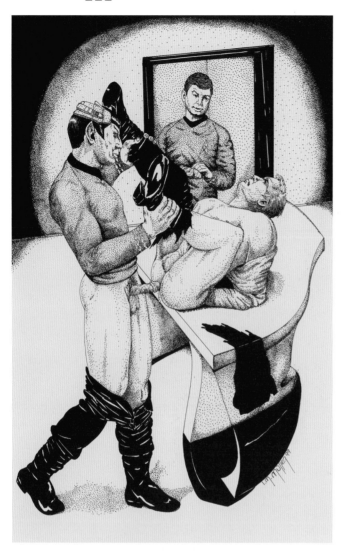

K/S + mind control inspired by *Spock's Brain*,
1968. Illustration: Marianne Miller

Cecilia Tan as Vulcan cheesecake.
Photo: D. Cameron Calkins

however. Their lesbian relationship was never merely subliminal.

CECILIA TAN: SPECULATIVE SM

Cecilia Tan is the founder and co-owner of the publishing house Circlet Press, devoted to "Erotica for Geeks since 1992," and a true groundbreaker in bringing explicit, sex-positive feminist BDSM into the fantasy and sci-fi genres. Susie Bright called her "simply one of the most important writers, editors, and innovators in contemporary American erotic literature." Cecilia received a Lifetime Achievement Award from the National Leather Association in 2004.

Circlet anthologies are filled with stories about telepathic dominatrixes, violent sex with cat-like aliens, and forest elves kept as battered sex slaves. The backlist is searchable by themes such as steampunk, furry, BDSM, and trans. Like so many of the people you'll meet at conventions, Cecilia is playful, intelligent, and resolutely sexually nonconformist.

Cecilia grew up masturbating to *Star Trek* and *Batman* at five. "Fantasy in the sense of 'fantasy and science fiction' became inextricably equated with fantasy as in 'erotic fantasy and daydreaming' and what you thought about when you jerk off." Cecilia found many of her favorite shows had a strong sexual component. "Catwoman is very clearly meant to be this erotic figure, and there's all this subtext in the show, about whether she and Batman are going to run off together, and whether their attraction for each other is enough to either turn her good or turn him bad. Even as a five-year-old I could tell that there was something really exciting and adult going on there."

Cecilia's earliest erotic fantasies involved some form of forced sex, a scenario mirroring the situations she saw on TV. "With *Star Trek*, when sex actually happened it was usually forced by the situation, and that's where the SM came in." Tan's early fantasies also ran along the lines of other literary genres, from pirates to westerns, "because

"Harry slams the book shut, hopefully too fast for Snape to recognise the wand-movement diagrams for Titillando Prostatis and Erecto Maximus."
—*from* Remedial Potions *by Acid and Sinick*

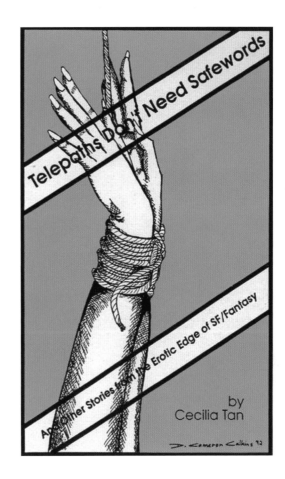

they're always getting into these situations of forced duress—they're captured or whatever. Although there's usually not actual sex in those stories, you still click to this situation where someone's not in control." For Cecilia, growing up in the suburbs, the only way she could imagine getting what she wanted was through some kind of coercion, "Where it didn't look like I actually went out and got it."

Cecilia's first self-published SM erotic sci-fi story came out in 1990, and was a sudden success. *Telepaths Don't Need Safewords* filled a deep need in a community forced to read sexless genre material. "What I discovered immediately when I published that first little chapbook was that, once again, I wasn't the only one. There were tons of people out there who were interested in erotic science fiction and fantasy. I would go to science fiction conventions and people would

chase me down in the hallways and ask me if I had any more of that book." Next thing she knew, Cecilia was receiving piles and piles of submissions—and Circlet Press was born. She describes her core audience as, "Those same weird perverts who are throwing SM parties at science fiction conventions and speaking on panels about polyamory and the influence of Robert Heinlein and Marion Zimmer Bradley on their multi-adult household."

Cecilia thinks science fiction has always offered alternatives to the mundane rituals of contemporary families and couples. (Sci-fi and fantasy fans often call non-fans and outsiders "mundanes.") Lesbians and separatists can read Marion Zimmer Bradley's *Darkover* novels and thrill to the idea of female-only warrior households where men are forbidden. People interested in linear marriages— where person A is married to person B and B

Sex toy inspired by macro fantasies

Cover of *Telepaths Don't Need Safewords*, Cecilia Tan's first BDSM fantasy book, 1990

Second Life, an online RPG, to try their hand at it. BDSM writer Michael Makai once suggested that Norman's writing may have helped to shape the rules now commonly used in the BDSM community. Cecilia laughs at the seriousness with which some of the Goreans take their play. "Of course, some of the more intelligent of us realize you can't slavishly follow a formula set down in a fictional work, any more than you can slavishly recreate Thomas More's *Utopia*."

Cecilia has noticed that manuscript submissions to Circlet Press seem to follow thematic waves, as if there's some sort of collective unconscious of sexual archetypes. In 1999, she was suddenly getting a whole slew of stories devoted to the tiny woman or tiny doll-girl concept. There are many variations of this theme, with the dolls living in men's pockets, flexible enough to fuck. "They can even crawl inside you and stimulate your prostate." Cecilia and Corwin discovered a sex toy that embodies this fantasy. "It's a silicone sleeve that you slide over the erect penis, and it's molded on the outside to look like a woman's body with no head and no legs. It's just her torso. And where you put your penis in is shaped like a little vagina with crenellations and everything! It's like the way a good dildo is, with little veins. The whole thing is silicone jelly, so it feels like gummy bears."

Today, gender transformation, which first showed up in sci-fi in the 1970s, is enjoying a resurgence. "If anything's changed, it's that stuff we were publishing in the underground 25 years ago is mainstream now."

Popular culture has caught up with Circlet press in some ways, but in other ways it has a lot to learn. Circlet published its first erotic vampire collection in 1997 called *Cherished Blood*, taking Anne Rice's *Vampire Chronicles* to the next level, with LGTB characters, powerful women, and explicit sex. Cecilia was tapping into an erotic subculture that had grown up in the suburbs among goth kids who dress up in costumes,

is married to C, but A isn't married to C—can read Robert Heinlein for inspiration. Science fiction has always appealed to secular humanists who want to imagine a world free from religion, where everyone fulfills their potential. It promotes speculation about future sexual options. Cecilia says the most likable qualities of sci-fi fans are that they really respond to these ideas and to making them real.

Certain fictional worlds have become models for elaborate, real-life SM relationships and play. John Norman's *Gor* books of the 1960s—macho potboilers set on a planet with brutish he-men and submissive slave girls—have inspired SM players who call themselves "Goreans." They religiously follow the protocols and vocabulary set out by the Gor series, especially when it comes to what costumes are permitted and in what situations, where the female slave can sit at what time, and how she should address her master. Those who can't play in real life go to

A wizard giant and young wizard from a familiar magic series. Illustration by Ponderosa121, "a poly, bi switch who female-identifies at least half the time"

share blood, and have complex polyamorous relationships in covens often dominated by a single charismatic older person.

For Cecilia, the most interesting vampire fantasies have them standing in for disenfranchised sexual minorities. "They can pass as normal, and yet they have some deep-seated need that cannot be satisfied by what's accepted by regular society. To me, that's a pretty strong parallel to the SM practitioner or to the gay or lesbian or trans person."

Yet the seemingly unending barrage of vampire romance today is often unimaginative and reactionary compared to the gender-fluid and culturally diverse worlds of Circlet Press. Many people don't realize that the *Fifty Shades of Grey* books that brought BDSM yet again into the mainstream were originally written as *Twilight* fan fiction. But the strictly hetero dominance and submission in *Twilight* and *Fifty Shades of Grey* reads more like abuse than BDSM to real-world BDSM practitioners, who have raised red flags about those books offering novices a bad idea about what constitutes good negotiation and safe practice.

If Cecilia has noticed one difference among her female and male readers, it's in the pace and style of the fantasies, not the content. "Women are more into delayed gratification. We just get hotter

"[Vampires] can pass as normal, and yet they have some deep-seated need that cannot be satisfied by what's accepted by regular society. To me, that's a pretty strong parallel to the SM practitioner or to the gay or lesbian or trans person."
—Cecilia Tan

Batman vs Joker battle, unknown DeviantArt artist

Gorean kajira slave in *nadu* "pleasure slave" position. Photo: Marcus J Ranum

and hotter and hotter the longer we wait... in a way, that's what the whole romance genre is about." She points out that the basic trope of a romance story is that the hero and heroine fall in love in the beginning of a book but are somehow separated—a situation common in the K/S slash stories as well. "And for whatever reason they spend the rest of the book trying to get together and then in the end they finally do." Many of the fetish narratives and scenarios I've come across—especially the more fantastic ones—are also about delayed gratification. The point isn't the orgasm as much as it is the process of getting there, the dramatic conflict.

In that sense, fetishists are deeply romantic.

FURRIES, YIFF, AND YIFFSUITERS

None of the other subcultures I covered in the original edition of this book has exploded quite like furries. In 1999, hardly anyone I knew had ever heard of it. Now, it's common knowledge that fur is an enormous fan community devoted to pop-culture characters that combine animal and human qualities. Some furries, called fursuiters, create their own costumes, often striving to achieve the professional-looking appearance of sports-team mascots and theme-park characters. Over the last decades, the furry movement has grown to the point where there are frequent regional conferences, countless web pages, newsletters, and even summer camps where furries can live out their own cartoon-animal identities. Today, when fursuiters show up in rap videos, everyone knows something edgy is going on.

I first came into contact with fur in 1994 at my first San Diego ComicCon. I owned a small underground publishing company at the time, and one of my associates invited me to a private party in a hotel room. There I met a woman in a sexy, tight-fitting, full-body cartoon bunny suit. The bed was covered with erotic drawings of anthropomorphic animals. My friend told me there was a plush toy in the back room filled

One of Robert Hill's self-made
fursuit alter egos, 1980s

Brokeback Mountain–inspired furry art
by Chewycuticle on DeviantArt

with cold cream for boinking; I can perhaps be forgiven for my mistaken assumption that furry was a specifically sexual subculture.

In 2000, the subject of the eroticism of fur was a seriously taboo subject within the furry community. Most furries saw their love of anthropomorphics as nonsexual, even spiritual, and preferred it that way. They were upset their community was being misrepresented in the media as a bunch of geeks getting into plushie orgies. My own forays into writing about the erotic side of fur were unwelcome at best, despite my enthusiasm and encouragement. A 2001 *Vanity Fair* interview, where despite my repeated insistence to the interviewer that fursex was just one small element of the larger

phenomenon, pushed many into full-on media blackout.

Those who were open about their interest in furry sex sometimes call themselves furverts to distinguish themselves from the nonsexual fans. Furverts not only want to become cute cartoon animals, they want to have sex with them as well—in character, in costume, in virtual reality, and in real life. The term "yiff" can be used to denote fursex, sexy fur imagery, or anything furry and erotic. ("Yiff" is said to be the sound an excited fox makes, especially when mating.) Costumes created for the purpose of erotic activities might be called murrsuits (sometimes as an insult) or yiffsuits.

Fursuit couple, 2002. Photo: Rick Castro, antebellum.blogspot.com

A cartoon universe is the perfect place for acting out sexual dramas. All sorts of weird, violent and surrealistically sexual things can and do happen in cartoonland—without guilt or repercussions. Underground comix artist Robert Crumb once told a *Comics Journal* interviewer he used to jerk off to images of Bugs Bunny in drag. Crumb went on to became famous for creating the lusty and entirely adult cartoon animal character Fritz the Cat, whose sexual adventures with ostrich-headed and alligator-headed women expressed the artist's own diverse and kinky sexual obsessions.

Costuming as a means of erotic self-transformation is ancient. Anyone who has ever been to Halloween parades or Mardi Gras knows that being in a costume (especially one with a full-face mask) gives one extra license to act sexually and provocatively. Trekker, comic book, and sci-fi conventions are modern updates of ancient costumed festivals. Costumes themselves can be erotic, because for the wearer they can heighten a sense of containment and bondage, and if made from materials like latex or plush, they can carry the sensual jolt of a true fetish.

Quite a few furverts combine their furry fantasies with any number of other kinky elements, from body inflation and macrophilia to ponyplay, cross-dressing, and BDSM. Thus you might find one furry with a latex inflatable unicorn alter ego, another with a cute werewolf identity that grows gigantic and rampages through cities, and yet another with the character of an assault-rifle-toting transsexual dominatrix snow leopard. Vore—as in carnivore—fantasies combine furry characters with cannibal/erotic eating/weight-gain scenarios. Some furverts seem to thrive on trying to be as outrageous as possible, and a certain amount of naughty playfulness and slapstick cartoon humor is inherent to furrydom. Today, you can follow Twitter users like Xydexx if you want to see NSFW animated gifs of cartoon foxes getting it on with lizardmen or she-bears.

The erotic appeal of the furry metaphor is fairly obvious: like many kinks, it immediately brings one back to a childlike state where sensuality, fear, and magic are felt more intensely. Playfulness is permitted and the deadening rules of the adult world don't apply. Cartoon animals in particular are perfect for expressing exaggerated emotional and psychological states: perky ears, fluffy tails, and shiny noses display lively eagerness and enthusiasm in a way adult humans aren't permitted to do. Jeremy Bernal, a furry artist, pointed out to me that animal characteristics are often used to create sexual stereotypes, such as a submissive rabbit or a sly, slinky fox. "Pulled-back ears suggest submission. Raised hackles or bared teeth show hunger and fearlessness." Animal body language is more blatant, their hungers and emotions more exposed and stylized. "In my opinion, this is the extra 'push' that draws people to furry erotica," Bernal adds. One of the appeals of being an animal is the freedom from human strictures. The Playboy mascot is a cartoon bunny for good reason.

Gay and bisexual men comprise a surprisingly high proportion
of furverts and yiffsuiters—some estimate as many as half. Some
gay men have long had an affinity towards Disney characters. The
gay subtext of Disney films is a well-known and popular source of
tittering gossip—look at Tarzan's loincloth, will you? Disney's show
tunes are camp heaven. Female Disney villains often seem more like
drag queens than cis women; think of *101 Dalmatians*' Cruella de Vil
or *The Little Mermaid*'s evil octopus-woman Ursula!

One of the founding fursuiters and furry artists, Robert Hill, once
worked as a costumed character at Disneyland. His favorite character to play was Eeyore, because he feels their personalities are quite
similar. Robert told me there was definitely some sex going on
between the characters when he was there. "There was that time
Br'er Bear gave Br'er Fox a cool blow job during a break…"

The Disney theme parks boast an extraordinarily strong gay
presence, not only on unofficial "gay days"—when busloads of
red-shirted queers proudly throng its Main Street, USA—but also
among the workers, especially costumed characters and performers.
Show tunes and make-believe worlds where things are brighter and
more beautiful over the rainbow are gay male traditions. (I once
took an amazing insider's tour of Disney World with a trans woman who had been working at the park for years—I was delighted
when she told me the person who played Tinker Bell in the nightly
fireworks spectacular was a gay man.) The most popular animal alter
egos in the gay furvert scene are well-hung centaurs, ravenous were-
wolves, and bears. Vanessa Ravenscroft, a professional fetish costume
maker, once built an animatronic werewolf costume for a gay male
client, complete with silicon dick.

PLUSH FETISH

Any childhood toy that has strong touchy-feely and smelly qualities
has strong fetish potential, so it makes perfect sense that some people grow up to become "plushophiles." Plushophiles—plushies for
short—are romantically and/or erotically attached to stuffed animals:
not taxidermy hunting trophies, but children's plush toys, like teddy
bears and that purple dinosaur you won at the carnival. Simply the
feel or smell of their favorite toy is enough to excite some plushies
to orgasm.

While most plushies are quite happy with the unique odor and
texture of polyvinyl plastic fake fur (in combination with their
own personal scent markings), others will only accept the fanciest
toys made with high-quality mohair blends. Some stuffed animals
are more sexually appealing—or "floofy"—than others. The most

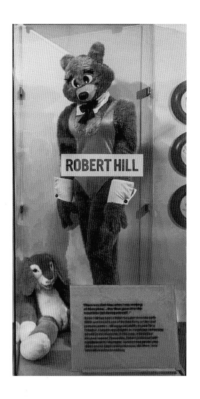

> *"There was that time
> I was working at
> Disneyland when Br'er
> Bear gave Br'er Fox
> a cool blow job during
> a break."*
> —Robert Hill

Robert Hill display at *KINK* exhibition,
Museum of Sex, 2006. Photo: Museum of Sex

FoxMajic, a plushie, with his favorite husky

desirable are those frozen in certain suggestive positions, such as hugging or begging (where the creature is posed with legs spread, ass raised, or both). The most universally popular partner among plushies was for years Meeko, a plush toy manufactured by Mattel and based on the raccoon from Disney's *Pocahontas*, so much so that its half-meter length is now a unit of measurement for plushies.

Galen, an out plushie who has sometimes been flamed within the community for his willingness to talk to the press, explains that unlike humans, toys never let you down. "I discovered plush sex long before I knew there was another adult in the world who loved stuffed animals as I did." At first Galen resisted the temptation to fuck his childhood toys, "Because I regarded my love for my plushies as purely innocent." Later he came to realize that consummating his love was innocent too, "and completely natural."

While some plushies are content to rub up against their favorite bedtime companion, others will actually modify the toy to make it suitable for more intimate acts. In fact, the unofficial motto of alt.sex.plushies is "In Plush We Thrust." They may rip open a seam and sew a fabric pocket into the inside of the animal, or they may sew on a penis-like attachment. The new orifice is called an "SPH" or "strategically placed hole." The SPA—or "strategically placed appendage"— may simply make the toy more realistic, or it may be used to penetrate its human companion. Vibrating plush toys produced to calm infants are also popular.

Galen feels that "giving the gift of love" to his plush toys is "a sacramental act." However, he recognizes that not all plushies want their toy to get spoogey (caked in semen or vaginal fluid). "If this concerns you, be sure to comb and dry the fur thoroughly right after sex, and untangle all the stuck-together plush." The plushie FAQ list advises the neophyte to "buy pairs for spares." Some male plushophiles may also place a fabric sleeve over their cock before insertion, to protect the innards of the stuffed creature from exces-

Strategically modified plush toys
by Hawtfur.com

sive soiling. This sleeve also protects them from the telltale "white fuzzies"—small particles of the toy's stuffing that can adhere to the penis. Bubble Gund vinyl-cleaning fluid is the brand most recommended by plushies for after-sex cleanup.

Narzil is one male plush fan whose extraordinary fiction story, entitled "A Night of Wishes," recounts the adventures of a college student named John who rediscovers his favorite childhood toy, a blue stuffed raccoon named Bouncer. Bouncer magically comes to life, grows to seven feet tall, and initiates various sex acts with the protagonist. "To his surprise, Bouncer carefully positioned the front of his muzzle to John's cock tip, then pressed his muzzle forward. John gasped…the inside of Bouncer's muzzle was like a tunnel, soft and warm and silken, made of some velvety cloth, glided smoothly and firmly across his skin." Bouncer then makes a wish for John to have a plushie costume of his own—a red raccoon full-body outfit with holes for nipples and ass that the toy can fuck him through. "All John could feel was the costume and his aching erection. Bouncer's voice giggled in his ear. 'Doesn't it feel good? You look so nice in the costume, John.'"

There is a significant overlap between plushies, furverts, and fursuiters. The plush toy and the fursuit costume share the same

"Be sure to comb and dry the fur thoroughly right after sex, and untangle all the stuck-together plush."
—Galen, plushie

FURRY IN BRIEF

CORE KINK:
plush

GENERAL THEMES:
pagan impulses

SUBTHEMES:
animal transformation

SUBGROUPS:
fursuiters (full-body costumes),
toonies (cartoon animals),
therians (spiritual "totem"
animals), plushies

RELATED KINKS:
ponyplay (Chapter 2), vore

SOMETIMES COMBINED WITH:
inflation/expansion, macro,
gender transformation

fake fur material and the same seams and rubber detailing on paws. For a plushie, being inside a fursuit is tantamount to being engulfed in the fetish object. Not surprising, then, that "A Night of Wishes" has the protagonist first wear a plushie-toy costume—and get fucked in it— then actually transform into a plush toy. In the storybook ending, John transforms into a true plush animal and goes to plush-toy heaven, where he is reunited with all of his lost childhood toys in a giant plushie orgy.

Plush fetish has entered the mainstream in a unique way: both Marvel and DC have created characters with plush proclivities. In Marvel's *Deadpool* (2016), the wisecracking antihero masturbates with a plush unicorn. Six months later, DC, not to be outdone, made *Suicide Squad*'s character Captain Boomerang a Brony with a pink unicorn fetish.

ROBOTS, DOLLS, AND MANNEQUINS

When I first found alt.sex.fetish.robots, I eagerly anticipated homemade piston-driven motorized love machines or Disney-esque animatronic space-age sex dolls, but most of these self-named technophiles' creations are strictly low-tech. They are perfectly happy fantasizing about playing with wind-up dolls, store mannequins, or people dressed up in android costumes. Some want to see a living person pretend to be mechanical or be forced to act like a robot. Others want to be transformed into mindless sex slaves through play hypnosis. For a few, it's the robot performance itself—especially the jerky, artificial, type of miming—which revs their engines.

Some robot fans simply want to own the perfect servile sex doll. Android69, a 20-something Navy seaman, explained to me: "She'll never get old, never tire, never have a headache, never have that time of the month, and she is always there to please YOU and ONLY YOU. Come on—what guy would not like this?" One man, who calls himself RobotMaster, wants a fembot he can program with a remote control. (Fembot = female + robot, a term popularized in the 1960s during the first wave of low-budget psychedelic sexploitation films like *Dr. Goldfoot and the Bikini Machine*, then revived in the Austin Powers films.) RobotMaster also imagines transforming a real woman into a mind-controlled toy, like the obedient suburbanites of *The Stepford Wives*.

RobotMaster is married to a woman who is occasionally willing to let him tell her exactly what to do during sex. "She was scared at first that I was into something very perverse and wrong, but

Plushie/furry illustration
by Richard Hernandez, 1993

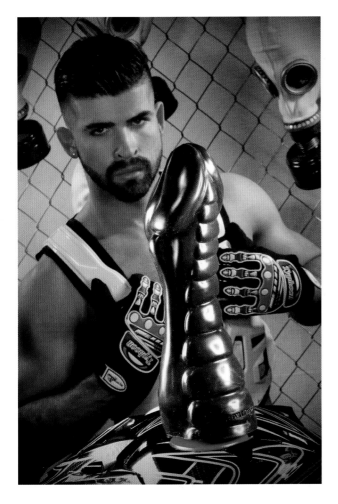

after we talked and I explained the way it ties into my hypnosis/mind control fantasies, she accepted it." RobotMaster's favorite way of acting these fantasies out, however, is online. "I ask women on the private show sites to move and behave robotically for me: sexy, robotic striptease; walking around like a robot; pretending to deactivate and reactivate again."

This is objectification in its purest form. Feminist objections aside, it is, in many ways, an adult version of how we played with dolls as kids. We made them perform for us. They mirrored our fears and desires. We could try things out with them and feel safe while we did it. RobotMaster's fantasies share some of the attractions behind taking the dominant role in BDSM—calling the shots, mastering the situation, having a play object.

Freyr is a gay man who enjoys robot role-play with lovers. "I especially like having the guy move around jerkily and talk in a robotic monotone. I like varying their speed, making them go slow, drawing out their speech to sound mechanical. Then having to wind them up again. Another aspect of this is having the robot complain about 'losing power' and needing to be recharged or rewound." He also pretends to take the robot apart and get a blow job from the disarticulated head. "I like taking off the feet and licking/sucking on them."

Robot fetishists aren't only men. One 40-year-old female robot fan came to her obsession through her love of the German techno band Kraftwerk. She dreams of building robots in the likeness of these already somewhat mechanical performers. "I want to be

The Cyborg Exploration sex toy, by Fort Troff. "The gnarly ridges and bumps will satisfy your INHUMAN cravings."

Fembot art by Meifembot, a Flickr user

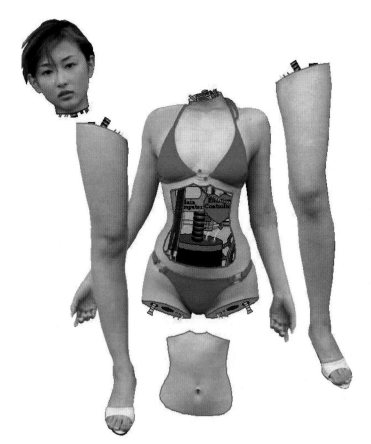

"During sex, she would say (in a monotone, robotic voice) 'My systems require a circuit overload,' or 'Master, overload my circuits.' Of course, 'circuit overload' occurred when we climaxed!"
—Solo, robot fetishist

Fembot art by Meifembot, a Flickr user

gang-banged by these ROBOTS as I KranK up their MusiK! I want to do to THEM what their MusiK does to ME… Machines can't LIE, CHEAT or otherwise HURT me the way humans always do." If there's one thing the robot-types seem to have in common, it's a mistrust of humanity in general, a sense robots are more emotionally reliable.

Like many female robot fetishists, she is a fan of Data, the android character from *Star Trek: The Next Generation*. Apparently, Data—like Mr. Spock before him—received more erotic fan mail than any other character on the show. (The savvy creators of the series made sure we knew early on he was "fully functional" in that regard!) Data is emotionally safe, and in some ways his social isolation and awkwardness gave him more humanity than the rest of the crew.

Some robot fans get aroused by anything that looks like a human but lacks a will of its own. One man has a powerful urge to masturbate to the Rockettes' performance of "Parade of the Wooden Soldiers." Another admitted to having a spontaneous orgasm at the sight of a mime pretending to be a mannequin in a store window at the mall. Several mentioned being fascinated by E.T.A. Hoffmann's early 19th century tale of a mechanical girl named Olympia and the man who falls hopelessly in love with her.

Robotdoll's Top Ten
Robot/Mannequin Sightings
in the Media

1. "Electric Barbarella"(1999): The video for the Duran Duran song from their album, *Medazzaland*. EB is a robot maid/pleasure doll bought by the band. The song is almost certainly the national anthem of the techno-sexual.

2. *I Dream of Jeannie,* "The Wedding" (1969): Jeannie replaces herself with a mechanical dummy. One of the finest examples of robotic motion on episodic television. (Robotdoll wrote a sequel — it's on the site.)

3. *Extreme Sex 3: Wired* (1994): Porn film. One scene involves sex with a wind-up puppet. Spectacular start-up sequence.

4. *Chitty-Chitty Bang-Bang* (1968): Yes, the kid's film. Sally Ann Howe masquerades as a wind-up music box doll, doing a very nice mechanical song number, even with sound effects as she moves.

5. *Dr. Goldfoot and the Girl Bombs* (1966): Directed by Mario Bava! Sequel to *Dr. Goldfoot and the Bikini Machine*, both starring Vincent Price in the title role. Highlights: A robotic dance number where dozens of girls clank their way around. One of the best examples of robot motion ever seen (and the benchmark Robotdoll has used ever since).

6. *Roboforce* (aka *I Love Maria*) (1988): Tsui Hark directs and appears in a film about a sexy robot woman who is found by some lunkheaded heroes and taught how to be good. The suit's a dream, the actress a delight.

7. Shields & Yarnell: This mime couple had a summer replacement show back in the 70s, and they appeared on a number of shows (including the second *Wild Wild West* reunion movie) as the mime robots, the Klinkers. There is little the author would not give to see this couple in a, shall we say, different locale.

8. *Star Trek*, "I, Mudd" (1967): robo-folks a-plenty. Great voices, great turn-on/off scenes. Chekov has a scene with two female robots that's positively brimming with techno-sexual undertones, where he laments that the girls aren't "real" and they assure him they are programmed to be female in EVERY way. In the next scene, he is smiling...

9. *Time Piece* (1995): Adult film. A woman has the ability to stop time. There's a lovely scene in an elevator where she uses another girl like a mannequin, posing her and playing with her.

10. Assorted Bob Hope Specials: Bob must be one of us, because he keeps doing robot girl sketches on his Christmas shows. Loni Anderson (hoo yeah) and Mary Lou Retton have both played robot girls destined for Santa's sack.

Bernadette Peters in *Heartbeeps*. Robotdoll's ideal woman

Twilight Zone still. A department store mannequin is allowed to come to life for one day a year

Shields & Yarnell, whose robot mime inspired a generation of technophiles

ROBOT ROLE-PLAY TIPS
by Robotdoll

START-UP/WIND-DOWN:
In some cases, the only moments the actors will act robotic is when they are being activated or deactivated. A little jerkiness in their arms and legs, some stiff action. If done well, this can be very erotic

VOICE:
The monotone quality of the voice can add to the arousal of the viewer. Many prefer a clipped, monotone voice

MOTION:
In the few classic examples of robot people, the movement of the actors is stiff and jerky. Best examples would be mime team Shields & Yarnell. Immobility is also very sexy; scenes where people are frozen/paralyzed are also appealing to the robot fetishist

There's something uncanny about mechanical dolls and robots that inspires sexual fascination. Mechanical dolls and robots appear to be both alive and dead, human and machine, powerful and helpless. In many ways, they represent ambivalence about sexuality itself: the sense we have no control over it, that we respond mechanically to stimuli, and that our sexual programming makes us helpless. Fetishes, especially, are a kind of hardwired sexual subroutine. Robots can be frightening on an existential level. Mastering a robot could be a symbolic way of mastering the fear of sex.

Not all robot fans want the dominant role. Foxdroid is a 25-year-old male bisexual who enjoys the fantasy of being transformed into a submissive female robot. "Most of my roboticization fantasies hinge upon some sort of abduction and deep mental reprogramming—there's definitely a Dominance & Submission aspect to it." To Foxdroid, it's about exploring an altered state of consciousness. "There's something sexy about the idea of your lover flooding you with mindless pleasure, with the press of a single button." Foxdroid has acted out his robot fantasies with both female and male lovers, usually with a costume made of silver fabric, PVC, metallic makeup and various odds and ends that create the futuristic effect. "We eventually got to the point where we referred to Toys "R" Us as a fetish shop! Anything that

Modifying pornography to match one's own fetish is sometimes called "rasturbation." Morph: Cybernarc

Cover of ebook available for Kindle devices

blinked or bobbled or glowed had potential as an alien sex toy." His favorite is the Touchstone, a little hemisphere of clear plastic with a touch-sensitive oil film that changes color with heat and pressure at the bottom. "It looks so much like some sort of xenotech control button when glued someplace strategic like the forehead—soooo sexy." Foxdroid's role-playing sex games last for hours and they remain in character during sex. "Monotones are very useful, and remain a major turn-on for me. It also took us a while to get the modes of speech right: 'Command. Protocol. Uplink. Established. This. Unit. Awaits. Your. Selection.' Sounds a hell of a lot sexier than 'Yes, Master!'"

Todd is a 26-year-old CAD designer who, at 12, began to create costumes for himself to wear while acting out Shields & Yarnell skits and masturbating. "The hardest part of this was (don't laugh too hard) hiding the pantyhose I stole from my mom… I found that I could make a neat-looking costume by sticking things like batteries, TV remotes, and electronic games under the pantyhose to give the appearance of having electronics in/on me."

Fembot is a female computer programmer who has monthly robot sessions with her boyfriend using her favorite fetish materials. (In robot play, sex is called interfacing, and sticky sex requires robots that have lubricant.) Sometimes she's a servile robot and other times she's a dominating one. "Once I confronted him in a latex dominatrix outfit and forced him to pleasure his robot mistress (I used a black dress with silver body paint—I even have a silver wig)."

Rotwang is a young German man obsessed with the female robot in Fritz Lang's *Metropolis*. His fetish comes from a fascination with masks and with the disquieting quality of a person in a costume. "It all boils down to 'the woman behind a mask' idea." Rotwang saw a picture of the *Metropolis* robot in an encyclopedia when he was little and instantly fell in love with it.

Robot "reveals" are a turn-on for some.
Images: Meifembot, Flickr

Anatomically-correct male doll
by sinthetics.com

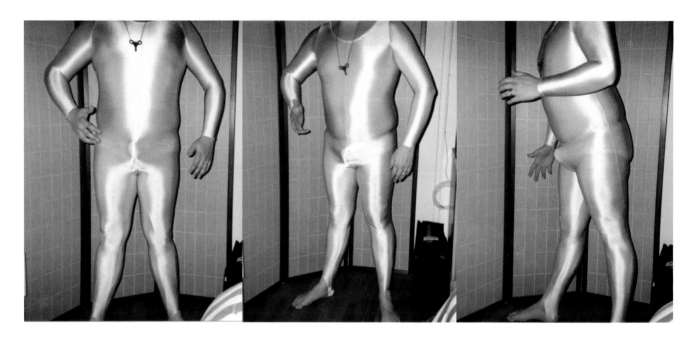

ROBOTS IN BRIEF

CORE KINK:
Lycra

GENERAL THEMES:
pagan impulses

SUBTHEMES:
object transformation

SUBGROUPS:
mind control, dolls, mannequins

SOMETIMES COMBINED WITH:
gender transformation

Rotwang is deeply jealous of plushies and ponygirls, because it's so easy to find a store that sells their fetish apparel. "Have you ever seen a shop that sells robot suits? No! I HATE THAT!"

For Robotdoll, the erstwhile "charismatic overlord" of alt.sex. robots, role-playing as a robot is a kind of meditation, an altered state of consciousness. "Your purpose for that moment is that moment." For him, much of the fun comes from the transcendent feeling of splitting himself into two seemingly contradictory parts: one is an aroused body and one is a pure mind. "There's this sense of detachment. You have to act kind of stiff and mechanical and motionless with this nice flat voice and this willingness to obey. At the same time in the back of my mind I'm terribly excited. I have to keep that inside. I don't want to ruin it by giggling in the middle. It's an amazing feeling."

SUPERHERO FETISH

Men who get turned on by role-playing with other men in full spandex superhero bodysuits is an emerging kink subculture. One man may play the strong, valiant, virtuous hero captured or kidnapped by a villain who ties him up and tortures him in various comic–book–tinged ways.

Superhero fetish isn't exactly new: Since 2001, EyeoftheCyclone. com has been delivering porn devoted exclusively to superhero bondage and wrestling. The photo sets are all presented in comic

Robotdoll at home in his silver Lycra bodysuit.
His wife uses the key around his neck to
"wind him up" in more ways than one

book cartouches, complete with sounds ("Ar-rgggggh!") and added effects like electricity or glowing Kryptonite—the latter used as a form of predicament bondage on a Superman-like hero. Instead of rope you might find bright red span-dex strips, cartoonish chains, or even an elaborate Spider-Man web, and WAM (wet and messy) su-perheroes with titles like "Slimed Spandex Strip" and "Glued in Goo," with size play and vore.

Although a few gay porn sites had tried to get into the superhero fetish market before this, Eye of the Cyclone worked because its founder "got it." He had the fetish himself and understood how important it was to pay close attention to the costumes, not just the hunks inside them.

Pablo Greene is the superhero-erotic-writing identity of a mild-mannered, university

Journalism professor. His BDSM-heavy, four-part erotic novel, *How to Kill a Superhero*, is a break-away success that has brought him fame even within the ironically hidebound world of the National Leather Association. The protagonist, Roland, starts off as a small, slender superhero-worshiping man who masturbates to comic books, but after a brutal mugging becomes a near-death experience, he discovers a mysterious book that unlocks his inner-superhero. Roland's sexual fantasies of being a kidnapped and tor-tured hero come true. Each time he performs BDSM superhero role-play, his body transforms. He grows taller and more muscular, his blond hair and blue eyes turn brown, he becomes hairier and more masculine. It's very hot while at the same time very "meta": only by truly accept-ing and exploring his own sexuality can he gain access to his superhuman powers.

Sidekink, a superhero fetishist who role-plays as various superhero sidekicks in predicament bondage

Transformation Fetish, the third installment of Pablo Greene's *How to Kill a Superhero* series

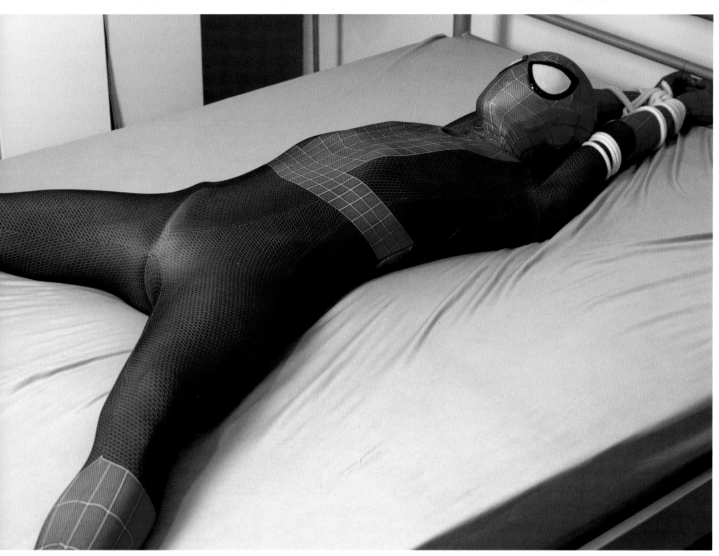

Pablo identified as gay at 11 or 12, but his fascination with male superheroes went back at least five years earlier. "The thrill and excitement of reading the comics wasn't sexual but it was something close to it," he said. Although it was definitely part of his erotic makeup, Pablo didn't really explore superhero role-play until his late 20s, after the end of his first serious relationship. He'd tried cyberchat, but that just wasn't enough. He wanted to meet in person, see others' costume collections, wear costumes, wrestle, and get tied up or maybe sometimes tie them up too, followed by plenty of sex.

Now his collection includes three different Spider-Man costumes, plus Superman, Robin, Punisher, and the Riddler. "I also have two custom suits made by the designer Shane Sprankel,

which feature the cover designs from books 1 and 2 in my series."

Pablo sees a connection between his superhero fetish and his Latino roots. He agrees it's partly about the machismo culture of masculine signifying, and in Mexico in particular the pop culture heroes of lucha libre wrestling, who often go perform acts of charity on the streets of impoverished neighborhoods.

But for Pablo it also has a lot to do with his Catholic upbringing: saints are like superheroes fighting for good, each with their own special powers and unique tales of suffering. Yet Pablo feels certain there is also something pagan at the core of his kink, pointing out that in Aztec,

Spidey in bondage, by soccerbondage

Maya, and other Mesoamerican cultures, individuals would be chosen to wear the costume of a god, thereby becoming that god for a year. The fact that those chosen ones always eventually get brutally sacrificed is a recurring motif in his books.

Pablo Greene's website, howtokillasuperhero.net, provides a forum for fellow gay superhero fetishists to discuss their personal histories and feelings about the kink. Spandex is clearly the core kink. One man wrote about joining a sports team in school just to have an excuse to buy a spandex unitard. Another, who goes by Sidekink, describes how he feels when he puts on a Lycra superhero costume: "I feel more confident in my sexuality and my sexual desirability than I ever do wearing regular clothes. They give me a power I don't normally have in real life. Being touched in those suits feels more electric, more sensuous. My inner negative thoughts—about my body, about if I'm good enough for a man, about my desirability—they melt away." Sidekink is happy to play the youthful sidekick who gets tied up, molested, and beaten. "Examining it as the sex nerd I am, I believe I most enjoy it for the juxtaposition and role reversal. The hero is strong, valiant, virtuous in the mythical comics. In these kinky scenes that dynamic is flipped on its head and he is now vulnerable, worshiped, erotic, and a person to be desired."

Another contributor, Captain Spandex, mentions Adam West's Batman and Christopher Reeve's Superman as huge influences in his childhood. "When they were onscreen in costume, my focus was absolute—I'd watch the hero's body, comic-made-flesh, as muscles and power radiated under spandex and cape." The skintight outfits of superheroes have always been erotic, the impossibly bulging musculature exaggerating every flex as if it were made of erections. But for Captain Spandex, there was something different about those two actors in particular. "They were icons of confidence and power that I worshiped because I felt these were

things I lacked in a childhood tainted by alcoholism and abuse."

One scene that gets repeated in the Eye of the Cyclone photosets is the unmasking of the hero. As Pablo explains it, "The eroticism of unmasking comes from the loss of control, loss of identity." There's also humiliation and embarrassment. "It's incredibly intimate…that moment when your human, vulnerable alter-ego is revealed." Another scenario is the superhero who has a friend who knows his secret identity. They might enjoy walking around in public together, with the exciting knowledge that only the friend knows how powerful the superhero really is. Pablo explains, "This role-play gets very emotional, because it's about trust. These are stories that most of us—maybe especially gay men—have lived. Having a secret identity that we can only share with people we really trust, and that trust is a huge kind of intimacy." Scenes like this can end in cathartic tears.

Pablo Greene, in a custom suit based on his *How to Kill a Superhero* books. Photo: Pablo Greene

Although the eroticism is clearly at its core about power play and bondage, superhero fans don't fit easily into the world of the old-guard gay leather scene, where having the right gear and clothes is strictly enforced. In the third book in his series, entitled *Transformation Fetish*, Roland attends a leather event and is ridiculed by the black-leather daddies for his shiny-silver spandex suit. Yet when the event is attacked by the hideous villain Crimson Hand, our protagonist saves the leathermen and becomes a true hero.

Things have changed. In 2014, Pablo was awarded one of the coveted book signing spots at the International Mr. Leather event organized by the Leather Archives Museum in Chicago. He didn't know what to expect, and was nervous how it would go over, but he sold huge numbers of his books and met others like himself. The next year at IML, Pablo started a meet-up—with no rules. "It was an anti-old-guard thing. You didn't have to have the gear. No one is kicked out for not having the right look."

In February 2017, Leather Pride Belgium featured a Mister Superhero Fetish event, complete with a beautiful poster proclaiming proudly: "Strength, agility, intelligence, elegance. These are the qualities that you must have if you want to participate in the exciting story of superheroes! Warm up your muscles and get your hot, tight suits at the ready—we're taking off."

SUPERHERO IN BRIEF

CORE KINK:
Lycra

GENERAL THEMES:
transformation, power play

SUBTHEMES:
growth

SOMETIMES COMBINED WITH:
predicament bondage, wet
and messy

Poster from the Mister Superhero Fetish
competition, Leather Pride Belgium 2017

Illustration: Leandrocomics.com

Sidekink:
Female Latex Masks

One of the more unsettling variations of the doll/costume theme is the women and men who enjoy wearing full-coverage latex masks that come in various models with names like "Dawn" and "Alice." They're supposed to be realistic, but they're eerie.

I had been corresponding via email for several years with Kerry, the straight male creator of the Female Mask Homepage, before I met him in person at the opening for the *KINK* show at Museum of Sex. In costume, he's over six feet tall. Because the mask completely covers his mouth he cannot communicate. He stood quite close to me, utterly silent throughout the event. I couldn't help but think of serial killer Ed Gein or *The Silence of the Lambs* character Jame Gumb putting on their female skin suits.

For the latex mask wearer, part of the appeal comes from being confined inside the latex material, but also from completely and perfectly transforming into the idealized female doll. Rogue, another straight, male latex mask fetishist, told me, "A woman in a mask is in complete control of her surroundings."

For many of the female mask fans, seeing women remove masks can be orgasmic: they collect clips from old TV shows like *Mission: Impossible,* where female characters pull off their disguises. The clips are often shown in slow-motion, so that the stretching and tension of the rubber is extended. Interestingly, the clips stop just before the new face appears.

Both Kerry and Rogue create costumes based on cartoon superheroines that they wear to comic book conventions. Rogue has also altered an inflatable female lovedoll into a full-body costume—latex meets inflation meets doll fetish.

TERMINOLOGY:
female mask

CORE KINK:
latex

GENERAL THEMES
transformation

SUBTHEMES:
gender transformation

RELATED KINKS:
robots, dolls, mannequins

SOMETIMES COMBINED WITH:
superhero

Rogue, a cis male latex mask fan, in one of his many superheroine costumes

An unmasking, from a video by Kerry, maskon.com

Kitty Meyer, a female mask fan, wearing one of Kerry's masks. kittyskornervip.com

Over the Edge:
Let's Talk About Limits...
and Never Stop Talking

Increasingly in the age of Instagram, tourists in national parks climb over fences and take ridiculous risks in the name of competing for the best selfie. They have no equipment, no hiking experience, and no knowledge of how to handle unexpected situations that may arise. In June 2016, an Oregon man visiting Yellowstone ignored prominent "DANGER" signs, left the boardwalk, and fell into a boiling-hot thermal pool at Norris Geyser Basin. His body was found days later. His sister told police that they were "hot potting"—looking for a new place to sit and soak. This man crossed a legal, ultimately deadly line in the name of pleasure.

It's always the tourists who want me to take them over the edge, beyond the fence. When I say I write about kink, vanilla people ask me about rape, pedophilia, bestiality, and necrophilia. Set these folks thinking about nonconformist sexuality, and they need to talk about non-consenting partners. It freaks me out, honestly. Vanilla folk seem to need to assume humiliation and degradation are key to every kink, but shame and fear are not, as we've seen, fundamental to every kinkster. Vanilla folk also often presume fantasies must only be blueprints for action, but that's just not the case. If you've read this book, you know even the most extreme scenario can be safe and fun with a little costuming, some negotiated role-play, and a strong imagination.

Some kinky people do seek out sexual activities that put them at risk. The subtitle of this book is "A Tour of the Erotic Edge," and as promised I've taken you to some edgy spots: trampling fans who crave such intense physical pressure that they risk breaking bones; feedees who choose to become fatter and fatter despite the effects on their mobility; even cannibal role-players who sliced off a bit of skin to eat, to make the fantasy seem that much more real. Like anyone who engages in extreme sports, these kinky folk are aware what they're doing comes with risks. They have taken the time to equip themselves with the right tools, educate themselves on how to handle unexpected situations, and weigh the consequences to the best of their abilities.

The BDSM community's guidelines on consent are clear. Children, animals and dead bodies cannot give consent; sex play with real kids, animals, or dead bodies is absolutely unacceptable. People who are drunk or high, mentally disabled, or who have certain untreated mental illnesses are unable to give meaningful consent. The ability to give meaningful consent can be compromised if one person in the situation has real power over the other, for example doctor/patient, employer/employee, teacher/student. And, especially in sexual play scenes that involve any sort of boundary pushing (such as initiating anal sex for the first time), everything must be negotiated in detail beforehand, because bottoms can get so high from endorphins during a scene they may give consent in the moment that they regret later.

"Safe, Sane, and Consensual" (SSC) evolved in the early days of BDSM as a set of guidelines for erotic play. SSC was valuable for clarifying the difference between BDSM and abuse to a skeptical public, but experienced players knew these guidelines could not replace lengthy, honest, and thoughtful negotiation between top and bottom. One person might see piercing or tattoos as unacceptable "permanent harm," whereas another might view it as personal adornment. Many in the BDSM community felt that edge play such as knife and breath play were way too dangerous even to be discussed, whereas others wanted to learn ways to engage in them safely. And, as the increasing popularity of BDSM brought an influx of eager, untrained novices, it became obvious that many of these BDSM tourists were getting in trouble: they assumed the rules would take care of any situation, that everyone agreed on definitions, and that safewords were all they needed. Some kinky folk who were interested in edge play were getting pushed out of the conversation, and their ostracism made it more difficult for them to get the information they needed to play safely.

In the early 2000s, dissatisfaction with SSC led to the development of a new rubric: RACK, or Risk Aware Consensual Kink. RACK accepts that risk can be essential element of the excitement, and that focus should instead be placed on knowledge and skill. RACK makes it possible to talk about edge play (needles, humiliation play, cultural trauma play, etc.) without shutting the conversation down as fundamentally unsafe.

No consensual activities should be marginalized; pushing anyone into secrecy is dangerous. If you go climbing over those fences without some real knowledge, you can get burnt. Most importantly, RACK proponents felt that their approach brought the emphasis back on negotiation. Just because needles were OK last week does not mean they're OK this week. Thorough conversations must happen before, throughout (when possible), and after a scene, *every time*.

In the last six years, the BDSM community has opened up the conversation on a particularly difficult subject: abuses of consent within the scene. For decades, most considered it more important to present a unified front of safety and sanity to a vanilla world. Anyone who spoke out publicly about tops who broke consent risked summary banishment. Novices often became the victims of known predators. Then, in 2001, International Ms. Leather Mollena Williams publicly came out and described a scene in which a prominent top pushed past one of her hard limits. Despite her specific prenegotiation that there be no penetration without a condom, he took advantage of her being in bondage to do exactly that. He claimed "just for a second" made it other than rape. It was rape. Later, at a panel discussion about consent, when Mollena asked the audience how many had experienced a top who pushed them beyond their negotiated limits, three-quarters raised their hands. Open discussion about this topic would have been unthinkable 10 years earlier, but now that the secret was revealed, the floodgates opened.

In 2011, the blogger kinkylittlegirl wrote, "We must get a better grip on the problem of abuse in our subculture, because it is at an all-time high, and part of that is examining consent much more deeply." The culture of secrecy was harming people. At a RACK panel in April 2011, one panelist contended that there were savvy predators who didn't care about consent and "just who knew how to hide behind the right language." When he suggested that these people should be named, "it drew a gasp of shock from the audience—and vigorous assent from the other panelists." Saikiji Kitalpha developed an extensive "red flag" list of behaviors that novices should watch out for in tops, one of which included isolating bottoms from the very BDSM community that could call them out.

Challenges to honest, open discussion remained. In early 2012, a group of young, queer, kinky people in New York City opened a thread on FetLife called "Confessions: TRIGGER WARNING" that allowed users to anonymously name other FetLife users (by their user names only) who they claim had violated their boundaries. Later, a hacker/activist called Maymay created a JavaScript plugin called the Predator Alert Tool that would pop up on your browser to alert if a particular FetLife profile was a known offender, and provide details of those accusations. The purpose of the thread and app was to make the community safer, but FetLife shut down both, citing the overarching importance of anonymity. "We do not allow accusations of criminal conduct when a conviction has not happened. If you can anonymize any accusations that come in from now on, we'll allow the thread to stay open. If not, we'll have to delete the thread completely."

Some cried foul, asserting that FetLife's motivation came down to money: patron memberships (the ones that supported the site financially) were held, they argued, overwhelmingly by the very kinds of people who had been accused. DisruptingDinnerParties' blog wrote, "In summary, we found that 15.3% of all users reported in [Predator Alert Tool] as having violated consent are currently paying supporters."

Some of the accused stepped forward and attempted to clarify where things went wrong. They either apologized for honest mistakes or pleaded their cases. Others simply refused to engage, calling the accusations censorship or libel. Members of the BDSM community are unlikely to bring charges against repeat predators, though. Rape convictions are notoriously difficult to obtain when the victim is part of a sexual subculture; mainstream legal understanding still hasn't caught on to the subtleties of meaningful consent, and a bottom who allows himself to be hogtied but not fucked will have little legal support in a rape case.

Then came the "Fetopalypse." In January 2017, FetLife's bank called to say the site would no longer be able to use their credit card gateway to accept donations and memberships, citing member content like incest fantasies, needles, zoophilia, blood, necrophilia, or scat. The banks didn't care whether this was fantasy role-play or not; they didn't want to have anything to do with it. In a panic, FetLife owner, Canadian programmer John Baku, deleted all threads with anything to do with these subjects. Even vampire fantasy threads were summarily destroyed without warning members. Suddenly, people who once had an outlet for their fantasies and a way to safely role-play their desires were out in the cold. Despite FetLife's attempt to win back the gateway's services, they still as of this date have no way of getting money to support their community. Watchers estimate they will go out of business before the year is out.

Perhaps the most disturbing legal development came in 2016, when the UK considered a Digital Economy Bill that would ban all forms of non-conventional pornography. *The Guardian* reported that this "classification…may include everything from female ejaculation to spanking (that leaves marks) and adult material involving urination or menstruation."

Kink may be scary to some, but the most dangerous thing of all is trying to pretend we can make it go away by shutting down conversations or by limiting access to information. No matter what, we have to keep talking and arguing. Pushing people to the margins will only cause more harm. Isolating someone for their kink is dangerous—being able to discuss, negotiate, argue, and explore within a safe and moderated setting is a healthy way to blow off steam. We have to stop assuming and start listening.

In Conclusion

We don't choose our kinks. Some messy combination of genetics and childhood environment sets us up with the erotic triggers—sensory, emotional, interpersonal—that get us off. Most people with a core fetish such as feet or leather say it feels as inherent to their psyches as a preference for male or female partners.

Not everyone is kinky, but I bet most of us have these erotic triggers. Perhaps your turn-ons are more typical: breasts overflowing tight bras, muscular asses pressing against denim jeans, potential partners playing hard to get, being naughty by having sex somewhere unexpected. No matter how kinky or how vanilla, we all have the capacity to enlist the emotional power of odor, the physical thrill of struggle, the interpersonal tension of conflict to intensify sexual excitement. We can use the Erotic Equation to amplify metaphors of power, engorgement, pressure, and orgasm.

Untold numbers of people suppress their own nonconformist leanings, preferring to hold at arm's length the transformative possibilities of ecstasy. They may fear stepping off the straight and narrow will lead them to the darkest parts of the erotic landscape. Yet honest and safe exploration is possible; other people have made this journey and left road maps. It's those who repress, then suddenly overindulge, who often lose a sense of reasonable limits. They mistakenly think that once they've broken out, they've entered a world without rules and boundaries. Nothing could be further from the truth.

We may not be able to choose our kinks, but we can choose what we do about them. Many people in this book enlist their kinks to fuel creativity. They explore their own erotic imaginations with honesty and integrity. Some choose to take on the sometimes difficult but often rewarding challenge of negotiating consensual play with other adults. Given the rise of kink communities both online and in real life over the last ten years in particular, it has never been easier to find knowledgeable professionals and safe, nonjudgmental public play spaces where novices can explore risk-aware consensual kink.

It has also never been easier to find kink-aware therapists and doctors who listen to their clients without judgment and help them negotiate how to experience joy without the crippling effects of culturally imposed shame. The best kink-aware therapists can help those with dangerous fantasies find ways to explore their desires without harm to themselves or others.

It's clear that over the last 20 years, kink communities have become far more open to the types of joyous play and silliness we associate with our childhoods. Safely exploring a need for play, mastery, and surrender through consensual kink can provide a powerful erotic engine for extraordinary, meaningful lives. As educator, artist, and writer Midori puts it, kink is "childhood joyous play + adult sexual privilege + cool toys…it's cops and robbers with fucking."

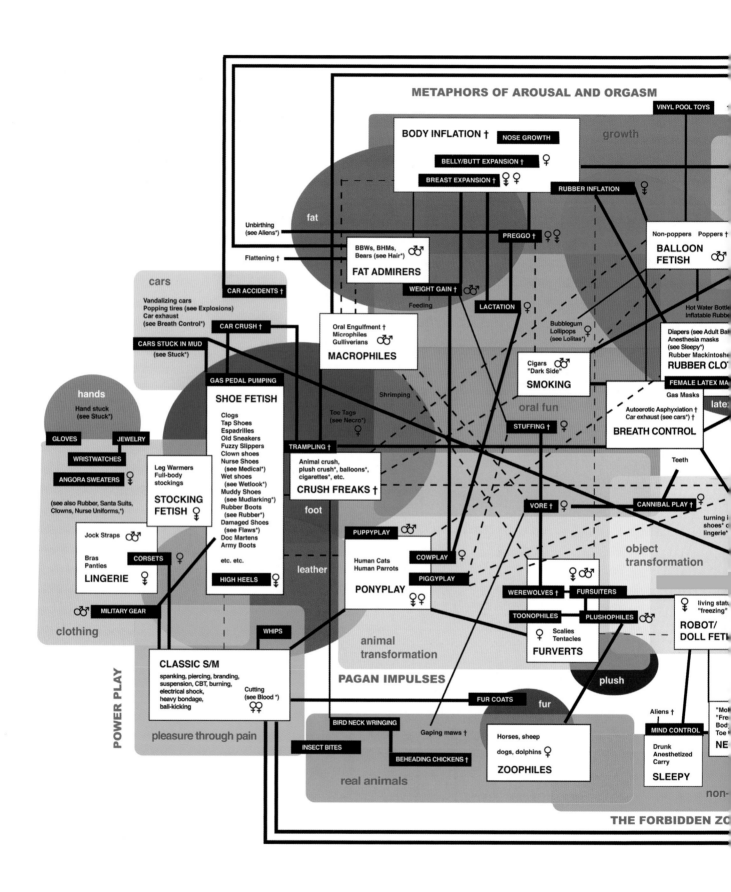

The Kinkmap

The Kinkmap is my attempt to plot the fertile and ever-mutating landscape of the erotic imagination. Core kinks such as feet, fat, leather, and rubber are the thematic story elements of narratives that employ metaphors of power, transformation, growth, and taboo, generating unique but interrelated kink families.

By shining a light on the many fascinating locations outside the conventional, I hope to render visible many people we have unnecessarily been taught to fear. It provides landmarks and shows connections.

Many different maps could have been made of this same information, but I created this map as a starting place for a vital discussion of the way sexual fantasy functions in our lives. No one needs to be lost or alone, and nothing is too scary to be discussed.

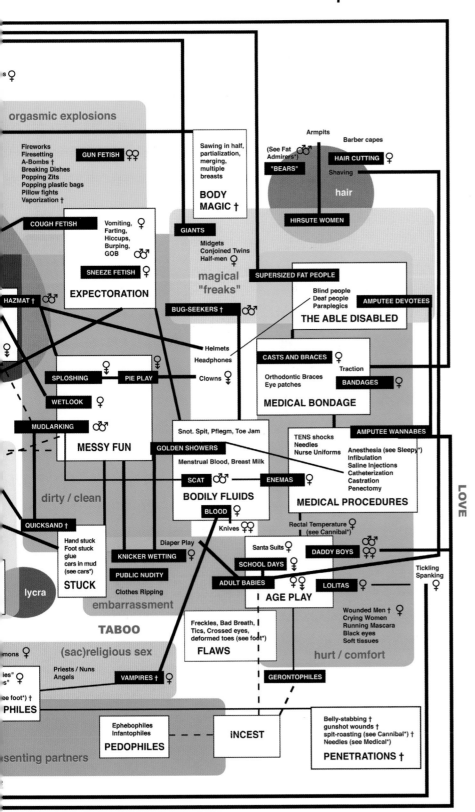

Please visit kinkmap.com
to follow this ongoing digital project

Selected Bibliography

Bacon-Smith, Camille. *Enterprising Women: Television Fandom and the Creation of Popular Myth.* Philadelphia: University of Pennsylvania Press, 1991.

Becker, Ernest. *The Denial of Death.* New York: Free Press Paperbacks, Simon & Schuster, 1973.

Blank, Hanne. *Big Big Love: A Sourcebook on Sex for People of Size and Those Who Love Them.* Gardena, CA: Greenery Press, 2000.

Brame, Gloria G., William D. Brame, and Jon Jacobs. *Different Loving: The World of Sexual Dominance and Submission.* New York: Villard Books, 1993.

Brame, Gloria G., and William D. Brame *Different Loving Too: Real People, Real Lives, Real BDSM.* Vancouver: Moons Grove Press, 2015.

DooLittle, Ducky. *Sex with the Lights On: 200 Illuminating Sex Questions Answered.* Boston: Da Capo Press, 2006.

Edmundson, Mark. *Nightmare on Main Street: Angels, Sadomasochism, and the Culture of Gothic.* Cambridge and London: Harvard University Press, 1997.

Ellis, Havelock. *Studies in the Psychology of Sex.* London: 1933.

Fiedler, Leslie. *Freaks: Myths and Images of the Secret Self.* New York: Simon & Schuster, 1978.

Fiedler, Leslie A. *The Tyranny of the Normal: Essays on Bioethics, Theology & Myth.* Boston: David R. Godine, 1996.

Foucault, Michel. *The History of Sexuality.* New York: Pantheon Books, 1978, 1980.

Freud, Sigmund. *Civilization and its Discontents.* New York: W W Norton & Co., 1989.

Freud, Sigmund. *Three Essays on the Theory of Sexuality.* New York: Basic Books, 1962.

Gamman, Lorraine, and Merja Makinen. *Female Fetishism.* New York: New York University Press, 1994.

Gamson, Joshua. *Freaks Talk Back: Tabloid Talk Shows and Sexual Nonconformity.* Chicago and London: University of Chicago Press, 1998.

Gates, Katharine. "Bullets for Broads," *Inappropriate Behaviour: Prada Sucks! and Other Demented Descants.* London: Serpent's Tail, 2002.

Gatewood, Charles. *Messy Girls!* Frankfurt: Goliath Books, 2015.

Greene, Pablo. *How to Kill a Superhero: A Gay Bondage Manual.* New York and Chicago: Beast Within Books, 2013.

Harrington, Lee, and Mollena Williams. *Playing Well With Others: Your Field Guide to Discovering, Navigating and Exploring the Kink, Leather and BDSM Communities.* Gardena, CA: Greenery Press, 2012.

Hanson, Dian. *Stanton: The Dominant Wives and Other Stories.* Cologne and New York: Taschen, 1999, 2015.

Herdt, Gilbert, and Robert J. Stoller. *Intimate Communications: Erotics and the Study of Culture.* New York: Columbia University Press, 1990.

I, Karl. *Pedal Pumping: The Fetish.* (ebook) The Pedal Pumping Organization, 2015.

Jenkins, Henry. *Textual Poachers: Television Fans and Participatory Culture.* New York and London: Routledge, 2012.

Krafft-Ebing, Richard von. *Psychopathia Sexualis with Especial Reference to the Antipathic Sexual Instinct: A Medico-Forensic Study*. Trans. F. J. Rebman. 1886. New York: Physicians and Surgeons Book Company, 1906, 1934.

Love, Brenda. *Encyclopedia of Unusual Sex Practices*. New Jersey: Barricade Books, 1992.

Masterleigh, Guy, ed. *Dianne's Days of Discipline*. London: Academy Incorporated Ltd, 2010.

Midori. *Wild Side Sex: The Book of Kink*. Los Angeles: Daedalus Publishing Company, 2015.

Miller, William Ian. *The Anatomy of Disgust*. Cambridge and London: Harvard University Press, 1998.

Money, John. *Lovemaps: Sexual/Erotic Health and Pathology, Paraphilia, and Gender Transposition*. New York: Prometheus Books, 1986, 1993.

Money, John. *Sin, Science, and the Sex Police: Essays on Sexology and Sexosophy*. New York: Prometheus Books, 1998.

Morin, Jack. *The Erotic Mind: Unlocking the Inner Sources of Passion and Fulfillment*. New York: Harper Perennial, 1996.

Penley, Constance. *NASA/TREK: Popular Science and Sex in America*. New York: Verso Books, 1997.

Rice, Anne [A. N. Roquelaure]. *The Claiming of Sleeping Beauty*; *Beauty's Punishment*; *Beauty's Release*. New York: Plume, 1983, 1984, and 1985.

Schechter, Harold. *The Bosom Serpent: Folklore and Popular Art*. Iowa City: University of Iowa Press, 1988.

Scorolli, C., S. Ghirlanda, M. Enquist, and E.A. Jannini. "Relative prevalence of different fetishes," *International Journal of Impotence Research: The Journal of Sexual Medicine*, 2007.

Shaffer, Peter. *Equus*. New York: Penguin Books, 1973.

Slocombe, Romain. *Tristes Vacances*. Lyon: Carton Editions. 1986.

Slocombe, Romain. *City of the Broken Dolls: a Medical Art Diary*. Velvet, 1997.

Sprinkle, Annie. *The Explorer's Guide to Planet Orgasm: for every body*. Gardena, CA: Greenery Press, 2017.

Stoller, Robert J. *Observing the Erotic Imagination*. New Haven and London: Yale University Press, 1985.

subMissAnn. *Pony Play with subMissAnn*. Los Angeles: (self-published), 2014.

Taormino, Tristan, editor. *The Ultimate Guide to Kink: BDSM, Roleplay, and the Erotic Edge*. San Francisco: Cleis Press, 2012.

Vilencia, Jeff, ed. *The American Journal of the Crush-Freaks*. Bellflower, CA: 1997.

Wilcox, Rebecca. *The Human Pony: a handbook for owners, trainers and admirers*. Gardena, CA: Greenery Press, 2008.

Williams-Haas, Mollena. *The Toybag Guide to Playing with Taboo*. Gardena, CA: Greenery Press, 2010.

Willie, John, and Eric Kroll. *The Complete Reprint of John Willie's Bizarre*. Cologne and New York: Taschen, 1995.

Author Katharine Gates and daughter
at the Coney Island Mermaid Parade, 2015.
Photo: Micah Atthemermaidstudio

Deviant Desires:
A Tour of the Erotic Edge

Text and images © 2000, 2017
Katharine Gates

A version of Chapter 10 originally
appeared in *The Village Voice.*

telephone
212.604.9074

e-mail:
info@powerHouseBooks.com

website:
www.powerHouseBooks.com

Second edition, 2017

Library of Congress Control
Number: 2017953725

ISBN 978-1-57687-844- 6

10 9 8 7 6 5 4 3 2 1

Printed in China

Published in the United States
by powerHouse Books,
a division of powerHouse Cultural
Entertainment, Inc.
32 Adams Street
Brooklyn, NY 11201-1021

Designed by
Eric Timothy Carlson

Edited by
David Steinhardt

Printing and binding through
Pimlico Book International